The Grand Tour of Beara

The Grand Tour of Beara

Compiled by

PENELOPE DURELL
&
CORNELIUS KELLY

CAILLEACH BOOKS

Published by
CAILLEACH BOOKS
Allihies, Beara, County Cork

ISBN 0–9537823–0–1

Cover design by Anissa Dampog
Cover illustration: The Sugarloaf Mountain (front) and Allihies Copper Mines (back) sketched by Georgiana Chatterton during her 1838 visit.
Typesetting by Carrigboy Typesetting Services, Durrus, County Cork
Printed by ColourBooks Ltd., Baldoyle, Dublin

Contents

Introduction

Visitors have been drawn to the Beara peninsula since prehistoric times and for centuries they have recorded their experiences and impressions of the area. In this anthology we bring together the accounts of fifty-one men and women who have visited Beara during the past five centuries; all appear exactly as published, without amendment or correction.

A variety of reasons brought these visitors to Beara. Some were on military or naval expeditions, while others were driven by a desire to explore and write about a remote area. They came to visit a diocese, observe plants, examine antiquities, study agricultural conditions, play the harp, establish a community, evangelize the poor, or caretake a castle. Their modes of transport were equally various: boat, ship, carriage, cart, coach, car, bicycle, horse or on foot. Those arriving by land came mostly via Bantry or Kenmare, the gateway towns to the peninsula. Arrivals by sea put in at Berehaven or at one of the many sheltered coves.

We open this collection with John Janes who, in 1593, found deliverance in Berehaven, after enduring a horrendous voyage to South America. We close with Chris Duff, who paddled here in his sea kayak 403 years later. In the intervening pages sea travel features in many of the accounts, a reflection of Beara's ancient tradition of maritime visitors that includes Milesians, Vikings, Spanish fishermen, French recruiters, pirates, privateers and shipwreck survivors. The sea continued to be a main highway until the middle of the 20th century, as journeys by road were slower and more arduous. Older residents still recall the Bantry Bay Steamship Company passenger service from Bantry railway terminal to Glengarriff, Bere Island and Castletownbere: the *Lady Elsie* plied the route from 1906 to 1936, succeeded by the *Princess Beara* until 1946. One passenger was Albert Thomas, en route to Dunboy in 1921 to take up his new post as butler and caretaker of Puxley's ill-fated mansion.

Before the end of the 17th century the peninsula's roads were little more than tracks and pathways through rugged terrain that would have seemed wild and inaccessible to the traveller. Oak, yew, arbutus, birch, alder and holly still flourished on the sheltered lower slopes until cut down for charcoal smelting. In the 1650s, Cromwellian soldiers marching to

Marie-Anne de Bovet remarked on the exposed nature of Irish cars, like this one that illustrated her 1889 book.

Dunboy forced the local people to finish the construction of the arched bridge at Ceim an Gabhair, Glengarriff: hence it entered local legend as Cromwell's Bridge. The soldiers also compelled others to build them a stretch of road below the Sugarloaf Mountain at Adrigole. By the end of the century the local administrative body, the Grand Jury of Cork, had created a pack-horse road along the south side of the peninsula to Berehaven – now partly incorporated into the Beara Way.

The first part of the 19th century brought major improvements in the road network, opening up the peninsula to many more travellers. By 1831 there was a new road to Castletownbere and within a few years, an extension over Knockoura to the copper mines at Allihies; Georgiana Chatterton took this route when she visited the mines in 1839. The following year saw the completion of the Allihies-Eyeries stretch. Although Castletownbere and Kenmare were connected by a road in 1845, the Caha Mountains, which divide the north and south sides of the peninsula, presented a challenge to anyone wishing to travel directly from Kenmare to Glengarriff. The terrain was boggy or too rough and steep for wheeled vehicles. For Prince Hermann von Pückler-Muskau, travelling at night in 1828, on foot with a baggage pony, the journey was 'indescribably difficult.' William Wordsworth, taking the same route on horseback the following year, complained of the three-hour ride over 'vile roads.'

All this changed in 1839 with the completion of the tunnel road across Esk Mountain under the supervision of engineer Alexander Nimmo. The construction of Ireland's first suspension bridge at Kenmare dramatically completed the link in 1841. The opening of the tunnel road put Beara on the tourist map. After the future Edward VII's visit to southwest Ireland in 1858, the Bantry-Glengarriff-Kenmare route became part of the popular Prince of Wales Tour to Killarney, along which passengers travelled in Bianconi coaches. The scenery, conforming with Romantic ideas of topographical beauty, held particular appeal for 19th century poets and writers. The then Poet Laureate, Alfred Austin, expressed the enchantment felt by many when he wrote of Glengarriff in 1894, 'I scarcely know how any one who goes there ever leaves it. For my part, I have been there ever since. It is a haven of absolute beauty and perfect rest.'

These days increasing numbers of visitors are drawn to the peninsula, where they can travel the entire Ring of Beara in a matter of hours. But even today, it is still possible to get a sense of the difficulties endured by earlier visitors. And undoubtedly there are and will be writers among today's visitors, like those in this book, recording their own responses to the striking landscape and the character of this special part of Ireland.

BEARA PENINSULA

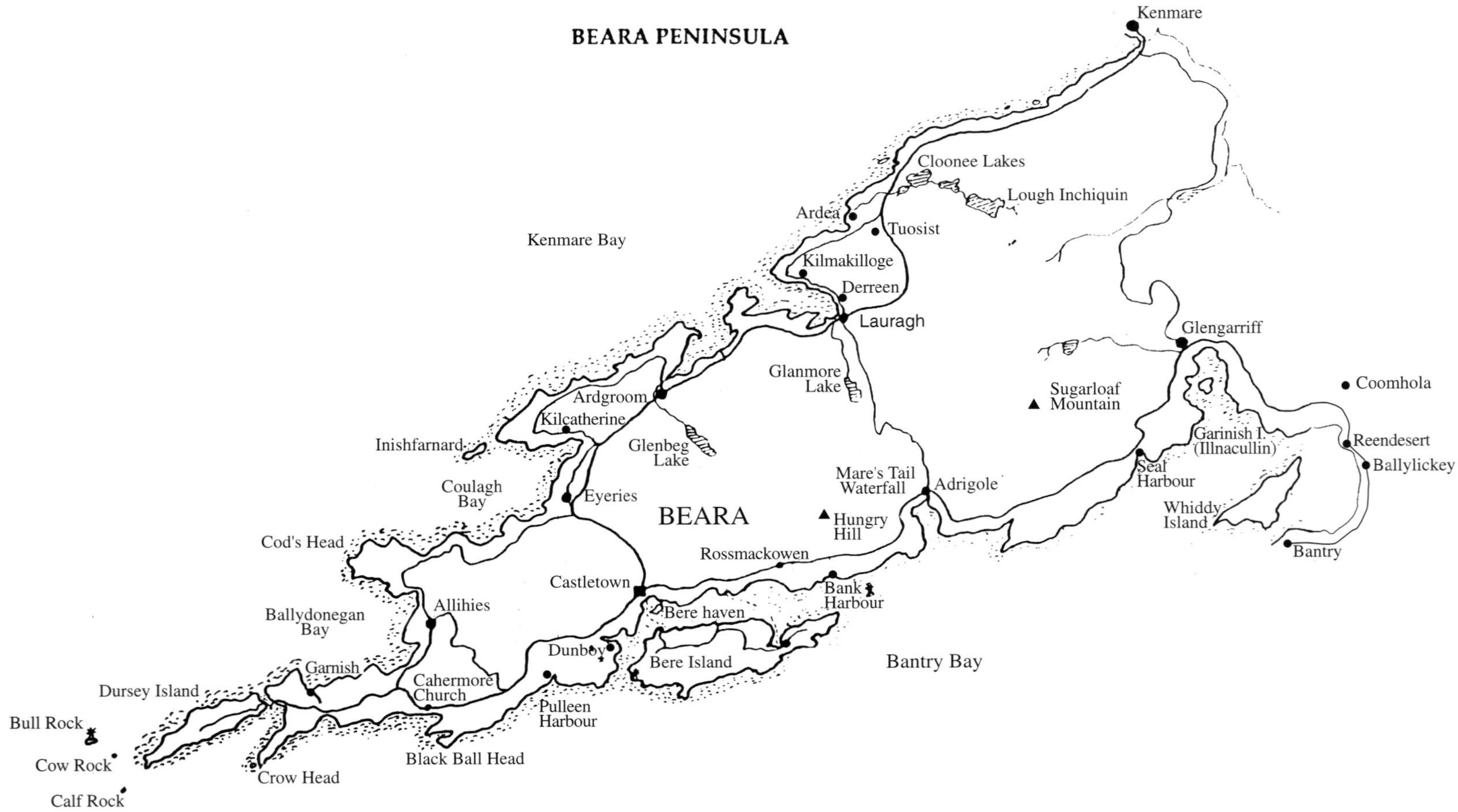

John Janes

1593

MERCHANT JOHN JANES accompanied the renowned navigator John Davis in 1585 and 1587 on two Arctic voyages in search of the North-West Passage, and wrote accounts of these journeys. In August 1591 he sailed from Plymouth as cargo superintendent on the *Desire*, commanded by Davis, with Thomas Cavendish's expeditionary fleet. This voyage (said to have inspired S.T. Coleridge's *The Rime of the Ancient Mariner*) included the accidental discovery of the Falkland Islands, passage through the Magellan Strait, storms, mutiny, desertion, Indian and Portuguese attacks, hunger, sickness and death. Finally, to supplement dwindling rations, the crew preserved thousands of penguins: but from these grew worms that started devouring everything except iron. Janes and his surviving shipmates were indeed fortunate to drift into Berehaven.

To be short, all our men died except 16, of which there were but 5 able to move. The Captain was in good health, the Master indifferent, Captain Cotton and myself swollen and short-winded, yet better than the rest that were sick, and one boy in health; upon us 5 only the labour of the ship did stand. The Captain and Master, as occasion served, would take in and heave out the top-sails, the Master only attended on the sprit-sail, and all of us at the capstan without sheets and tacks. In fine, our misery and weakness was so great, that we could not take in nor heave out a sail; so our top-sail and sprit-sails were torn all in pieces by the weather. The Master and Captain, taking their turns at the helm, were mightily distressed and monstrously grieved with the most woeful lamentation of our sick men. Thus, as lost wanderers upon the sea, the 11th of June 1593 it pleased God that we arrived at Berehaven, in Ireland, and there ran the ship on shore, where the Irish men helped us to take in our sails, and to moor our ship for floating; which slender pains of theirs cost the Captain some ten pounds before he could have the ship in safety. Thus without victuals, sails, men, or any furniture, God only guided us into Ireland, where the Captain left the Master and three or four of the company to keep the ship, and within 5 days after he and certain others had passage in an English fisher-boat to Padstow in Cornwall. In this manner our small remnant by God's only mercy were preserved and restored to our country, to Whom be all honour and glory, world without end.

From *Hakluyt's Voyages*

Thomas Stafford

1602

AFTER THE BATTLE OF KINSALE, Sir George Carew, president of Munster, and his forces came to Beara to subdue the chieftain Donal Cam O'Sullivan Beare and his allies who were still resisting English rule. In 1633 *Pacata Hibernia*, a military report of the Munster campaign, was published under Carew's authorship. It is generally assumed, however, to have been written by Thomas Stafford, who is reputed to have been his natural son. This eye-witness account covers the fateful days in June 1602 when Dunboy Castle was under siege.

The seventh, the President drew his forces to a neck of land within a mile of Donboy, opposite it, an arm of the sea passing between the castle and the camp, whence the President, taking Sir Charles Wilmot and one hundred foot for a guard with him, stole out of the camp and marched directly to the castle to view it and the grounds adjoining, in doing whereof some small shot was bestowed upon them, but no other hurt done than Sir Charles Wilmot's horse shot in the foot. There they found, contrary to the reports of all men who had seen the same, a fair place of good ground, and of capacity sufficient to encamp in, within twelve score of the castle, and yet out of sight of it by reason of a rising ground interjacent; and also, upon the top of a small ascent in the midst of the rocks, a fair green plot of ground, not a hundred and forty yards distant from the castle, like a natural platform, of just sufficient largeness to plant the artillery upon. At their return, the report being made, it was hardly believed. For the Lord Barry, the White Knight, Cormack MacDermond, Captain John Barry, and Owen O'Sulevan, who was born and bred in the castle – all of them, being in the camp, constantly averred that there was no other than rocky ground near it, and surely I conceive they did think it to be so, supposing that the plots of ground aforementioned were too little to lodge in and to plant the artillery. Further, the President assured them that, with God's favour, he would plant the ordnance without the loss of a man, and, within seven days after the battery had begun, to be master of all that place. Hereat the whole army much rejoiced, for the general opinion was that it would be a long siege; but afterwards, as you shall hear, the President kept his promise aforesaid. The same day, seven great shot were made from the castle to the camp, but no harm was done.

The eighth, we planted two falcons, taken out of the Queen's pinnace, upon a point of land on the north side of the castle, hard by our camp, which beat upon the enemy, who were then carrying turf and earth to advance their works. And the same day the hoy was brought aground, and two culverins were unshipped and put into boats, and two spies sent by the enemy into our camp were taken and hanged. And we also sent soldiers to the wood to cut gabion stuff and to bring the rafters of an old church to make joists for the platform to plant the ordnance on.

The ninth, the Sergeant-Major, Captain George Flower, was sent by sea to take view of the Spanish bay near Donboy, to see whether there was any good landing for the ordnance there, and found the ground rocky and unfit for draught.

The tenth, Captain Francis Slingsby, whom I cannot too much commend, in the hoy with the demi-cannon, and the three boats laden with two culverins and one demi-culverin, passed the point underneath the castle, within one hundred feet of the same, whence their great shot were made at the hoy, but all without harm, for his muskets so plied the artillery that the gunners durst scarcely stand by the same. And the same day we landed the two culverins and the demi-cannon, and encamped within musket-shot, but not within sight of the castle, by reason of a rising ground aforesaid which shadowed us, although oftentimes their great and small shot came over the camp and amongst us into the same.

The ordnance could not be drawn from the place where we landed to the place where we made our quarters, but there was a small creek very near the castle of Donboy, which being once entered into, they might ride in safety, being then covered with a hill between them and the castle, but all the way of their coming thither was open to the play of the ordnance of the castle, until they were within that creek, whose mouth was not above forty yards distant from the castle. The President commanded the ordnance be shipped into boats, and to carry them into that creek, which, by the help of dark nights and still rowing, was effected undiscovered. But the cannon and culverins were of such weight that no boat there could carry them, and none durst venture in the hoy to carry them by night. In this difficulty Captain Slingsby desired the President that he would commit that to his charge and give him but thirty shot, and he would (by God's grace) carry that ordnance by daylight into the creek or sink by the way, if his Lordship would please to venture the ordnance; which was accepted and performed the same day without the loss of a man, though many shot were made from the castle; for he had placed all his shot in the hold upon the ballast, so that the deck was breast-high above them, so that they had only their pieces and head and shoulders above the deck to play with their small shot; and that he that steered the hoy might be in safety (which much concerned the effecting of that service by his safe conducting) he placed him in the hold, and ordered it so that with two cackles he might steer the hoy either to starboard or to port as he was willed above by the captain, who stood aloft by the mizen-mast to order her course as he saw cause; but it was so fine and fresh a gale of wind that though they sailed above half a league in play of the ordnance and small shot of the castle, yet she made that way that they could not above twice discharge and lead their ordnance before she attained the creek, where she was then in security from any further annoyance of the castle.

The eleventh, we entrenched our camp, mounted our ordnance, and drew them all into the Market-place; and the same day, about eight o clock in the evening, the Lord President gave direction to have a demi-culverin drawn within shot of the castle, which made but two shot that night and was withdrawn. The Spanish cannoneers, finding the shot, willed the Irish to be of good courage, for that piece would do them no harm. He also caused two minions to be landed out of the Queen's ship, and placed them upon a point of ground on the north-west side of the castle, which overlooked it, to annoy the rebels whilst we were about our work. The same night we began our approaches, the care whereof the President imposed upon Captain Francis Slingsby, a discreet and dexterous gentleman, making him trench-master, who performed with commendations the charge which was laid upon him, having all the day before employed a great party of men in the wood, which was a long mile and a half distant from the camp, to fetch more wattle to make gabions, and was constrained to send a strong guard with them for their defence. This day the enemy made a sally out of the wood upon some of our guards, but were immediately repulsed.

The twelfth of the same, understanding that the enemy had fortified the Island of the Dorseys, and carried thither three pieces of Spanish ordnance, and placed a strong ward of forty choice men in the same, reserving that as their last and surest refuge, the Lord President made special choice of Captain John Bostock, and sent him with Owen O'Sulevan and Lieutenant Downings (officer to Sir Francis Barkley), and gave them (as also to Captain Thomas Fleming, who had command of her Majesty's pinnace) secretly in charge that, now, while their army was occupied in besieging Donboy and making their trenches and approaches, and the enemy secure from any suspicion that we would give any attempt elsewhere, they should presently take Her Majesty's pinnace and four boats, and put into them one hundred and sixty foot men and set sail for the Island of the Dorseys, which charge they effected accordingly, and arrived there with the forces early the next morning, and being on land drew to the north point of the island, where they found the walls of a ruined chapel. Captain Bostock, under the safety thereof, lodged Lieutenant Downings and a party of men, and then returned on board the Queen's pinnace to give direction

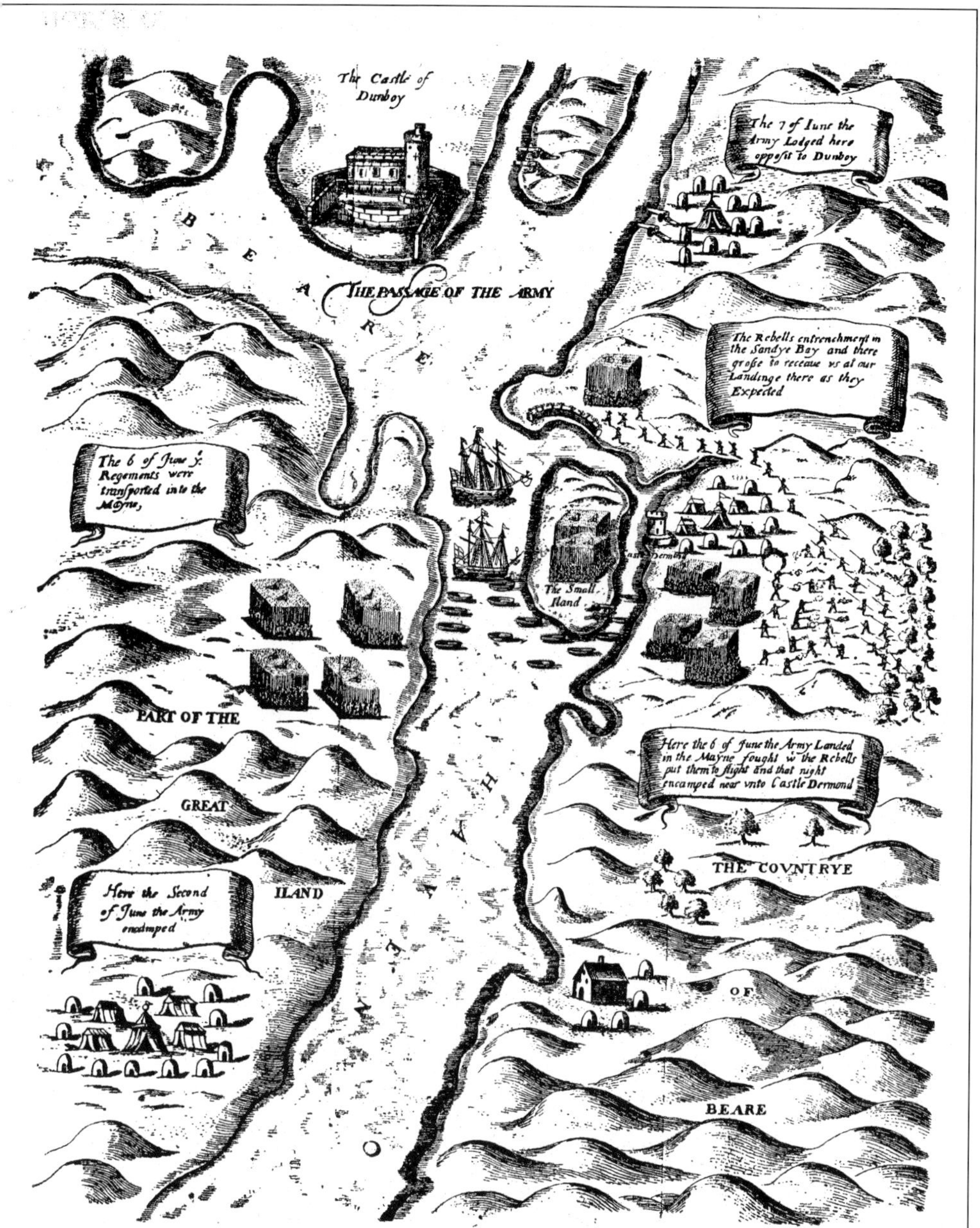

'Map of army on the Beare Country' from Pacata Hibernia, *the military report of Carew's Munster campaign.*

what he would have done, and thence took the boat of the pinnace and rowed about the island to discover a fit landing place for himself and the rest of his soldiers; then, coming back to the pinnace, so often as the tide served he caused the pinnace to warp up nearer the place, and appointed thirty soldiers and a serjeant to attend her, and sent to Lieutenant Downings, on shore, advising him that, at the very instant that he should land in the eastern part of the fort, he should give an attempt on the north side. Then he divided his men into three boats, and the pinnace beating upon the fort with her ordnance, he and Lieutenant Downings (at the other two places first agreed upon) assailed the outermost fort, which, after a good defence made, their resolution and valour carried, and there they possessed themselves of three iron pieces of the Spanish ordnance, and forced the rebels into their second fort, where they entertained a good fight for the space of two hours. But our men, being encouraged with their first good fortune, gave on them so eagerly that the enemy, amazed, rendered themselves, and presently all their weaponed men came forth and delivered him possession of the fort, which was a place of exceeding great strength; and in the same, at the yielding up thereof, was the wife of Owen O'Sulevan, who since February last had been held prisoner by O'Sulevan Beare. There were found within the fort seven barrels of powder, with a small proportion of lead, and above threescore shot for their great ordnance, as also a quantity of wheat, oil and vinegar. In the island there were taken five hundred milch cows. Of the rebels, four were killed and two hurt, who with all the rest were brought into the camp and afterwards executed. The fort, for that it was conceived to be an unnecessary charge, and unmeet to be held, the Lord President caused Lieutenant Downings to ruin and lay it even with the ground.

The same night the Lord President, the Earl of Thomond, Sir Richard Percy, Sir Charles Wilmot, Captain Francis Slingsby, and Captain George Kingsmill, with others standing round together in conference, a musket shot came amongst them from the castle and shot Captain George Kingsmill through the left hand and broke many of his bones.

The thirteenth, about midnight, Tirrell, with the rebel forces, came as near our camp as he durst, and gave us a hot alarm, pouring shot into our camp, shot through many of our tents and cabins, which did us little or no hurt, who being resisted from the north side of our camp, where a little sconce was the same day raised to hold a guard in, the charge whereof was imposed on Lieutenant Jeffrey, and good seconds sent from us, they ran away. This day Sir Samuel Bagnall arrived at the camp by sea, and brought letters to the President from the Deputy, commanding him to send all the forces to his Lordship, except those of the old list of Munster. He also brought with him a letter from Don Juan de Aquila, which had come by a merchant of Dublin to the Lord Deputy's hands.

The fourteenth and fifteenth our men were busy making gabions and drawing the trenches nearer the castle, Captain Francis Slingsby being, as aforesaid, trench-master.

The same day the President, the Earl of Thomond, and Sir Charles Wilmot, taking a guard of foot with them, rode, for recreation, out of the camp towards our last camping-place, and riding softly by the seaside, all three in rank, having left their foot behind them, they espied a gunner in the castle traversing a piece of ordnance. 'This fellow,' said the President, 'will make a shot at us.' The word was no sooner spoken than fire was given. The President, knowing that gunners always lay before a moving mark, reined his horse and stood firm. The Earl and Sir Charles started forward, and the ball grazed their horses' heels, beating some of the earth upon them. The President, glad to see them past danger, laughing, said that if they had been as good mechanical cannoneers as they were commanders they would have stood firm as he did. Also this day a whole culverin was drawn out of the camp and certain shot were made. The balls being found, the gunners liked it not, and began to fear their success. The day following, the whole culverin having being formerly withdrawn, certain shot were made out of the demi-culverin aforesaid. Upon sight of the shot they much rejoiced, supposing that our culverin had received some mischance, and scorned at any offence we could do them.

The sixteenth, the gabions, trenches, and platforms were finished, and in the night the demi-cannon and the two culverins were drawn down and planted against the castle, within 140 yards.

The seventeenth, about five o'clock in the morning, our battery, consisting of one demi-cannon, two whole culverins, and one demi-culverin, began to play, which continued without intermission till towards nine in the forenoon, at which time a turret annexed to the castle, on the south-west part thereof, was beaten down, in which there was a falcon of iron placed, upon the top of the vault, that continually played at our artillery, which also tumbled down. With the fall of the tower many of the rebels were buried therein. That being ruined, the ordnance played on the west front of the castle, which, by one o'clock in the afternoon, was also forced down. Upon the fall thereof the enemy sent out a messenger offering to surrender the place if they might have their lives and depart with their arms, and a pledge given for the assurance thereof; nevertheless they continued shooting all the while the messenger was coming between them and us, whose message being delivered, the Lord President turned him over to the Marshal, by whose direction he was executed. And then, the breach being in our opinion assaultable, the Lord President gave command to have it entered; whereupon the Captains of the Lord President's regiments, which were commanded by Captain Henry Skipwith, lieutenant-colonel thereof, who were to give the assault, cast the dice for the point, and who should give seconds; and it fell to Captain Doddington's chance, and to be seconded by Sir Anth. Cooke, their lieutenants, Francis Kirton and Thomas Mewtas, to give on first, and the rest of the regiment to second them. The Earl of Thomond's regiment was to second the Lord President's, and during the assault the two regiments of Sir Richard Percy and Sir Charles Wilmot were commanded to stand in arms in the Market-place, as well to assure the camp as also to answer all other occasions. All things being thus disposed of, Lieutenant Kirton, according to the direction, giving on first, in entering the breach was, at the push of the pike, on the top of the same, who, although he received three shot and hurt in the right arm, yet with valour and resolution kept the place and made it good till Lieutenant Mewtas came up to his second, and both they until the Lord President's colours and the rest climbed up and placed their ensigns upon a turret of the barbican, reinforced with earth and faggots of great thickness, to which was added a large spur on the south-west part of the castle, of the height of sixteen feet, as in like manner all the turrets and curtains of the barbican were reinforced, at the top whereof they barricaded themselves with barrels of earth, and at the first approach there were within it some of the enemy with a falcon of iron, whom our men forced to quit the place and to retreat into a turret adjoining upon the south side, which was ramparted with earth some sixteen feet high, flanking the first, it being well manned, and therein a demi-culverin and a saker of brass loaded with hailshot; the one whereof they presently discharged upon our men that were possessed of the south-west turret and spur, and going to load her again, their gunner was slain at his piece; whereupon, being for the present deprived of the use of those ordnance, and the place we possessed playing directly into it, they were forced to retreat under the safety of the east part of the castle, which was standing, where the enemy had placed pikes at the corners of the walls to receive them; the way between it and the curtain of the barbican being but six or eight feet broad, which passage they so well defended that we could neither annoy them nor go betwixt the two turrets aforesaid without disadvantage and apparent danger of great loss, where the shelter of the wall and the narrowness of the passage deprived both us and them of all use of shot, and there for the space of an hour and a half it was disputed with great obstinacy on either side; the enemy still making good defence, and beating with shot and stones upon us from the stairs and likewise from that part of the castle which stood from the top of the vault, and from under the vault, both with pieces and by their throwing down stones, iron balls, and other annoyances, wherewith many of our men were slain and wounded, and we oppressing them in all those places by all means we might, and still attempting to get up to the top of the vault by the ruins of the breach, which was maintained by the enemy so that we were divers times forced down again. And whilst in each of these places our men were thus employed, Captain Slingsby's sergeant, who had got to the top of the vault of the south-west tower by clearing the rubbish thence, found that the ruins thereof had made a way that led to a spike or window that looked into it and commanded that part of the barbican of the castle which the enemy possessed and defended, he having been there two hours before he discovered the same, by which passage our men, making their descent to the enemy, and gaining ground upon them, they being then in desperate case, some forty of them made a sally out of the castle to the seaside, whither our men pursuing them on the one side, and they being crossed by Captain Blundell with a small party of men (on the outside of the barbican) on the other side, we had the execution of them all there, saving eight who leapt into the sea to save themselves by swimming. But the Lord President, supposing before that they would in their extremity make such a venture to escape, had appointed Captain Gawen Harvy and his lieutenant Thomas Stafford, with three boats to keep the sea, who had the killing of them all; other three leapt from the top of the vault, where our soldiers killed them, amongst them a notable rebel called Mellaghlen Moore, being the man who first laid hands upon the Earl of Ormond, and plucked him from his horse when he was taken prisoner by Owhny MacRory, was slain.

After this, the courage of the enemy decreasing with their numbers, and not able nor daring to make such defence as they did before, we gave a new assault to the top of the vault, where having a difficult ascent, the shot from the foot of the breach giving good assistance, after some hours' assault and defence, with some loss on both sides, we gained the top of the vault and all the castle upwards, and placed our colours upon the height thereof, the whole remainder of the ward, being threescore and seventeen men, being constrained to retire into the cellars, into which we having no descent but by a straight winding stony stair, they defended the same against us, and thereupon, upon promise of their lives, they offered to come forth, but not to stand to mercy. Notwithstanding, immediately after a Friar born in Youghal, called Domnick Collins, who had been brought up in the wars of France, and there under the league had been a commander of horse in Brittany (by them called captain Le Branch),

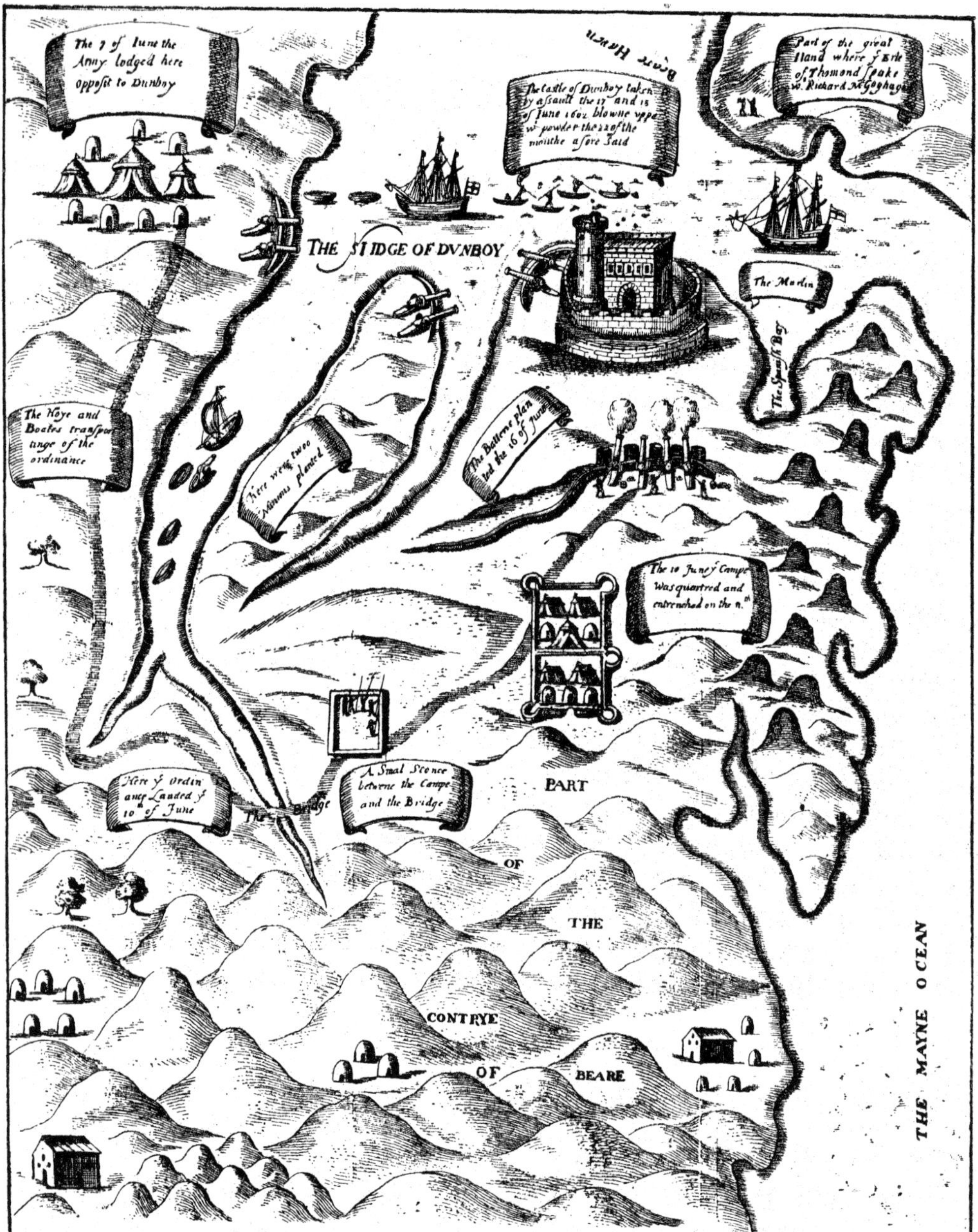

Map of The Siege of Dunboy showing the English army positions.

came forth and rendered himself. The sun being by this time set, and strong guards being left upon the rebels remaining in the cellars, the regiments withdrew to the camp.

The eighteenth, in the morning, three and twenty more likewise rendered themselves simply to Captain Blundell, who the night before had the guard, and afterward their cannoneers, being two Spaniards and an Italian (for the rest were slain), likewise yielded themselves. Then MacGoghagan, chief commander of the place, being mortally wounded with divers shot in his body, the rest made choice of one Thomas Taylor, an Englishman's son, the dearest and most intimate man with Tirrell, and married to his niece, to be their chief, who having nine barrels of powder, drew himself and it into the vault, and there sat down by it with a lighted match in his hand, vowing and protesting to set it on fire and blow up the castle, himself and all the rest except they might have promise of life, which being by the Lord President refused, for the safety of our men his Lordship gave directions for a new battery upon the vault, intending to bury them in the ruins thereof, and after a few times discharged, and the bullets entering amongst them into the cellar, the rest that were with Taylor, partly by intercession, but chiefly by compulsion (threatening to deliver him up if he were obstinate), about ten o'clock in the morning of the same day constrained him to render simply, who, with eight and forty more, being ready to come forth, and Sir George Thornton, the sergeant-major, Captain Roger Harvy, Captain Power, and others entering the vault to receive them, Captain Power found the said Richard MacGoghagan lying there mortally wounded (as before), and, perceiving Taylor and the rest ready to render themselves, raised himself from the ground, snatching a lighted candle, and staggered therewith to a barrel of powder (which for that purpose was unheaded) offering to cast it into the same. Captain Power took him and held him in his arms, with intent to make him prisoner, until he was by our men, who perceived his intent, instantly killed, and then Taylor and the rest were brought prisoners to the camp.

The same day fifty-eight were executed in the Market-place, but the Friar Taylor, and one Tirlagh Roe MacSwiny, a follower of Sir Tirlagh O'Brian, and twelve more of Tirrell's chief men, the Lord President reserved alive, to try whether he could draw them to do some more acceptable service than their lives were worth. The whole number of the ward consisted of one hundred and forty-three selected fighting men, being the best choice of all their forces, of which not one man escaped, but were either slain, or executed, or buried in the ruins, and so obstinate and resolved a defence had not been seen within this kingdom. On our part we lost in the place Thomas Smith, Captain Francis Slingsby's lieutenant, and some others: and many of our men were burnt with powder and fireworks, which the enemy cast amongst them as they were in fight. Men of note hurt: Captain Doddington, shot with two bullets in the body, but not mortally; his lieutenant, Francis Kirton, shot in the arm and thigh; divers sergeants and sixty-two soldiers maimed and wounded, of which some are dead since, and others like to follow. And amongst the rest Sir Anthony Cooke, Sir Garret Harvy, Captain Skipwith, and Captain Roger Harvy received several bruises with stones and iron bullets flung upon them, but, being well armed, they received no great hurt. In the castle we gained ten pieces of ordnance, whereof four were brass, two of them being broken by our battery; and another piece of brass was likewise broken by our ordnance before any part of the castle fell, which the prisoners say is so deeply buried in the ruins that the search of the metal is not worth the labour. All the carriages were by the fall of the castle and by our artillery so broken that not one of them was left serviceable. Moreover, there were of powder nine barrels, and some great shot, but their whole store, by reason of the ruins, we could not well find out. There were also in the castle some quantities of wine, vinegar, oil, corn, beef, and hides, which the soldiers made pillage of.

The nineteenth, proffer was made by the traitor Tirrell to do some acceptable service that might redeem the lives of his men, so that their execution might be respited, which was for that time forborne. And the same day all our ordnance, and the Spanish pieces that we gained at Donboy, were put aboard and shipped, as also our boats sent to the Island of the Dorseys to fetch Lieutenant Downings, our men, and the ordnance thence, which were in number twelve, viz. demi-culverin one, sakers four, minions five, falcons two.

The twentieth, Tirrell, understanding, as is said, that his men's lives were respited, sent his trusty servant Laghlin Odallye to the Lord President to signify to him that he would perform any service that should be within his power to purchase the lives and liberties of his followers. Answer was returned him, and a stratagem propounded in the effecting thereof, that he should obtain pardon and liberty for himself and his dependents, but the reply which he made thereto was that he would ransom the prisoners with money, if that might be accepted, but to be false to the King of Spain, whom he termed his master, or to betray the Catholic cause, he would never; upon which answer his twelve men, before respited, two days afterwards were executed. The reason why he so suddenly swerved from his first promise of service was the hopes which he received by Owen MacEggan, the Pope's Bishop of Ross, lately arrived at Ardea, in the Bay as aforesaid of Kenmare. The President, therefore, perceiving that they conceived great hope of Spaniards, advised the day following with the chiefs of the army as to what course was best to be taken with the Castle of Donboy, half ruined, who were all of opinion that a garrison which should be left there could not defend themselves or give any great annoyance to the Spaniards, if they should fortune to land there; for being so remote from all seconds and succours, were unavoidably left to ruin. And besides, though the Spaniards came not, the service that they could do in that country would not countervail Her Majesty's charge in maintaining them. Therefore they resolved to bestow the powder which was recovered in the castle to blow up the same; committed to the charge of Captain Slingsby.

The two-and-twentieth, the castle of Donboy was accordingly blown up with powder, the outworks and fortifications being utterly destroyed; and the same day Lieutenant Downings, with our men and boats, returned from the Dorseys to the camp, and also twelve of Tirrell's chief men, formerly spoken of, were executed.

But Taylor, and Domnick Collins the Friar, were carried prisoners to Cork, where being found, by due proof, that Taylor was one of the principal murderers of his captain, George Bingham at Sligo, besides being guilty of an infinite number of other foul and traitorly acts, he was shortly afterwards, without the city of Cork, not far from the north gate, hanged in chains; and the Friar, in whom no penitence appeared for his detestable treasons, not yet would endeavour to merit his life either by discovering the rebels' intentions (which was in his power) or by doing some service that might deserve favour, was hanged at Youghal, the town wherein he was born.

The same day, also, all our carriage and baggage being laid aboard, at the entrance into our boats, because we were not able to carry the cows, horses, and mares which we had taken, being at least six or seven hundred heads, the President commanded they should be killed, which was performed.

The three-and-twentieth we shipped our whole army back from Donboy, who all arrived that day in the Great Island, and thence the Earl of Thomond and Sir Charles Wilmot and both their regiments, were transported by shipping to Killaminog, being the place we encamped in, as we went, in Mounterbarry.

From *Pacata Hibernia*

Thomas Dineley

1680

THE ANTIQUARY THOMAS DINELEY was born about the middle of the seventeenth century at Southampton, where his father was controller of customs. He was educated by the dramatist James Shirley and at Gray's Inn in London, but abandoned his studies to take up a post in the Low Countries. Keenly interested in foreign countries, Dineley kept illustrated journals of his travels there and in France. In 1680 he toured Ireland, but the account of his Irish travels was not published until 1870. Dineley died at Louvain in 1695.

Description of Bear-Haven. Is scituate twelve miles to the northward of a promontory or foreland commonly called Missenhead or Caronhead; that which is properly the Haven is the sea which cometh between the great Island and the main or countrey called Bear or O'Sullevan Bears countrey. At the entrance into the harbour it is not above the shot of a musquet over from Dunboyne castle to the great Island; being entered, the tides are slack, good anchorage, and convenient places to bring ships on ground, smooth water. At low water mark it is five fadoms deep; towards the north end it groweth much larger, a league over, and large enough to lett all the men of War of England, Holland, and France, ride therein safe, nay, I may say of the whole world.

The great Island, seven miles long, & the maine, forme ye Haven, which at its south end joins with the bay of Bantry.

When the famous Castle of Dunboyne, belonging to O'Sulevan Beare, was tenable and fit to offend and defend, it had the command of this admirable Haven.

The Fishery here in ye Reign of Queen Elizabeth, viz., anno Dni. 1588, was worth to ye Lord of the Haven (afterwards Rebell), O'Sulevan Bear, (who was likewise owner of the castle Dunboyne), 500li sterling p annu. paying but small duties to him. The coast so abounds in Fish, that few places known exceed it.

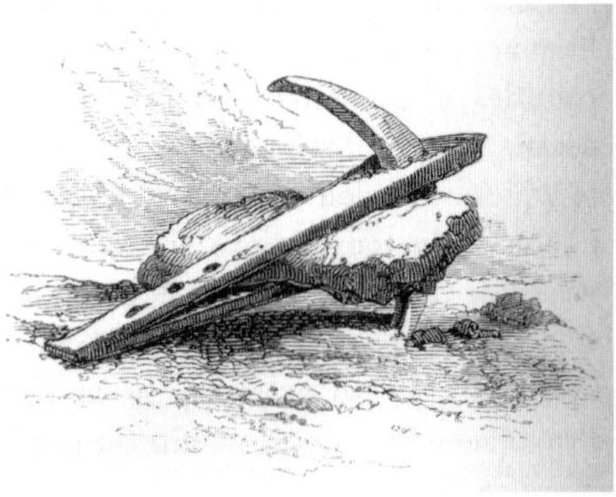

From *Observations in a Voyage through the Kingdom of Ireland*

Bantry, at the end of the 19th century, looked considerably more attractive than John Stevens' description.

John Stevens

1689

JOHN STEVENS WAS COLLECTOR of excise at Welshpool in Wales when William of Orange came to the throne. Being Jacobite in sympathy, he followed James II to France. On 2 May 1689, the day after the Battle of Banty Bay, Stevens landed in Bantry with the Jacobite forces. He was at the Battle of the Boyne and in Limerick during the Siege. When Limerick fell, James's supporters were given the choice of the oath of allegiance or exile on the continent. Along with most, Stevens chose the continent, where he spent the rest of his life as a translator of Spanish and Portuguese histories.

Thursday the 2nd: we landed at Bantry, which is a miserable poor place, not worthy the name of a town, having not above seven or eight little houses, the rest very mean cottages. The least part of us could not be contained in this place, so most were sent two or three miles round to no better cottages to quarter. Two nights that we continued here I walked two miles out of town to lie upon a little dirty straw in a cot or cabin, no better than a hog-sty among near twenty others. The houses and cabins in town were so filled that people lay all over the floors. Some gentlemen I knew who took up their lodging in an old rotten boat that lay near the shore, and there wanted not some who quartered in a sawpit. Meat the country brought in enough, but some had not money to buy, and those who had for want of change had much difficulty to get what they wanted, the people being so extreme poor that they could not give change out of half a crown or a crown, and guineas were carried about the whole day and returned whole. Drink there was none, but just at our landing a very little wort hot from the fire, which nevertheless was soon drunk; and good water was so scarce that I have gone half a mile to drink at a spring. About half a mile from this is the old town of Bantry, much like the new. Upon a hill over the town and creek is a fort built by Cromwell, now gone to decay but never of any considerable strength.

From *A Journal of My Travels in Ireland since the Revolution*

Dive Downes

1700

BORN IN NORTHAMPTONSHIRE IN 1653, Dive Downes studied at Trinity College, Dublin. Soon after being appointed to the bishopric of Cork and Ross in June 1700, he undertook a visitation of his diocese, and recorded his observations in a journal which is preserved in the Trinity College library. This document is a rich source of information about the Beara peninsula at that period. Married four times, Downes died in 1709, on the same day that his daughter Anne was born.

Monday, June 10, 1700, I went from Bantry to Beerehaven in a hooker, and returned to Bantry on Wednesday, the 12th of the same month.

Dunbwy, als. Beerehaven, lies due west of Bantry. I went from Bantry to Beerehaven by sea. In the way, on the N. of the bay, is Glengarriff, Sugarloaf hill and Daad O'Huologhan, als. Hungry hill, which is the highest in that country. We landed at Daad O'Huologhan. In a small wood at the bottom of the hill on the south side we saw above a hundred of the arbutus trees. O'Sullivan Beere lives in a cabin at the foot of the hill. Part of Daad O'Huologhan is in the parish of Kilkaskan and part of it in the parish of Killaghaneenah.

Parish of Killaghaneenah reaches from Bantry bay to Kinmare river, 'tis in breadth about 3 or 4 miles and 12 miles in length. The Island of Beerehaven is in this parish, and also the Dorses and Beerehaven, als. Dunbwy. There was a chappel in Beerehaven Island called Ballinikilly, the walls are standing uncovered, on the N. side of the Island. We saw it as we passed by it in the bay. Two English families and near 30 Irish families in this island. About 10 Irish families in the Dorses. No English. There was a chappel in the Island of Dorses called Kilmichil, some of the walls are standing. In the whole parish of Killaghaneenah are about 15 Protestant families, five of them French and five Scotch which are Dissenters, and five English families which are Conformists. In the parish of Killaghaneenah are about 80 plowlands.

Arbutus.

A Popish schoolmaster, Major Carthy, teaches Latin in this parish. No Protestant school nearer than Bantry.

The Lord Altham, Earl of Corke, and Mr. Gookin, by lease, and Captain Boid have the lands of this parish, and Mr. John Davys, Mr. Hutchins, Capt. Boid, Mr. Fountain, Sergeant Grahams, Mr. Thos. Dyer and a waiter live in this parish.

The Countess of Castlehaven has the Rectory, 'tis worth about £18 p. an., she has the bulk of all the tythes. The Vicar's part, by the addition of bookmoney, is worth about £25 p. an.

The tides at the change and full of the moon rise about 10 feet at Beerehaven. No Divine Service nearer than Bantry. About 20 plantation acres of glebe lie around the Church of Killaghaneenah. Set for £20 p. an. The lands of this parish are generally very coarse mountains, rocky and boggy, that part that lies towards the Dorses is much better than the rest. In our way to Kilmannah, near Beerehaven, we saw iron mine in ye road, they use at the iron works at Croomholla in Mr. Wallis's iron works.

At Dunbwy, als. Beerehaven, there was a castle in Qn. Elizabeth's time, it was made a fort in Cromwell's time. Beerehaven Island, 5 miles in length, within a small mile of the main, it makes a good harbour, but there are some rocks under water near the entrance into Beerehaven called the Cotts. There are 10 beds of escallops and oysters in the bay at Beerehaven.

There were no Protestants before the late troubles neither in this nor in the parishes of Kilmannah nor Kilkatierin nor Kilkaskan. Now there are a few Protestants in Killaghaneenah, the Papists are humbled and are become amenable to law, which they scarcely were before.

On the south side of Daad O'Huologhan towards the bottom of the hill near the sea, grow at least a hundred of the arbutus or Cane Apple trees, called in Irish apples Cahannah, some of them 24 or 26 foot high. This tree grows like a shrub, severall branches growing out of the same stock. The old trees have no leaves only at the top. The high trees had no fruit, but the suckers that grow at the roots of the old trees had fruit on them unripe, but no blossoms, nor ripe fruit, the suckers of 4 or 5 foot high bear fruit. The old bark pulls off, and a new bark grows under it. The trees at a distance look reddish, the edges of the leaves being reddish. The ground on which the trees grow is very rocky, the roots shoot themselves into the clefts of the rocks. The earth is blackish, and boggy, but 'tis thought to be fat earth. In the same woods grow oaks, birch, hazel, crab trees, heath, fern and furzes and holly, which seems to thrive better than the rest. Commonly heath grows at the roots of the Cane apple trees.

Teige O'Sullivan is popish priest of this parish of Killaghaneenah, Kilmannah and Kilkatierin. He has been here about 20 years.

Oghigianag, an Irish Saint, is Patron of this parish, his day is observed on the 15th of August, the Assumption of the B. V.

We saw several eagles upon the lands of Beerehaven. There are many wolves there. Bantry bay is for the most part 2 leagues broad. 'Tis seven leagues from Bantry to Beerehaven. We were 12 hours agoing thither, but we returned in seaven. It would be very fit that a minister should be placed at Beerehaven, if there were a competent maintenance for him. He might serve Killaghaneenah, Kilmannah, Kilkatierin and Kilkaskan.

At Dunbwy, als. Beerehaven, was formerly a castle belonging to O'Sullevane. Afterwards by the government there was a fort made there, 'tis now ruinous.

In this parish and in Kilmocomoge and in Killaghaneenah they formerly paid 40s. tythe for every saine, but now they pay nothing. Mr. Holmes sued the parishioners in 1663 in the Bp.'s Court for the tythes of fish, upon which they afterwards paid 40s. per saine. Col. Beecher opposes the paying of tythes for the saine. They pay for drift nets the 20th fish in these parishes.

At the mouth of the Harbour of Beerehaven the channel betwixt the W. point of the Island of Beerehaven and the mainland is not half a mile broad. There will be at least 20 saines out in Bantry Bay this season, 2 boats and 15 men to each saine.

On Tuesday, being St Barnaby's day, I confirmed four persons in Mr. Hutchins' house at Beerehaven. I gave amongst the Protestants 4 common prayer books, and 1 of Tillotson's 6 sermons and 5 little books.

On Tuesday, 11th of June, I went to view the Churches of Kilmannah, and returned to Beerehaven at night. The same day I viewed the church of Killaghaneenah. The church of Killaghaneenah stands within a small mile of Dunbwy, als. Beerehaven, the walls are standing uncovered, it would be the most proper church to be rebuilt for the parishes of Killaghaneenah, Kilmannah, Kilkatierin and Kilkaskan, and the minister to live at Dunbwy, als. Beerehaven.

On Tuesday, 11th of June, 1700, I went from Dunbwy, als. Beerehaven, to view the Church of Kilmannah.

Camomile.

Kilmannah Church, 3 miles from Bantry. We went to it over Knockooragh, from which hill we saw the Dorses, the Cow, a steep rock off Dorses, the Skellix Islands, and Hog Island beyond Kinmare river. In the Skellix a fowl of as big as a goose breeds.

No Protestants here in this parish.

This parish lies to the N.W. of Beerehaven, it extends northward to the river of Kinmare. 9 plowlands and 9 gnives in this parish, some of it is the best land on this side of the Bay of Bantry. The sheep grow fat here, they often die with excess of fat. There grows camomil in great plenty upon the hills here, on which the cows and sheep feed.

The Lord Altham has all the lands of this parish.

About 12 acres of glebe near the church, to the S. of it, and about 2 acres about 500 yards from the church on the south-west is glebe. Captain Boyd pretends to a house on the 12 acres near the church, but without any reason, for as much as I can hear. The intire Rectory belongs to Mr. Holmes, 'tis worth about £7 p. an. This parish and several other plowlands are in the mannor of Altham.

The parish church stands on the N.W. side of Beerehaven, near the mouth of Kinmare river, the greatest part of the walls are standing, it was built of stone and clay, it is about 50 foot long and 16 broad. The land for about a mile square about the church is good, the rest of the country is very coarse mountain, rocky and boggy. The Dorses are west of this church at about 4 miles' distance. The Dorses is in the parish of Killaghaneenah. Off of the Dorses is the Cow and Calf, 2 rocks in the sea. There are the ruins of a house near the church, but not reckoned to belong to the church. There is a cabin near the church where the Rector's house stood. There is no churchyard but a little spot on the S. side of the church. There was, as it is said, formerly a house for monks here, and from thence it was called Kilmannah, Monagh signifies monk in Irish. The 13 March, Mochery, als Mochevoge's day, is observed in this parish.

Kilkatierin parish lies to the east of Kilmannah towards Bantry, it extends to Kinmare river. It is bounded on the west and south and east by the parish of Killaghaneenagh, on the N. by Kinmare river, some part of this not far from the church is separated from the rest of it by Killaghneenagh parish.

The Lord Altham has all the lands of this parish.

All the inhabitants of this parish are Papists.

About 12 plowlands in this parish very coarse land. Glebe in 3 parcels about 10 acres plantation measure. There are the ruins of a chappel at Coulagh in this parish. The intire Rectory belongs to Mr. Holmes. 'Tis worth about £7 per annum.

The last of January in this parish they observe St Katierin's day, it is said she was an Irish saint in St Patrick's time. In most of these parishes they observe the day of the Saint of the parish. The families of O'Sullevans, O'Donegans, etc., have their peculiar saints.

The Church of Kilkatierin to the N.E. of Dunbwy, als. Beerehaven towards the river of Kinmare. Part of Kilkatierin lies at some distance from the rest of the parish.

Kilkaskan parish is bounded on the west with part of the parish of Killaghneenagh, on the south with Bantry bay, on the N. with part of Kerry, on the east with Kilmaccomoge. The Church of Kilkaskan about a mile from the shore of Bantry bay about half-way betwixt Bantry and Beerehaven. Bonane and Dromfennah, in the County of Kerry, are in this parish. The Vicar enjoys this portion of the tythes of these towns, and so does the Archdeacon. The east side of Daad O'Huologhan is in this parish.

The Earl of Anglesey has all the lands of this parish that are in the County of Corke, set in a long lease which Mr. John Davys enjoys. The Bp. of Corke has Drumfennah. The Archdeacon of Rosse has half the tythes of this parish, the Vicar the other half. The Vicar's part is worth about £10 p. an. No glebe in this parish.

There are the ruins of a chappel at Dromfennah, and a little piece of glebe near the chappel worth little or nothing.

All the inhabitants in this parish are papists except one Downing, a convert, who lives in Bonane.

John Mulconry is popish priest of this parish, he has been there about 20 years.

McKaskan the Patron of this parish.

Dr. Michael Boyle, Bp. of Corke, was in possession of many chiefries in this parish, viz., out of 4 plowlands and a half in Kilkaskan, and out of most of the other lands. These lands were forfeited by O'Sullevane, and his estate was passed in patent to the Earl of Anglesey.

Ald. Lynchy of Kilkaskan saies he formerly paid to the Bp. of Corke a chiefry of 3s. p. an. for 9 gnives of Drumfennagh. The other 9 gnives are held as 'tis said, by patent.

On Wednesday, 12th of June, 1700 I left Dunbwy, als. Beerehaven, and returned by boat to Bantry.

From *Bishop Dive Downes' Visitation of His Diocese*

Jaques Fontaine

1704

A HUGUENOT REFUGEE FROM persecution in France, the Reverend Jaques de la Fontaine (1658–1728) lived first in England and transferred to Cork with his family in 1694. He tried his hand at a number of ventures before establishing a farming and fishing community at Bank Harbour near Berehaven in 1699. The Fontaines experienced many vicissitudes during their nine years in Beara, and eventually moved to Dublin. For his children Fontaine wrote an account of his family history and eventful life, which included the following incident from their time in Beara.

Early in the morning of the first day of June 1704, a French privateer hove in sight; she floated gently towards the house in a perfect calm. She had on board four of my Irish neighbours to act as guides, in addition to eighty men of her own. She mounted ten guns. I watched her progress, and thought the intention was to bring her to the south of my house, so that her guns would bear directly upon the front, and have full scope at high water. I would prevent this if it were possible, and so I mustered all the men I could find, exactly twenty in number. I gave the Protestants muskets and the Papists

Jaques Fontaine.

clubs, on their shoulders, which made them, at a distance, look like armed men. I ordered them to follow me and do as I did. We went round the little cove, stooping very low as if we wished to hide ourselves, though in reality I made choice of the highest ground in order that we might certainly be seen from the privateer. I then placed all the men behind a large rock near the shore, while I stood alone on top of it, within sight of the vessel. I ordered them all to appear on one side of the rock, as if they were peeping out of curiosity, while I was looking the other way; then I turned and made angry gesticulations as if I were finding fault and striking some of them, and, at the same time, I told them all to show their heads on the other side of the rock. I turned again and appeared to be very anxious that they should conceal themselves. The enemy having seen, as they thought, forty men behind the rock did not deem it expedient to effect their landing at a point so well guarded: thus my manoeuvre produced exactly the effect I intended it should, and they turned about towards the mouth of the creek on which my house stood; and there they were opposite to one corner of the house, from which point their fire would be comparatively without effect. They dared not venture up the creek for fear of getting aground at low water. When I saw that they had decided upon their position, I took my men back by a low path, and this time I made them really hide themselves, so that those in the vessel could not see one of us returning from the rock. I took the Protestants into the house to assist in our defence, and sent the Papists away. The privateer cast anchor about a long musket shot from the house, and the lieutenant landed with about twenty men. I had seven men with me, in addition to my wife and children; four or five of these were of very little use. I placed them all at different windows; I posted myself in one of the towers over the door, and as the lieutenant was advancing, with every appearance of confidence in his mien, I fired at him with a blunderbuss loaded with small leaden balls, one of which entered his neck above the shoulder-blade, and another his side. He took aim at me before he fell, but his fire was too high. While I was gone to fetch another loaded piece from the next room, his men took him up, crossed the ditch, and carried him back to the ship. The captain, furious at such unexpected resistance from a minister, sent twenty more men ashore, with another commander and two small cannon; these they placed under cover of the rocks and hedges, and cannonaded the house from the north, while the guns on board the vessel fired at us from the south-east. I must acknowledge that, being unaccustomed to this sort of music, I felt some little tremors of fear when the first cannon ball struck the house; but I instantly humbled myself internally before my Maker, and having committed myself, both soul and body, to His keeping, my courage revived, and I suffered no more from fear. I put my head out of the window to see what effect the ball had produced on our stone wall and when I perceived it had only made a slight scratch I cried out with joy, 'Courage, my dear children, their cannon balls have no more effect on our stone walls than if they were so many apples.'

An officer was then in my house, with whom I had been conversing the evening before on what would be my prospect of success if I were to defend myself on such an occasion as the present, and he thought I should have no chance, because, he said, a cannon would overthrow my house with as much ease as if it were a castle of cards; and this opinion of his, I verily believe, occasioned me the apprehension of which I have just now spoken, but which was only perceptible to myself and my Heavenly Father, who in answer to my petition, had dissipated my fears. John MacLiney, a brave Scotchman, who was stationed at a window which overlooked the cannon on shore, having fired repeatedly without any apparent effect, at last put a double charge of powder into his musket, and killed a man who was pointing the cannon. This obliged them to alter the position of their battery, and they moved their cannon to the foot of the wall, and sheltered themselves behind a rock about thirty paces from the north-east corner of the house, where everyone was protected from our fire, except the men who reloaded the cannons. The new position was much more favourable for us, because, being at one corner of the house, they could not strike the walls or injure anything but the slates on the roof. During the whole battle there were two or three hundred Irishmen collected on a neighbouring height, watching the conflict, rejoicing in the anticipation of our defeat, and waiting impatiently for the moment when they might come down and help to plunder. A Frenchman, named Paul Roussier, a brave man and a skilful soldier, was in the garret opposite to the enemies' battery; he constructed a sort of rampart of sheeps' fleeces, then made a hole through the slates, and from thence he fired without the slightest intermission, a fresh loaded piece being handed to him from below directly after he had fired: and he killed one of them. They, on their part, kept up a continual fire with the cannons against the house, and the pirates from the vessel fired with small arms upon our windows, which we had barricaded with mattresses and large books. At the commencement of the action some of our muskets were a little out of order. The officer who was loading for Paul Roussier had put in the ball before the powder (by which you may judge of his confusion), and seeing my wife enter the room, who was here and there and everywhere, carrying ammunition and giving encouragement both by her words and her manner – he went up to her, and taking her by the hand he said: 'Alas, my dear lady, we are undone; it would be the height of folly to attempt to resist any longer when our arms are in bad order; here are no less than three

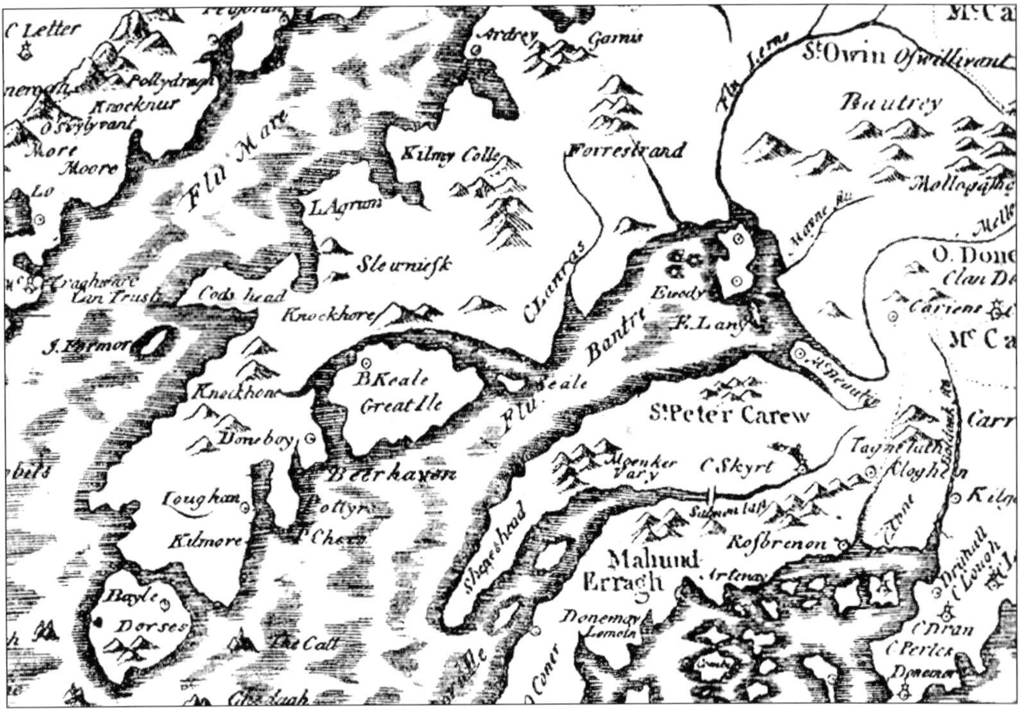

Beara, in a 17th century map from Thomas Stafford's Pacata Hibernia, *published in 1633.*

useless muskets' (observe we had eighteen muskets, two blunderbusses, and several pistols). My wife replied with her usual composure: 'We are in the hands of the Almighty, and nothing can befall us without His permission. I trust he will not suffer us to fall into the hands of these wicked men. We must not lose our courage; but try if we cannot repair what is defective.' She then came to me where I was on duty, and told me to go into the parlour directly to encourage the people, and do away with the alarm caused by this faint-hearted gentleman. I went immediately and examined the three muskets; one wanted a flint, another had some dirt in the touch-hole, and the third had two cartridges in it, one on top of the other, and a ball below both, next to the touch-hole. I laughed at him a little, and from that time there was no further complaint of arms being out of order. My wife was so entirely free from fear, that when she went to fetch a needle for me to broach the muskets from a place where the balls where coming in at the window like hail, she did not think of stooping until I called out to her to do so. The children were a good deal alarmed when the balls struck the roof and made the slates fly, which she perceiving said to them: 'Courage, my children, we are in the hands of God, and it is not fear that will ensure our safety; on the contrary, God will bless our courage. If you cannot fire yourselves, you can load the muskets for your father and others, who are older and stronger than you are; drive away all fear, if you can, and leave the care of your persons to God.' This address of hers to the children had a great effect upon the older persons present, and seemed to inspire them with new courage and confidence. Ere long, however, we had serious cause for anxiety; our powder was becoming so scarce that we felt as if we ought to be sparing in the use of it. We were in great perplexity: if we did not continue the same fire, we thought the enemy would perceive the difference, and attack with fresh vigour; to go on at the rate we were using it we had not more than enough for three hours; we had only twelve pounds at the outset. 'Great God! it was then that Thou discouraged our enemies and showed us their backs.' Claude Bonnet, a French soldier, seeing one of them run away, went forward to take aim at him, and just at that moment a ball from the enemy struck against the house, rebounded, and entered the fleshy part of his arm, without touching the bone. This showed us that if we had been spared, it was to God that we owed it, and to Him we should return our thanks. My dear wife was the surgeon; she had him laid upon a bed without any noise, and applied the first dressing to the wound with her own hands.

The battle lasted from eight o'clock in the morning till four in the afternoon, and during that whole time there was never the least cessation in the firing, except for a few minutes when the first man was killed. We had no one wounded but Claude Bonnet, and one of the children from a piece of slate striking against his thumb. The enemy had three men killed and seven wounded, as we learnt afterwards from the Irishmen who were on board. When the assailants had returned to the vessel, we visited the stations they had occupied, and found a quantity of blood, which they had evidently tried to hide by treading earth and leaves into the ground. The privateer remained at anchor for some time, and we were afraid they meditated a second attack, for which we were badly prepared, being so near the end of our powder; but we determined that if they did land again that we would only fire when we could take aim. While we were waiting the development of their plans, we took some nourishment, which was much needed after our fatigue. I had given each one a large glass of sherry when we entered the house on our return from the rock first thing in the morning; and after that, during the whole action, I did not permit anyone to take a drop of wine, or spirit, or strong beer. We had the satisfaction in a short time of seeing them draw up their anchor and sail away; and we returned thanks to God for our glorious deliverance. I immediately wrote a full account of the affair to Lord Cox, then Lord Chancellor of Ireland, and to the Duke of Ormond, who was Lord Lieutenant.

From *A Huguenot Hero of Berehaven in 1704*

Charles Smith

1750

BORN IN WATERFORD, CHARLES SMITH (c.1715–1762) worked for many years as an apothecary in Dungarvan before making a name for himself as a county historian. He wrote his first book, *The Antient and Present State of the County of Down*, in collaboration with Walter Harris. Published in 1744, it was the first-ever Irish county history on a large scale. That same year Smith founded the Physico-Historical Society in Dublin to provide topographical materials for a series of county histories. He went on to publish histories of Waterford, Kerry, and Cork, from which this excerpt is taken.

Bear and Bantry compose but one barony; it is very large but barren and desolate, there being but two or three resident Clergy in the barony; but what it wants in the goodness of the land is amply made up by the noblest bays in the world, that of Bantry being capable of containing all the shipping in Europe: this bay is also called Bear-haven, and has given title of Viscount to the family of Berkley, who were Viscounts Fitz-Harding of Bear-haven. A branch of the O'Sullivans in Spain have also assumed the title of Counts or Earls of Bear-haven: It at present gives title of Viscount to the Right Hon. Walter Chetwynd, created Viscount Chetwynd of Bear-haven, and Baron of Rathdown, in the county of Wicklow, Anno 1717, the 3rd of George I.

The town of Bantry is seated at the bottom of this extensive bay, on the E. side. It was formerly called Ballygobbin, as also the Old Town, to distinguish it from another settlement more to the N. called the New Town, where Ireton had a fortification erected, with 4 regular bastions, which caused the inhabitants to build near it; but when this fort went to decay, they returned by degrees to the Old Town, called Bantry, from its being the chief settlement of this half barony. A few years ago, when the Pilchards frequented this bay, it was a very thriving town, but for want of imployment is again fallen into decay. Near it stood a Franciscan abbey, founded Anno 1460 by Dermot O'Sullivan, now entirely demolished. In many creeks round this bay are several fish palaces, as they are called, built for saving, preserving, and salting of Pilchards, of which commodity several thousand pounds worth have been sent from hence to Spain, Portugal, and Italy; but of late years there has not a single Pilchard appeared on the coast. The Sullivans had formerly several good seats round this bay; that of Rinedizart was demolished by a ship of war in Oliver Cromwell's time: They had another at Black-Rock, where there is now a good house of Samuel Hutchinson, Esq; Three rivers fall into this bay from the N. viz. Moyallab river, being the most eastern, next to Bantry, which empties itself down a steep rock into the bay, neither salmon nor trout can go up into it, so that it is quite destitute of either; the Ouvane, i.e. the middle river, and the western river called Curloom. In the town of Bantry is a barrack for a foot company, and a decent parish church; it formerly gave title of Baron to Roper Viscount Baltinglass. The bay of Bantry is 26 miles long, and in most places above a league broad; in the midst of it are 40 fathom water: There are few strands round it, the coasts being all high stupendous rocks. The entrance of this bay is formed by the mountains of Bear-haven to the N. W. and Sheep's-Head point to the S.E. On the larboard hand lies the island of Bear-haven; all the W. side is one continued chain of lofty mountains, running far up the country to the N. and dividing the counties of Cork and Kerry; they were antiently called Vallis Juncosa, and were the retreat of the antient Irish, soon after the arrival of the English, from whence they scarce stirred till the divisions of the houses of York and Lancaster obliged many of the latter to quit the country; upon which the Irish came once more into the lower grounds to the great annoyance of the remaining English. The island of Whiddy, antiently Fucida Insula, lies opposite the town of Bantry; it is a pleasant spot of a triangular form, and the soil is excellent: In it Richard White, Esq; (whose property it is) has a deer park, where are both a fresh and salt water lake at no great distance from each other. The deer are very fat, and this island produces as large mutton as any in the county of Limerick, where the largest in Ireland is said to be; and it is not unpleasant to see the small Bantry mutton (also exceeding fat and good in its kind) compared to this of Whiddy Island, which bears no proportion to it as to bigness. In this island are good orchards, and also a profitable hop-yard; it abounds with hares, as the owner suffers none to be killed. Near Whiddy Island are some small ones, viz. Horse-Island, Hog-Island, Chapel-Island, and Coney-Island, and all these fatten lean horses in the spring season to admiration.

From Bantry to Bear-haven by land, there is nothing remarkable, except the iron furnaces at Comolin, which have been in a thriving condition for some years past, but wood begins to grow very scarce. In the bay of Glangariff, and towards the N. W. part of Bantry bay, they dredge up large quantities of a coral sand, found to be a most excellent manure, and lasts in the ground above 20 years. At Ross Mac-Owen, midway between Bear-haven and Bantry, lives Mr. Murtough O'Sullivan, a person well known in those parts; he and his elder brother, who is commonly called Mac-Fineen Duff, who lives near the river of Kinmare, are the chief remains of the O'Sullivan family in this country. There is in Spain a descendant of O'Sullivan Bear, who is enobled and called there Count of Bear-Haven; and is also said to be hereditary Governor of the Groyne.

Not far from Ross-Mac-Owen is one of the largest and highest waterfalls in this kingdom. This cataract is very visible from the town of Bantry, at least 14 miles distant from it: The water is collected from various small rivulets and springs, forming a large lake on the top of a vast high rocky, and almost perpendicular mountain, called Hungry Hill, which is at least 700 yards above the level of the bay of Bantry. The water cascades from the top of this mountain in a beautiful sheet, at least ten yards broad, which expands as it falls; about half the height of the mountain it dashes perpendicular on a prominent rock, from whence a mist arises almost a third part of the hill, which in some particular stations, the sun's rays playing on it, and meeting with the eye of a spectator, must make a charming appearance; these kind of mists in such positions generally reflecting the colours of the Iris; hence it falls from rock to rock, till it has passed the rugged declivity of Hungry-Hill; and before it gains the ocean, it has another fall cascading in an arch over a lower hill, all which make a fine sight as one sails up and down the bay. But those who are curious will not murmur at the labour they may have in visiting every part of this noble cataract. . . .

Castle-Town, alias Castle-Dermot, is a small village of little note, opposite to the island of Bear-haven, which is about 6 miles long, is very coarse, mountainous, and rugged, yet is of great use in defending this noble bay from the fury of the S.W. winds; so as vessels within the island may ride secure . . .

S.E. from Castle-Dermot stood the celebrated castle of Dunboy, which in the year 1602 was taken by Sir George Carew, after a most obstinate and vigorous defence. Crossing a rude uncultivated country to the W. the river of Kinmare (as it is called, though really a large bay of the ocean) appears. The E. side of the mouth of this river is in this county, and farther up both sides belong to that of Kerry.

From hence one has a prospect of the Durseys, antiently called Bea Insula. This island is very strong by nature, because of the difficulty of landing which is convenient but by one narrow entrance, that might be defended by a few hands, and was formerly fortified with a castle, by some mistaken for the ruins of an abbey; besides, it is impossible to arrive at this spot but in a dead calm; the least gale of wind raising such billows, as it is very dangerous for any boat to come near the shore. This seemingly impregnable place was chosen by the Irish, after the defeat of the Spaniards, for their last refuge, if Dunboy should be taken by the English. They committed the custody of it to Connor O'Driscoll, son and heir to Sir Fineen O'Driscoll, who procured three pieces of Spanish ordnance to be conveyed into this island, with stores, ammunition and 60 men, which fortified it (as they imagined) against the most potent enemy; but they were soon obliged to surrender it to Captain Rostock, who demolished the forts, and brought off the garrison prisoners to the camp at Dunboy, where they were all executed. This island is exceedingly rough and coarse, and is about three Irish miles long.

From the S. part of Bantry bay to the N. there are but two passages by which one can go into Kerry; that on the N. end is a most rugged, dangerous one, called the Priest's Leap, and well known in this country, from whence the road leads over the mountain of Mangerton, justly esteemed one of the highest in Ireland. Among these wild tracts are here and there some yew trees remaining of a very large size, they were formerly in greater plenty; as was also the Arbutus or strawberry tree, which is celebrated to flourish in such soils.

By the 18th century the Mare's Tail Waterfall at Hungry Hill had begun to attract visitors from afar.

Arbutus fairest in wild tracts arise.

There were plenty of red deer in this country, but they are of late becoming exceeding rare.

From *The Antient and Present State of the County and City of Cork*

Arthur O'Neill

C.1752

ONE OF THE LAST ITINERANT harpers, Arthur O'Neill was born in County Tyrone in 1734. He became blind in early childhood and was taught the harp to prepare him for the career he was to follow. He won each of the three harp festivals held at Granard in 1781, 1782 and 1785. In 1808 O'Neill was appointed resident master of the newly formed Belfast Irish Harp Society. The venture lasted for only five years, after which O'Neill returned to County Tyrone, where he died in 1818.

Arthur O'Neill.

I travelled the principal part of the County of Cork without anything occurring worth relating. I spent one Christmas with a gentleman that lived in Berehaven named Murtagh MacOwen O'Sullivan, who lived in a princely style. My boy came to me one morning when in bed, who desired me to bless myself. I asked him why so. 'Och Sir! there is a pipe of wine and two hogsheads of some other liquor standing up in the hall with the heads out of them and a wooden cup swimming in each of them for anyone that wishes to drink their skinful.' I mention this merely to record the hospitality of the gentlemen of the province of Munster.

Lord Kenmare, the principal proprietor of Killarney, the lake and the surrounding country, took it into his head to give a Milesian entertainment, that is, to entertain at Christmas time every Milesian that could be found that bore the name of an Irish chieftain, which names are, the O'Neills, the O'Briens, the MacCarthys, the O'Donoghues, the O'Driscolls, the O'Connors, the O'Donovans, the O'Sullivans, the O'Connor Kerry, the MacNamaras, the O'Keeffes, the O'Meaghers, the O'Learys, the O'Callaghans, the O'Connells, the O'Mahonys, the MacGillacuddys, and some others of the Milesian race that my memory at present will not enable me to mention. At the feast there were one or more of every name (already mentioned) present but an O'Neill, which Lord Kenmare observed and mentioned. 'Och,' says my patron, Murreetagh MacOwen O'Sullivan, 'upon my honour I can soon fill up that gap for you, as I have now at my house a young man from the north who is blind and plays on the harp very well for his years, and from what I can understand from his own lips he has a good claim to represent on this occasion the O'Neills.' 'Well, send for him,' says my lord. I was sent for and was without any ceremony seated amongst them in the Great Hall before dinner. Hundreds of questions were asked me concerning my descent, and on my giving them satisfactory answers I was dubbed and deemed an O'Neill, for they all said I had a very genteel mug (a good face), etc., etc.

When dinner was announced, very near two hundred of the O's and Mac's took their seats, and poor self being blind I done what blind men always do – I groped a vacancy near the foot of the table; and such a noise of cutting, carving, roaring, laughing, shaking hands, and such language as generally occurs between friends who only see each other once a year, I never before or since witnessed. While dinner was going on I was hob-nobbed by almost every gentleman present. But when Lord Kenmare hob-nobbed me he was pleased to say, 'O'Neill, you should be at the head of the table, as your ancestors were the original Milesians of this Kingdom.' 'Oh, my lord,' says I, 'it's no matter where an O'Neill sits, and let it be at what part of the table I am, it should be considered the head of it.' A universal burst of applause ensued, and my arm was almost shaken from my body by all present, and I believe it was in consequence of my reply to his lordship, which they remarked came by instinct to an O'Neill; and damn the O'Neill that ever was born or that will ever yet be born as well as myself but was drank by all the Milesians then present.

From *Carolan: The Life, Times and Music of an Irish Harper*

Richard Pococke

1758

HAMPSHIRE-BORN RICHARD POCOCKE (1704–1765) followed family tradition and became a clergyman. He is known for fostering technical instruction in Ireland, but his true avocation was travel – in continental Europe, Egypt, the Middle East, England, Scotland and Ireland – of which he kept records. As bishop of Ossory, he undertook a tour of Cork and Kerry in the summer of 1758. Accompanied by a valet and groom, he travelled on horseback and by boat. Pococke's observations were recorded in informative letters to his sister Elizabeth. Two centuries elapsed before this correspondence was first published, after Cork County Librarian Pádraig Ó Maidín came across it in the Bodleian Library, Oxford.

Beerhaven Aug. 2 1758

Dear Madam,

About eight miles from this place is the Sound between the land & Durray Island, which is about 200 fathoms over, but a boat cannot cross except it is very Calm weather & when there is no great swell. This Island is about three miles long & a mile wide; the Cliffs are high to the north & there is a descent to the South; it is a fine pasturage, & consists of nine small plough lands & belongs to [ ] who have property on the adjoyning continent; in the 3 parishes are 800 families, & only about 8 of them Protestants, & notwithstanding the laws can be executed here better than in other parts of Kerry. In the heigth of the Island are fine Springs of water which never fail. They begin to fill to prevent Moss; they keep here Sheep & black Cattle, but they often fall off the Cliffs; they swim 'em over tyed to boats: They have a small berry, not seen any where near, & is probably the same I saw at 3 Castle head, I observ'd London pride growing about Beerhaven. There are near twenty Roman families in this Island, some of them natives of it. The Privateers kept this island in Queen Annes wars & water'd there, & the Government the Proprietors £50 a year for the rent of it, & all the people fled from it. On the Continent Privateers made contracts with the inhabitants who left their Cattle to be taken away by them, which they might otherwise have easily drove off; & they had such possession of Barhaven as to come & clean their Ships there. In the Island they draw up small boats at the place when they land, for there is no Creek or harbour. The large fishing boats harbour in Kilcuchine Bay, if I mistake not in the Cove call'd Lough Lan cove to the South east. About 7 or 8 leagues to the South west of Dursey, is a rock call'd Lae rock, about 30 fathom under water, here the fishing boats fix with a stone in summer in fair weather, & fish with lines for Hake, Cod & Ling which lay on the rocks: the Proprietors of the boats give 'em seven shillings for the first, & twenty for the others: Maiden Ling are about four feet long & Ling grow to seven feet in length; maiden ray are the small Skeat, & here they throw away this last kind both young & old: A

Richard Pocock.

small whale came ashore dead on this Coast some years agoe, the whale bone was about four feet long. When they can't fish off the rock they come & fish in the Sound or somewhere under the Shelter of this Dursey; but the fish caught off the rock is greatly preferable to it. They can legaly send no fish to France but Salmon, all the rest goes to Spain, or is run into France. It is to encourage their own fishery. People live here to a great age, notwithstanding they drink drams imoderately, living on fish & potatoes & the sea air may make this custom less pernicious, especially to some particular constitutions. They sit and drink Spirits as others drink wine: But the smallpox is very mortal among them: supposed to be owing to the first diet. A sort of scurvey also which sometimes comes near to a Leprosie is frequent among them. They have great notions of Fairies in all these parts, which take place of Witches in other places. Instead of laying a dead body tyed up in a sheet or blanket in which they are buryed without a Coffin. They lay the body on a form under a table & throw a Sheet over it. All workmen, tho' only making a ditch or threshing & all Sorts of Handicrafts in a private house or fields have the Shameful custom in these parts more than in any other, of holding a String or something a cross the way & begging money, more than in any other parts of Ireland, tho' it is pretty frequently done in the Country places. I am &c.

Beerhaven Aug. 5 1758

On the 31st we set out in a sail & row boat from Bantre & came in three leagues to Adragile harbor into which several streams fall from the high rocky mountains. We came here to see the famous Waterfall wch has been so much spoken of & is to the west. When we first saw it, it appear'd like a vein of Sparr in the rocky mountains; we walk'd about 2 miles to it. The whole mountain is call'd Hungry Hill, the top of which is computed to be 700 yards above the sea, but I do not think it so much, the upper part is very steep, it may be about one third of the heigth; at the foot of this eminence is a lake on that part of the mountain call'd Coumgira (the crooked clog) the water comes from the lake first in a gentle declivity; it may be two hundred & fifty feet perpendicular, it may then fall down the rock which is very steep about as much more to a Shelf, which may be 100 feet broad, from this it may fall down about 450 feet down the rocks near perpendicular & after that it may be 100 feet in a gentle descent, & is not seen; it divides into several very narrow Streams close to each other, but when there is much water, it seems to have spread to the south it may be ten yards or more most part of the way down. The rock is beautiful on each side cover'd with Shrubs & particularly to the South, where it forms four or five hillocks all down the side of the hill with shallow valleys between 'em: Men went up to the Shelf to throw down Stones, which made a great noise, & in speaking to them we observ'd an Eccho, which I think repeated six syllables & one syllable four or five times, like the Eccho near Milan: they call the waterfall Mounlare (Mares stale). There is a fall to the north after rain which they call Eskimileen (Poets hillock) & another to the South which now Flow'd, it is a gentle declivity & is call'd (Geravilen) Rough Island. On an eminence above the rivlet to the South I saw four or five Stones, which they told me form'd a circle, the place is call'd Gustinereha, & was doubtless an ancient Druid Temple. We saw also some Strong Chalybeat Springs, which seem'd in taste to have a mixture of Sulphur. Camomile grows here: We had civilities shown us by a widow, the daughter of an old Proprietor, so we thought proper to take our provisions to her house, & accept of whatever civilities she could show us. We took boat & soon came up with the east point of Beerhaven Island which is two leagues long & about a mile broad, (there are many families in it: here are houses & no foxes, & a great number of foxes & no houses on the Continent, being destroy'd all by the foxes) forms the harbour of Beer haven, which is of that length & about half a league broad, & would hold all the fleet of England; the passage in at the west end of it is about half a mile broad & is rocky & unsafe without a Pilot. There is no Village at this harbour, only small houses; they have a small Stone bridge here of red Coral, of which I could not get a Specimen. I went to see the remains of the Shores Castle of Dunboy to the south of the harbour, to which the Irish fled as their last resort in 1602, & when they were attack'd by Sr George Carew who planted 3 batteries against it, one on an eminence near it, & the two others on eminences to the north side of the harbour; here he took twenty five of the heads in the rebellion, who were all hang'd. I went to see the creek of Poleen two miles to the south west, where a rivlet call'd Copel rising out of several lakes abounding in trouts, forms a beautifull Cascade, falling down an easy descent in several Streams, for about 30 feet perpendicular heigth. On the west side of this Creek is some free stone in an hill over which the road leads to the Dorteep Island; on the east side of the Creek is a Cave, into which they can go only at Spring tydes, when there is no swell in the sea; it is said to be 50 yards long, forty feet broad & 20 high. This Creek is a good fishing place; they draw the Sein to a little Island in it, the harbour being rocky all around. The Mountains have good pasturage on them, & they make huts & keep their cattle on the mountain in summer & live on new churn butter & milk. They marry very young, the women at 13, the men at 16, &

those of condition are call'd Gentlemen of good families, chiefly the Sulivans, have a way of portioning their daughters by what they call Coleprits; they go round all their relations & friends who give each family an Head of black cattle, they call it lending; for the compliment is return'd as occasion offers; but if they take of their inferiors it is only understood to be purchasing their protection & friendship & no return is made; the mother & sisters go about to get Sheep & this goes for the fortune of the Daughter, & they make up from 40 to 200 head of Cattle in this way. These Gentlemen have about 300 acres each, most of it let out, & the Tenants are entirely at their command, & are heads of these little Clans, which have been of late reduc'd to great poverty. For one of the Principal of them, Martogh Oge O Sulivan who had been a forreign officer & outlaw'd & proclaimed for a rescue for a seizure, & returning was told, that one Puxley the Surveyor (by whose widow I was entertain'd) had said he would take him: On which about five years agoe he & two more shot him from a smith's forge, as he was going to Church, he liv'd about three hours. Part of the army were sent to take the assasins but miscarried & went off; & return'd upon them in a wet night, where 20 of 'em were asleep in a house, they set fire to the house & all of 'em escap'd except the true Martogh being kill'd on the spot, & the two others taken & quarter'd at Cork, & the three heads were set up publick place. This broke the Combination, & they have been since kept under by the excessive high rents they are oblig'd to pay. The three Parishes united here, which make up the whole County of Cork, consist of a hundred Plough lands which may be about 1000 acres each; the land is let for about one Shilling an acre; Twelve Geneva's make plough land & four Cusses a Geneve. Another told me that 36 acres make a Geneve, which is about 250 acres to a plough land; but there are ploughlands of 1500 acres, so that the quantity may probably make up 250 acres. They have a Custom of Shooleing or corstuming about, the former is rather an expression of Spunging, the latter of visiting those you entertain again, – that is those of a family who are very poor, go from house to house, & must have the best of every thing, which is a great oppression on the poor people. I am &c.

Berehaven in August 1888, three hundred and thirty years after Richard Pococke's visit.

Milltown in the County of Kerry Aug. 12 1758

On the 2nd I set out on horseback from Beerhaven, to cross the head of land northwards. In the way to the Church we pass'd a narrow defilee between rocks, over which are the ruins of a smiths forge, from which Martogh oge Sulivan shot Mr. Puxley, he first saw blood on his hands when he was wounded & thought his own pistols had gone off; the second volley came on him as soon as he pass'd the rock & twenty balls were found in him. As soon as it was over Maclogh & his two bravoes went & stood behind the rocks near in sight of everybody, & drank a bottle of Brandy, he then went to Mass, & said, if any one was sorry for Puxley death they might go & cry over him, concerning which I am thus particular, because it was the most villanous, audacious & extraordinary act, that probably was ever committed. Passing on I saw on an eminence a circle of stones, & near us to the right, two stones near each other & about twelve feet high, being larger than I had seen, except the single stone near Roaring water. I was inform'd of one about 15 feet high, a mile from Roaring water in the way to Bantry. They say there are many of these circles in these western parts, as there are in Cornwall; which is a proof that the Druid worship provail'd more to the west than in other parts of these Islands. We came to a rivlet call'd the Inches near the sea on the north side of the land. This rivlet forms a beautiful cascade, in three or 4 falls thro' the rocks, the whole making a cascade about 30 feet perpendicular. I observ'd several very strong chalybeat springs, not far from the sea; and at Beer they have found Lead ore, of which I have a specimen, but they do not pursue it: To the north of this river are the ruins of Martogh Oge's house, which was never repair'd, after it was burn't. When the army first came, he was always on the neighbouring mountains & saw them looking after him, & with his companions made a jest of them, but the last affair was very well conducted by Mr. Fitzsimmonds, the nephew of Mr. Puxley & is now in the same office; They came by water, landed near the house & surrounded it, & the besieg'd fir'd upon them, so were forc'd to burn the house. We came to Coolagh bay where a row boat & sail met me, & I embark'd for Kerry.

From *Richard Pococke's Irish Tours*

Arthur Young

1776

ARTHUR YOUNG (1741–1820) spent much of his life in Suffolk, where he carried out numerous agricultural experiments on his farm. He founded and for many years edited the monthly *Annals of Agriculture*, and was regarded as the most prolific and influential agriculturalist of his day. In 1776 he went to Ireland to research a book. Unfortunately his servant stole his trunk along with his travel journal, so Young had to recreate his entire trip from memory. After the death of his beloved youngest daughter, Young was a broken man, finding solace in religious fanaticism.

September 25th, the road to Nedeen, through the wildest region of mountains that I remember to have seen; it is a dreary, but an interesting road. The various, horrid, grotesque, and unusual forms in which the mountains rise, and the rocks bulge; the immense heights of some distant heads, which rear above all the nearer scenes, the torrents roaring in the vale, and breaking down the mountain sides, with here and there a wretched cabin, and a spot of culture yielding surprize to find human beings inhabitant of such a scene of wildness, altogether keep the traveller's mind in an agitation and suspence. These rocks and mountains are many of them no otherwise improvable than by planting, for which, however, they are exceedingly well adapted.

Arthur Young.

Sir John was so obliging as to send half a dozen labourers with me, to help my chaise up a mountain side, of which he gave formidable account; in truth it deserved it. The road leads directly against a mountain ridge, and those who made it were so incredibly stupid that they kept the strait line up the hill, instead of turning aside to the right, to wind around a projection of it. The path of the road is worn by torrents into a channel, which is blocked up in places by huge fragments, so that it would be a horrid road on a level; but on a hill so steep that the best path would be difficult to ascend, it may be supposed terrible; the labourers, two passing strangers, and my servant, could with difficulty get the chaise up. It is much to be regretted that the direction of the road is not changed, as all the rest from Cork to Nedeen is good enough. For a few miles towards the latter place the country is flat on the river Kenmare; much of it good, and under grass or corn. Passed Mr. Orpine of Ardtilly, and another of the same name at Killowen.

Nedeen is a little town, very well situated, on the noble river Kenmare, where ships of 150 tons may come up. There are but three or four good houses. Lord Shelburne, to whom the place belongs, has built one for his agent. There is a vale of good land, which is here from a mile and a half to a mile broad; and to the north and south, great ridges of mountains said to be full of mines.

At Nedeen, Lord Shelburne had taken care to have me well informed by his people in that country, which belongs to the greatest part to himself. He has about 150,000 Irish acres in Kerry; the greatest part of the barony of Glanrought belongs to him, most of Dunkerron and Ivragh.

The country is all a region of mountains by a vale of flat land on the river; the mountains to the south come to the water's edge, with but a few variations, the principle of which is Ardee, a farm of Lord Shelburne's: to the north of the river, the flat land is one-half to three-quarters of a mile broad. The mountains to the south reach Bear-haven, and those to the north to Dingle Bay; the soil is extremely various, to the south of the river all are sand stones, and the hills loam, stone, gravel, and bog. The north there is a strip of lime-stone land, from Kilgarvan to Cabbina-cush, that is six miles east of Nedeen, and three to the West, but is not more than a quarter of a mile broad, the rest, including the mountains, all sand stone. As to its rents, it is very difficult to tell what they are: for land is let by the plough-land and gineves, 12 gineves to the plough-land; but the latter denomination is not of any particular quantity; for no two plough-lands are the same. The size of farms is various, from 40 acres to 1,000 less quantities go with cabbins, and some farmers are taken by labourers in partnership. Their tillage consists of potatoes measured by the peck of 84lb., manure for them with sea weed, three boat loads to an acre, each at 16s. 3d, the poor people use nothing else; but those who can afford it, lay dung with it. These potatoes are the first crop. Thirty pecks plant an acre, and it takes from twenty to thirty men to set an acre in a day.

From *A Tour in Ireland*

Theobald Wolfe Tone

1796

THEOBALD WOLFE TONE (1763–1798), the son of a Dublin coach-maker, studied at Trinity College and was called to the bar. He became secretary of the Catholic Committee in 1790 and the following year co-founded the Society of United Irishmen. Impatient with English rule, Tone turned to the French Republic for help. When discovered, he was obliged to take exile in America. He travelled to Paris in 1796 and persuaded the government to invade Ireland. That December they dispatched an expedition under Admiral Hoche, but foul weather scattered the fleet. Though Tone never set foot on Beara, this excerpt from his journal was written while his vessel, the *Indomptable*, was riding at anchor off Bere Island.

December 22, 1796: This morning, at eight, we have neared Bantry Bay considerably, but the fleet is terribly scattered; no news of the *Fraternité*; I believe it is the first instance of an admiral in a clean frigate, with moderate weather, and moonlight night, parting company with his fleet. Captain Grammont, our first lieutenant, told me his opinion is that she is either taken or lost, and, in either event, it is a terrible blow to us. All rests now upon Grouchy, and I hope he may turn out well; he has a glorious game in his hands, if he has spirits and talent to play it. If he succeeds, it will immortalise him. I do not at all like the countenance of the État-Major in this crisis. When they speak of the expedition, it is in a style of despondency, and, when they are not speaking of it, they are playing cards and laughing; they are every one of them brave of their persons, but I see nothing of that spirit of enterprise, combined with a steady resolution, which our present situation demands. They stared at me this morning when I said that Grouchy was the man in the whole army who had least reason to regret the absence of the General, and began to talk of responsibility and difficulties, as if any great enterprise was without responsibility and difficulties. I was burning with rage; however I said nothing, and will say nothing until I get ashore, if ever I am so happy as to arrive there. We are gaining the Bay by slow degrees, with a head wind at east, where it has hung these five weeks. To-night we hope, if nothing extraordinary happens, to cast anchor in the mouth of the Bay, and work up to-morrow morning; these delays are dreadful to my impatience. I am now so near the shore that I can see, distinctly, two old castles, yet I am utterly uncertain whether I shall ever set foot on it. According to appearances, Bouvet and Grouchy are resolved to proceed; that is a great point gained, however. Two o'clock; we have been tacking ever since eight this morning, and I am sure we have not gained one hundred yards; the wind is right ahead, and the fleet dispersed, several being far to leeward. I have been looking over the schedule of our arms, artillery, and ammunition; we are well provided. . . . Messieurs of the État-Major continue in the horrors; I find Simon the stoutest of them, and Fairin, Chérin's aide-de-camp, the worst; he puts me in mind of David in the 'Rivals,' 'But I am fighting Bob, and damn it, I won't be afraid.' I continue very discreetly to say little or nothing, as my situation just now is rather a delicate one; if we were once ashore, and things turn out to my mind, I shall soon be out of my trammels, and perhaps in that respect I may be better off with Grouchy than with Hoche. If the people act with spirit, as I hope they will, it is no matter who is General, and, if they do not, all the talents of Hoche would not save us, so it comes to the same thing at last. At half-past six, cast anchor off Bere Island, being still four leagues from our landing-place; at work with General Chérin, writing and translating proclamations, &c., all our printed papers, including my two pamphlets, being on board the *Fraternité*, which is pleasant.

December 23rd. Last night it blew a heavy gale from the eastward with snow, so that the mountains are covered this morning, which will render our bivouacs extremely amusing. It is to be observed, that of the thirty-two points of the compass, the E. is precisely the most unfavourable to us. In consequence we are this morning separated for the fourth time; sixteen sail, including nine or ten of the line, with Bouvet and Grouchy, are at anchor with us, and about twenty are blown to sea; luckily the gale set from the shore, so I am in hopes no mischief will ensue. The wind is still high, and, as usual, right ahead; and I dread a visit from the English, and altogether I am in great uneasiness. Oh! that we were once ashore, let what might ensue after; I am sick to the very soul of this suspense. It is curious to see how things are managed in this best of all possible worlds. We are here, sixteen sail, great and small, scattered up and down in a noble bay, and so dispersed that there are not two together in any spot, save one, and there they are now so close, that if it blows to-night as it did last night, they will inevitably run foul of each other, unless one of them prefers driving on shore. . . . The day has passed without the appearance of one vessel, friend or enemy, the wind rather more moderate, but still ahead. . . . I am now so near the shore, that I can in a manner touch the sides of Bantry Bay with my right and left hand, yet God knows whether I shall ever tread again on Irish ground. There is one thing which I am surprised at, which is the extreme *sang-froid* with which I view the coast. I expected I should have been violently affected, yet I look at it as if it were the coast of Japan; I do not, however, love my country the less, for not having romantic feelings with regard to her. Another thing, we are now three days in Bantry Bay; if we do not land immediately, the enemy will collect a superior force, and perhaps repay us our victory of Quiberon. In an enterprise like ours, everything depends upon the promptitude and audacity of our first movements, and we are here, I am sorry to say it, most pitifully languid. It is mortifying, but that is too poor a word; I could tear my flesh with rage and vexation, but that advances nothing, and so I hold my tongue in general, and devour my melancholy as I can. To come so near, and then to fail, if we are to fail! And every one aboard seems now to have given up all hopes.

December 24th. This morning the whole État-Major has been miraculously converted, and it was agreed, in full council, that General Chérin, Colonel Waudré, Chef d'État Major of the Artillery, and myself, should go aboard the *Immortalité*, and press General Grouchy in the strongest manner, to proceed on the expedition, with the ruins of our scattered army. Accordingly, we made a signal to speak with the Admiral, and in about an hour we were aboard. I must do Grouchy the justice to say, that the moment we gave our opinion in favour of proceeding, he took his part decidedly, and like a man of spirit; he instantly set about preparing the *ordre de bataille*, and we finished it without delay. We are not more than 6,500 strong, but they are tried soldiers, who have seen fire, and I have the strongest hopes that, after all, we shall bring our enterprise to a glorious termination. It is a bold attempt, and truly original. All the time we were preparing the *ordre de bataille*, we were laughing most immoderately at the poverty of our means, and I believe, under the

Ardnagashel House was home to the family of Tone's friend Hutchins from 1800 until 1947. It was destroyed by fire in 1958.

circumstances, it was the merriest council of war that was ever held; but '*Des Chevaliers français tel est le caractère.*' Grouchy, the commander-in-chief, never had so few men under his orders since he was Adjutant-General; Waudré, who is Lieutenant-Colonel, finds himself now at the head of the artillery, which is a furious park, consisting of one piece of eight, one of four, and two six-inch howitzers; when he was a Captain he never commanded fewer that ten pieces, but now that he is in fact General of the artillery, he prefers taking the field with four. . . . It is altogether an enterprise truly *unique*; we have not one guinea; we have not a tent; we have not a horse to draw our four pieces of artillery; the General-in-chief marches on foot; we leave all our baggage behind us; we have nothing but the arms in our hands, the clothes on our backs, and a good courage, but that is sufficient. . . . But this infernal easterly wind continues without remorse, and though we have been under way three or four hours, and made I believe three hundred tacks, we do not seem to my eyes to have gained one hundred yards in a straight line. One hour and a half of good wind would carry us up, and perhaps we may be yet two days. Damn it! damn it! I learn from a pilot whom I found aboard the Admiral, that my friend Hutchins lives within two miles of Bantry, and is now at home, so perhaps I may see him to-morrow; I wonder what kind of a meeting we shall have? When I saw him last he was a right good fellow, but so many changes happen in twenty months! At all events, he will be, I dare say, not a little surprised to see me with a blue coat on my back, and a national cockade in my hat. At six, cast anchor, having gained I think not less than fifty yards, to speak within bounds. The rapidity of our progress is the more amazing, when it is considered that we have been not much more than eight hours in covering that space of ground, and besides, we have a cool refreshing breeze from the east, which is truly delightful. Well, time and tide wait for no man. I may now say with the Probationary Odes, 'Sometimes it blows, sometimes it freezes, just as it pleases.' Well, let it blow and be hanged! I do not wonder to-night at Xerxes whipping the sea; for I find myself pretty much in the mood to commit some such rational action. To return to our expedition; the more I think of it, the more I find it amusing; as Johnson says: 'the negative catalogue of our means is extremely copious.' In addition to what I have mentioned already, we have no horses for our cavalry. Huzza! I apprehend we are to-night 6,000 of the most careless fellows in Europe, for everybody is in the most extravagant spirits on the eve of an enterprise, which, considering our means, would make many people serious. I never liked the French half so well as to-night, and I can scarcely persuade myself that the loungers of the Boulevards, and the soldiers I see about me, are of the same hemisphere. To judge the French rightly, or at least to see the bright part of their character, you must see them not in Paris, but in the camp. It is in the armies that the Republic exists. My enemy, the wind, seems just now, at eight o'clock, to relent a little, so we may reach Bantry by to-morrow. The enemy has now had four days to recover from his panic, and prepare to receive us; so much the worse, but I do not mind it. We purpose to make a race for Cork, as if the devil were in our bodies, and when we are fairly there, we will stop for a day or two to take breath, and look about us. From Bantry to Cork is about forty-five miles, which, with all our efforts, will take us three days, and I suppose we may have a brush by the way, but I think we are able to deal with any force that can, at a week's notice, be brought against us. . . . It is inconceivable how well that most inconceivable of all writers, Shakespeare, has hit off the French character in his play of *Henry V*. I have been struck with it fifty times this evening; yet it is highly probable he never saw a French officer in his life. Well, I have worked hard to-day. . . . I have written and copied fifteen letters, besides these memorandums. . . . I have but one observation to add: there is not, I will venture to say, one grenadier in the Compagnie Bloom that will not sleep to-night in his hammock more contentedly than the Archbishop of Dublin in a down bed. I presume our arrival has put several respectable characters in no small fuss, but time will show more of that.

December 25th. These memorandums are a strange mixture. Sometimes I am in preposterously high spirits, and at other times I am as dejected, according to the posture of our affairs. Last night I had the strongest expectations that to-day we should debark, but at two this morning I was awakened by the wind. I rose immediately, and, wrapping myself in my greatcoat, walked for an hour in the gallery, devoured by the most gloomy reflections. The wind continues right ahead, so that it is absolutely impossible to work up to the landing-place, and God knows when it will change. The same wind is exactly favourable to bring the English upon us, and these cruel delays give the enemy time to assemble his entire force in this neighbourhood . . . Had we been able to land the first day and march directly to Cork, we should have infallibly carried it by a *coup de main*, and then we should have a footing in the country; but as it is – if we are taken, my fate will not be a mild one; the best I can expect is to be shot as an *émigré rentré*, unless I have the good fortune to be killed in the action; for most assuredly if the enemy will have us he must fight for us. Perhaps I may be reserved for a trial, for the sake of striking terror into others, in which case I shall be hanged as a traitor, and embowelled, &c. As to the embowelling, '*je m'en fiche*'; if ever they hang me, they are welcome to embowel me if they please. These are pleasant prospects! Nothing on earth could sustain me now but the consciousness that I am engaged in a just and righteous cause. For my family I have, by a desperate effort, surmounted my natural feelings so far, that I do not think of them at this moment. . . . Our first capital error was in setting sail too late from the Bay of Camaret, by which means we were obliged to pass the Raz in the night, which caused the loss of the *Séduisant*, the separation of the fleet . . . and, above all, the loss of time resulting from all this, and which is never to be recovered. Our second error was in losing an entire day in cruising off the bay when we might have entered and effected a landing with thirty-five sail, which would have secured everything; and now our third error is having our commander-in-chief separated from the État-Major, which renders all communication utterly impossible. I see nothing before me, unless a miracle be wrought in our favour, but the ruin of the expedition, the slavery of my country, and my own destruction. Well, if I am to fall, at least I will sell my life as dear as individual resistance can make it. So now I have made up my mind. I have a merry Christmas of it to-day.

December 26th. Last night, at half after six o'clock, in a heavy gale of wind still from the east, we were surprised by the Admiral's frigate

Only one boat reached shore during the failed French expedition: a century later, an artist imagined the scene.

running under our quarter, and hailing the *Indomptable* with orders to cut our cable and put to sea instantly; the frigate then pursued her course, leaving us all in the utmost astonishment. Our first idea was that it might be an English frigate, lurking in the bottom of the bay, which took advantage of the storm and darkness of the night to make her escape, and wished to separate our squadron by this strategem; for it seems utterly incredible that an Admiral should cut and run in this manner, without any previous signal of any kind to warn the fleet, and that the first notice we should have of his intention should be his hailing us in this extraordinary manner with such unexpected and peremptory orders. After a short consultation with his officers (considering the storm, the darkness of the night, that we have two anchors out and only one spare one in the hold), Captain Bedout resolved to wait at all events till to-morrow morning, in order to ascertain whether it was really the Admiral who hailed us. The morning is now come, the gale continues, and the fog is so thick that we cannot see a ship's length ahead; so here we lie in the utmost uncertainty and anxiety. In all probability we are now left without Admiral or General; if so, Chérin will command the troops, and Bedout the fleet, but at all events there is an end of the expedition. Certainly we have been persecuted by a strange fatality from the very night of our departure to this hour. . . . Of forty-three sail, of which the expedition consisted, we can muster of all sizes but fourteen. There only wants our falling in with the English to complete our destruction; and, to judge of the future by the past, there is every probability that that will not be wanting. All our hopes are now reduced to get back in safety to Brest, and I believe we will set sail for that port the instant the weather will permit. . . . Notwithstanding all our blunders, it is the dreadful stormy weather and the easterly winds, which have been blowing furiously and without intermission since we made Bantry Bay, that have ruined us. Well, England has not had such an escape since the Spanish Armada, and that expedition, like ours, was defeated by the weather. . . . I hope the Directory will not dismiss me the service for this unhappy failure, in which, certainly, I have nothing personally to reproach myself with; and, in that case, I shall be rich enough to live as a peasant. If God Almighty sends me my dearest love and darling babies in safety, I will buy or rent a little spot and have done with the world for ever. I shall neither be great, nor famous, nor powerful, but I may be happy. . . . This infernal wind continues without intermission, and now that all is lost I am as eager to get back to France as I was to come to Ireland.

December 27th. Yesterday several vessels, including the *Indomptable*, dragged their anchor several times, and it was with great difficulty they rode out the gale. At two o'clock the *Revolution*, a seventy-four, made signal that she could hold no longer, and, in consequence of the Commodore's permission, who now commands our little squadron, cut her only cable and put to sea. In the night the *Patriote* and *Pluton*, of seventy-four each, were forced to put to sea, with the Nicomede flute, so that this morning we are reduced to seven sail of the line and one frigate. Any attempt here is now desperate, but I still think if we were debarked at the mouth of the Shannon we might yet recover all. At ten o'clock the Commodore made signal to get under way, which was delayed by one of the ships, which required an hour to get ready. This hour we availed ourselves of to hold a council of war, at which were present Generals Chérin and Hardy and Humbert, who came from their ships for that purpose; Adjutant-Generals Simons, Chasseloup, and myself; Lieut.-Col. Waudré, commanding the artillery, and Favory, Captain of Engineers, together with Commodore Bedout, who was invited to assist; General Hardy, as senior officer, being President. It was agreed that, our force being now reduced to 4,168 men, our artillery to two four-pounders, our ammunition to 1,500,000 cartridges and 500 rounds for the artillery, with 500 pounds of powder – this part of the country being utterly wild and savage, furnishing neither provisions nor horses, and especially as the enemy, having seven days' notice, together with three more which it would require to reach Cork, supposing we even met with no obstacle, had time more than sufficient to assemble his forces in numbers sufficient to crush our little army; considering, moreover, that this province is the only one of the four which has testified no disposition to revolt; that it is the most remote from the party which is ready for insurrection; and, finally, Captain Bedout having communicated his instructions, which are, to mount as high as the Shannon and cruise there five days, it was unanimously agreed to quit Bantry Bay directly, and proceed for the mouth of the Shannon in hopes to rejoin some of our scattered companions; and when we are there we will determine, according to the means in our hands, what part we shall take. . . . The wind, at last, has come round to the southward, and the signal is now flying to get under way. At half after four, there being every appearance of a stormy night, three vessels cut their cables and put to sea. The *Indomptable*, having with great difficulty weighed one anchor, we were forced at length to cut the cable of the other and make the best of our way out of the bay, being followed by the whole of our little squadron, now reduced to ten sail.

From *The Autobiography of Theobald Wolfe Tone 1763–1798*

Jacques Louis de Bougrenet

1797

In 1792 a Breton Royalist, Jacques Louis de Bougrenet, Chevalier de La Tocnaye, fled to England to escape the French Revolution. Though he spoke no English on arrival, he soon managed to persuade several wealthy patrons to buy subscriptions to a book he proposed to write – an account of a walk around Great Britain. On completing this project he was encouraged by a wealthy Irishman, Burton Coyningham, to do the same thing in Ireland. He spent nine months on his walk and, armed with letters of introduction, rarely had to stay at inns. While travelling through Dunmanway, he found two hundred French soldiers there on parole after the recent invasion attempt.

Crossing a rather wild bit of country I came to Bantry, where I was received by Mr. White in a most hospitable manner. Bantry is a poor little town, situated at the end of a superb bay of the same name, which has been much on the tongue lately on account of the appearance there of the French fleet. The Bay of Bantry must be about forty English miles in length by fifteen or twenty wide; it is at all parts very deep, except in the neighbourhood of the little town, and is everywhere surrounded by a sterile mountainous and rocky country, in which, nevertheless, one may find from time to time some charming little spots. Mr. White was good enough to take me in his boat to the Port of Glengariff, between Bantry and the island of Bear. This is a most ancient little spot. The way is literally sown with rocks, which are covered with plants and shrubs of every species. I went with my host a little way into the country to a small house belonging to him, and found to my surprise a well-wooded and romantic little valley in the middle of these rocky and arid hills. Plant life is here very vigorous. I have seen pretty large oaks and other trees growing in crevasses of rocks hardly large enough to admit a finger; surely they must draw their subsistence from the moisture of the air.

Between Glengariff and Bear Haven is seen a very high cascade, of nearly perpendicular fall from a mountain which has got the name of the 'Hungry Hill,' and not without reason. The island of Bear, where the French stopped for a few days, is at the mouth of the bay and, although pretty large, has very few inhabitants – it is a mere mass of mountains and rocks. Whiddy is another island not nearly so large but very productive, with some of the best land in the country. At different places I saw the walls of buildings which had been erected in connection with the sardine industry, this little fish having formerly frequented this bay; but it has been said that they ceased to appear after the naval battle here between the French and the English in the time of King William III. At present the fish is never seen here, and it is almost entirely unknown in England or in Ireland, even under its English name of pilchard.

Cape Clear, the most southern point in Ireland, is only about twenty miles distant from Bantry, but as a visit to it would have necessitated a return over the same ground, I dispensed with the journey. I have never been so near the country of my birth since the day of the fatal emigration. The thought came to me that in one or two days, with a favouring wind, I might go from here, and land on my own property and calm the anguish of my relatives. Could I have believed years ago that ever my compatriots should one day look upon me as their enemy . . . their enemy! No, never. I could blame them, detest their atrocities, suffer by their follies and blind rage; I shall be a wanderer, miserable, without a stone on which to rest my head, and France will always be France for me. Always to my native land shall my thoughts return until the last day of my life, always my most ardent wishes shall be for her welfare.

I quitted with great regret the hospitable roof which sheltered me here. It was a sorrow for me to turn my back now on the south and set my face northward, but I had reached the end of the land. I climbed to the top of the high mountain by which is the only approach to Bantry from the west, and which is called 'The Priest's Leap.' The tradition of the good women of the country on this subject is, that a holy priest, coming from Co. Kerry to Bantry to visit a sick person, learnt on the summit of this mountain that the sick one was dying. Fearing to arrive too late to give him his passport for the other world, he knelt down and prayed, and immediately leaped from the summit of the mountain to his destination, a distance of five miles.

They will show you, near the town, the rock on which he alighted, and on which you will see the print of his knees, of his fingers, and of his nose. Assuredly this is proof positive. Nevertheless, I fear that there are hardened unbelievers in the world who will not believe the story – so perverse is the human heart.

After having travelled about a dozen miles among these wild and absolutely deserted hills, the eye is suddenly gratified by the appearance of a little cultivated valley round the village of Nedeen. The guide who came with me to take back my horse had never passed this way before, and on the lonely way he seemed sad and troubled. But when his eye caught sight of this little corner of the world, he cried out suddenly, 'Oh, at last, here is a place with a natural look!'

Lately the name of Kenmare has been given to the village situated in this valley, out of compliment to Lord Kenmare, for in this country, as well as in Great Britain, more than elsewhere do riches attract admiration and respect. One or two miles before arriving at this place there is to be seen in a peat moss, a hundred feet or so from the road, an isolated rock; it may measure about thirty feet in height by fifteen or twenty on each face. It has a circumference of about sixty feet, and it is a stone absolutely different from any found in the country on this side of the river.

It is an enormous block of limestone which by some natural convulsion must have been thrown about four miles from the place from which it was torn. I went over to see it, and went round it; I even climbed with trouble to the top of it and found that formerly there had been on it a little tower, of which the ruins remained. It is covered with plants of various kinds – little shrubs, hollies, ivies, &c. – while the peat which surrounds it produces nothing but heath.

The inhabitants of the country pretend that a certain giant, whose name I have forgotten, amused himself by carrying this piece of limestone to a granite country and a smaller block of granite to the other side of the river, where he placed it in limestone territory. There is, really, a similar sized block of granite on the other side. This phenomenon could only be explained by supposing a great convulsion of the earth; but how terrific must have been the explosion which was capable of throwing a stone weighing more than one million pounds a distance of five or six miles!

The large bay, which is called Kenmare River, looks very imposing from this point. Two peninsulas approach in the middle and form a safe harbour for vessels. There is no country so well provided with deep and safe bays as the south of Ireland.

From *A Frenchman's Walk through Ireland 1796–7*

Isaac Weld

1800

DUBLIN-BORN ISAAC WELD (1774–1856) first achieved fame with a book of his travels in North America. In 1800 he visited the southwest of Ireland, navigating lakes in a boat made from paper and climbing to the summit of the then almost unknown Carrantuohill. His *Illustrations of the Scenery of Killarney and the Surrounding Country*, published in 1807, with his own drawings, enhanced his reputation as a topographer. Keenly interested in Irish industries, Weld played a key role in the inauguration of the Royal Dublin Society's triennial exhibitions.

From Reen we proceeded by land to Beare-haven, crossing in our route the summit of Hungry-hill, or mountain, as it should rather be called, the most elevated land in this part of the country. It abounds with lakes, one of which, very near its summit, affords large quantities of trout; whilst others, situated lower down the hill, yield none: this difference is probably rather to be ascribed to accident, than to any material difference in the qualities of the water.

The prospect from the summit of Hungry-hill is extremely extensive. Every creek and inlet on Bantry-bay appears as conspicuous as on a map; and beyond the mountains, which bound it on the east, are seen Cape Clear, and a long extent of the southern coast: in the opposite direction Kenmare-river opens to view, and the vast mountains of Kerry.

Isaac Weld.

The country between Hungry-hill and the town of Beare-haven was much better cultivated than that towards the head of the bay, and the population appeared more numerous. Agriculture has been much promoted, throughout this country, by the Cork merchants; who have built store-houses in suitable positions along the coast, where clerks are stationed to purchase corn, whenever the farmers of the adjacent districts find it convenient to bring it for sale; and in general they prefer disposing of their grain in this manner, to the labour and uncertainty of carrying it to a distant market. The low grounds are devoted to tillage; and on the hills are fed numerous herds of cows, from whose produce butter of the best quality is made, which is all sent to Cork. It is in this part of the country that the small breed of cattle is preserved, of which mention has already been made. The bulls are extremely fierce: in two or three instances we found whole villages in arms, to drive them back to the hills, which they had left in order to attack their rivals at the opposite side of the valley: they challenge each other with dreadful bellowings; and when they meet, the conflict is obstinate and sometimes fatal.

Beare-haven was formerly defended by a strong castle, and was a place of no small importance in the fifteenth and sixteenth centuries, when the Irish chieftains maintained a frequent intercourse with Spain. The town stands in a convenient and pleasing position, on the banks of a small inlet of the sea; but the houses are poor, and few in number. The only objects of peculiarity here seem to be the tombs in the church-yard, which were of a pyramidal form. The church was in ruins, and the few families of the established religion met at the house of the clergyman: the case was the same at Reen.

At Beare-haven we again embarked on the sea, with an intention of proceeding to Dursey-island, at the extremity of the long peninsula which separates Bantry-bay from Kenmare-river. The aspect of the coast below this place was bleak and desolate; it bore no trace of cultivation; and the only human beings we saw for many miles were a few aged individuals who sat fishing on the rocks. Immense flocks of sea fowl hovered over the waves in quest of prey; and, as the boat passed under the shore, thousands

Kerry bull.

more of various kinds, that lay concealed in the hollows of the cliffs, alarmed at our approach, took wing, and flitted around us with loud screams of the most discordant nature imaginable. These savage sounds, combined with the hoarse roar of the billows and the gloomy aspect of the tall impending piles of black rocks, gave something of horror to the scene, which was not relieved by the boundless prospect of the vast Atlantic, or by the consideration that we had committed ourselves to its waves in a frail and leaky boat. More than six hours had elapsed from the time of our departure from Beare-haven; when, perceiving that our rowers were exhausted with fatigue, that the flood tide opposed their progress, and that Crow-head, which terminates the peninsula, still lay at a great distance, we intimated our desire to be put on shore at a place where the cliff appeared accessible: but the men requested us to confide a little longer in their exertions, assuring us that, if the tide had risen to a certain height, the voyage would soon be over. On asseverations which had so often proved fallacious much reliance was not to be placed: in this instance, however, we were agreeably surprised by perceiving the boat almost immediately directed towards a break or chasm in the cliff, which afforded, as we were informed, a short passage into Dursey-sound. It was so narrow as barely to admit the boat; and on each side was guarded by walls of rock of vast height, which, approaching at the top, obscured the light of heaven, and cast an awful gloom over the water below. On entering it, the ocean was soon lost to our view; but the roaring of the waves continued to resound through the vaults of the passage, and, increasing as we advanced, intimated that seas still more agitated than those which we had left lay beyond it; but it was merely the effect of the echoes, for, in a few minutes, we found ourselves in a calm sheltered basin, whose shores, well cultivated, and studded with houses, appeared highly grateful to an eye wearied by the long-continued view of barren rocks and immeasurable expanse of ocean. This basin is situated between Crow-head and Dursey-island.

Dursey-island is about three miles long, and two wide. It contains several villages, and in some parts is tolerably well cultivated. The inhabitants, like most others on this coast, are well provided with food and raiment, and seem to be a very contented happy race of people. One would wish, however, that the pursuits of honest industry were more attended to than smuggling and shipwrecks, the principal sources of their wealth at present. The numberless insulated rocks on this coast are productive of the utmost danger to vessels which are so unfortunate as to be drifted towards the land during the night: at the distance of miles from the main shore we perceived several, which did not appear larger than the hull of a small vessel.

The most curious of the rocks within sight of Dursey are those called the Skeligs, which were once the seat of several monasteries and chapels, whose remains are still visible. They are quite barren, but abound with springs of good water. It is said that they consist entirely of marble; a remarkable circumstance, if true, as the other islands are composed of argillaceous and siliceous rocks, and no calcareous matter is found on the opposite coast much nearer than the lake of Killarney. The Gannet, or Solan goose, breeds on these rocks, and is never seen, if current report is to be believed, on any other part of the coast of Ireland.

Dursey island affords specular iron ore, of which we found many beautiful specimens adhering to quartz, in flat hexaëdral crystals; searches were formerly made for the ore, in different parts of the island, by sinking deep pits, which still remain; but of the quantity that was procured we could learn nothing.

At this place we were met by O'Sullivan McFinan Duff, who conducted us in a boat to his house, which is agreeably situated at the head of an inlet, about fifteen miles from the mouth of Kenmare-river. This gentleman is regarded as the chief of the O'Sullivans in this district, and, as a mark of respect, is simply addressed by his surname. The O'Sullivan-more, or head of the eldest branch of the family, according to their genealogy lately printed in London, is an English baronet: the O' was dropped some time before the family settled in England.

Of the Ardea branch of this family some particulars were communicated to me by Mr. Beltz of the Herald's College, of a nature so extraordinary, that I shall make no apology for inserting them in this place.

In the twelfth year of the reign of Queen Elizabeth, Sir Owen O'Sullivan, in order to establish a substantial title to the countries he then held, surrendered them to the crown, and received a formal grant thereof by patent. This measure gave rise to a long suit at law between Sir Owen and his nephew Donel McDonel O'Sullivan; the latter of whom endeavoured to prove that his uncle had usurped the possession at the death of his (Donel's) father. Sir Owen, on the contrary, pleaded that the possession of the estates had fallen to him by the laws of Tanistry, and had been afterwards irrevocably established by the letters patent.

The suit terminated in a commission being issued under the great seal, dated at Dublin the 18th July, in the thirty-fifth of the reign of Queen Elizabeth, directing Sir Thomas Norreys, vice-president of Munster, and others, to partition and plot out, by certain limits and boundaries, the territories, hereditaments, castles, &c. of Beare, Bantry, Ardea, and others, belonging to the O'Sullivans; which partition was effected by an instrument dated at Mallow 15th January, 1593. The castle and dependencies of Beare were allotted to Donel; and Bantry, &c. to Sir Owen; saving only to Sir Philip O'Sullivan, younger brother to Sir Owen, the castle of Ardea and its dependencies. Attempts, however, were made, a few years afterwards, to wrest the castle of Ardea from the lawful possessor, pursuant to the old custom of tanistry; whereupon an appeal was made to the lord-deputy of Ireland; and, upon the petition of the injured party, a copy was granted of the above-mentioned instrument of partition. Sir Philip's heir was secured in his rights; and the family continued to maintain possession of the castle, until it was forfeited during the civil wars.

In the year 1802, Mr. Beltz, having had occasion to visit the south of Ireland, stopped at the house of O'Sullivan McFinan Duff; where, inquiring, through curiosity, if any of the Ardea branch of that family remained in existence, he was informed that a cottager, in very humble circumstances, lived in the neighbouring mountains, who was reputed to be the lineal descendant of Sir Philip. Desirous of an interview with him, a message was sent to that effect: the ruins of Ardea castle, on the banks of Kenmare river, were fixed upon as the place of rendezvous; and, pursuant to appointment, the man, accompanied by his whole family, appeared there on the allotted day. Aware, in some measure, of the object of the interview, he had brought in his hand a bundle of parchments and papers, which he opened and spread on the grass. They were all in a mouldering state, and nearly obliterated by the damp and smoke of his cabin. Of their purport he knew nothing: no person, he said, to whom he had ever showed them, not even the priest of the parish himself, had been able to read them; but, as they had been handed down from father to son, for many generations, he had preserved them with a scrupulous care to the best of his ability.

By the beginning of the 20th century progress had come to Adrigole in the shape of improved roads and telegraph poles.

Mr Beltz, prior to his examination of these writings, wished to assure himself of the identity of the person who brought them: he therefore put numerous questions to him, each of which was answered with such precision, that no doubt could remain of the man being the actual lineal descendant of Sir Philip O'Sullivan. It appeared that he was the seventh in descent from Sir Philip, which, allowing thirty years for each generation, made up a period of two hundred and ten years; nearly agreeing with the date of the first settlement of the family at Ardea. Mr. Beltz then took up one of the parchments, and, to his surprise, found that it was the actual copy of the deed of partition which had been granted to Sir Philip's heirs, upon petition to the lord-deputy of Ireland, in the year 1613. He next discovered the original draft of the petition, with several other writings equally ancient, which it would have been impossible to have decyphered, owing to their mouldy state, if he had not happened previously, whilst passing through Dublin, to have taken copies of the same in the record office.

That writings of such a nature should thus be preserved for almost two centuries, and that an illiterate man, whose family for generations had not enjoyed a condition above that of peasants, should be able to give such a detailed account of his genealogy, is a circumstance to which a parallel would not readily be found, except amongst the Irish. As to Mr. Beltz, who was able to explain these writings, and to tell so much more of the history of the family than the poor man himself knew, he was regarded as a prophet, and found no small difficulty in disengaging himself from the importunities of the people.

Kenmare river is very improperly so called: it is an inlet of the sea, which deserves the name of a bay or haven; and it is difficult to determine how it came to be otherwise called, as no river falls into it of sufficient importance to have given it a name. It is about thirty English miles in length, and varies in breadth from two to seven miles. The shores are diversified by numerous creeks and coves; and it abounds with islands, many of which are extraordinarily beautiful. In some places the mountains rise abruptly from the water; in others, a considerable extent of sloping ground intervenes between them. The views on every side are highly picturesque; but the most striking parts of the scenery are where the lofty peaks of the Kerry mountains are seen through valleys, rising in the distance, and gradually receding behind each other till they are lost in the air. Kenmare river is more sheltered than any of the other estuaries of the south-west coast; so that the water, notwithstanding its great expanse and the influence of the tide, remains commonly very tranquil, and sometimes, by its smooth and glassy surface, adds much to the beauty of the scenery. Some parts of the shores are well cultivated; but, on the whole, they are very thinly inhabited. . . .

Nedheen is the principal place of trade on Kenmare river: it is a very small town; and, though we observed some new houses, has, on the whole, an appearance of decay. Perhaps this is to be attributed to the very bad state of the roads which lead to it; and if so, it will probably not recover very soon, as it seems the object of the inhabitants of Kerry rather to direct their new roads towards the Blackwater, which is a more convenient place for shipping, and better situated for supplying the inland district with foreign commodities.

There is an abundance of excellent limestone at Nedheen, by means of which the hills around might be all readily improved; and, if the occupiers received good encouragement, agriculture would flourish, and the country probably wear a very different aspect from what it does at present.

From *Illustrations of the Scenery of Killarney and the Surrounding Country*

Edward Wakefield

1808

EDWARD WAKEFIELD (1774–1854) started out as a farmer in Essex. In 1814 he established himself as a land agent in London and soon earned a reputation as an authority on agriculture. At the suggestion of John Foster, former chancellor of the Irish exchequer, Wakefield wrote *An Account of Ireland, Statistical and Political.* He devoted four years to the task, and the book was well received, being described as 'the best and most complete work on Ireland since Arthur Young's Tour.'

On the 26th of October, 1808, I went to Bantry, proceeding through Kenmare, across the mountains, and bidding farewell to Killarney, Mucross, and its various unrivalled beauties. The views among these mountains are bold, wild, and romantic, but as I had seen them in their most majestic appearance from the top of Mangerton, if I except the nearer sight of the channel between the two lakes, which afforded me great satisfaction, I was not so much struck as I expected.

At Kenmare I crossed the river of that name, and passed through a country equally mountainous, abounding with scenes as rude and wild as the imagination can paint, to the head of Bantry Bay. On approaching towards it, but before it comes in sight, the road proceeds quite to the top of a mountain, between which and another of great height, is a glen, where the scenery is much heightened by the peculiarly barren and rugged appearance of the opposite mountain. Here the eye is sometimes attracted by a solitary herd of goats browsing among the heath below; while cultivation, gradually extending up the sides of the hills, forms a pleasing contrast with the desert and more prominent features of the prospect. In this neighbourhood is a place called the 'Priest's Leap,' but on what account I was not able to learn.

From Bantry to Glangarriff, the road passes through mountains. Mr. White's house is an excellent mansion, built in the modern taste, and surrounded by woods rather the production of nature than of art. It stands at the edge of the harbour, which is one of the finest indentations of Bantry Bay, so perfect in its form, and so depressed at the bottom of the lofty and extensive mountains by which it is surrounded, that it looks like a bason beneath you, and though it appears small to the eye at some distance, it is not so in reality. The mountains are separated, rough, and craggy; though inferior in height to McGillycuddy's Reeks in Kerry, which hang over the upper lake of Killarney, they possess, in a considerable degree, a terrific grandeur of the same kind. This place is beautiful in the true sense of the word, as it is not indebted to art for any of its embellishments.

The eastern side of the harbour, on which this house is built, is well planted with arbutus, holly, and birch, growing in the most luxuriant manner: at every turn you perceive a glen, and each step presents new, varied, and enchanting scenery, the beauty of which is set off to great advantage by the sight of the immense mountains above, and those which surround you on the opposite side of the harbour, and which being barren and untenanted, have in their aspect something uncommonly wild. The oak and the birch do not attain here a large size, but the different tints produced by their foliage add greatly to the richness and variety of the scene.

Geraniums, myrtles, and many of the most tender plants, remain out of doors the whole year, under the shelter of a rock, which protects them from the cutting sharpness of the north-easterly winds. The mildness of the climate has no small influence on the scenery of this delightful spot, as the deciduous trees remain stripped of their leaves only during a very short period of the year. The most captivating features of the prospect immediately round the harbour, where the woody glens are seen to the greatest advantage, are by this genial temperature much improved, and a sort of almost perpetual bloom and verdure are maintained.

There are here no straight highways, presenting one open view before you. The road winds round the harbour, a new mountain or a new view every moment bursting into sight, which renders the ride to Coolranny Bridge, in particular, one of the most delightful that can be conceived.

From this place I ascended the Gowl Mountains, at the gap of which I saw the Bay of Bantry in its full extent, with the mountains on the opposite shore, and in the distant prospect Cape Clear rising above them all. Hungra Hill, which was now in full view, appears to me to be wrongly placed in all the maps which I had an opportunity of examining, previously to the publication of that by Mr. Arrowsmith. I regret much that my time would not allow me to ascend it, as I am told that it commands the most extensive prospects any where to be seen. The fall of water down its sides, during rainy seasons, is exceedingly grand. When at Bantry I had the pleasure of viewing it, although twenty miles distant.

I cannot quit this neighbourhood without recommending to every traveller whose object may be to see the romantic, beautiful, or sublime scenes of nature, to pay particular attention to this part of Ireland. Killarney is spoken of as the ultimatum of every thing worth visiting in the United Empire; but highly as I think of it, though gratified and delighted by its enchanting and extraordinary scenery, I cannot help saying, that I consider Glangarriff, and the adjacent country, if not exactly its rival, at any rate a place of uncommon beauty; interesting in no small degree; possessing charms various and striking; embracing scenes suited

When Marie-Anne de Bovet visited, a sudden downpour provided a wealth of waterfalls.

to almost every taste; and, upon the whole, such as must always arrest the notice and excite the admiration of those who seek for nature in her most favoured retreats. The mountains exhibit as much of the terrific in their character and shapes, and want nothing but a greater height to render them as celebrated as those of Kerry. But though these mountains have less elevation, the wide expanse of water, and the views connected with so noble a bay as that of Bantry, make up for this defect, and create an interest, which those who feel it cannot well describe. For my part, Glangarriff and its numerous beauties made such a deep impression on my mind, that the picture is still lively, and will not easily be effaced.

From *An Account of Ireland, Statistical and Political*

Horatio Townshend

1810

BORN AT ROSS, COUNTY CORK, Horatio Townshend, or Townsend, (1750–1837) studied at Trinity College, Dublin, and Oxford University before taking holy orders. He was appointed vicar at Rosscarbery in his native county, where he lived the rest of his life. An accomplished agriculturalist, he farmed for many years at Courtmacsherry. Townshend's most important work, *A Statistical Survey of the County of Cork*, was published in 1810. He was also the author of *A Tour Through Ireland and the Northern Parts of Great Britain* (1821) and some ephemeral verse.

Bear island, very high, rocky, and coarse, standing a little within the mouth of the bay, braves the fury of the western waves, and forms, by the shelter of its large body, a most secure and spacious haven. Safe in its more retired situation at the upper end of the bay, the island of Whiddy presents a surface of gentle inequalities, covered by a soil of uncommon richness and fertility. The grandeur of the scene, in which this noble expanse of water bears so conspicuous a part, is greatly enhanced by the rugged variety of the surrounding mountains, particularly those on the west side, which far exceed the rest in altitude and boldness of form. Among these, Hungry-hill, rising with a very steep ascent from the water, raises his broad and majestic head, easily distinguishable from a great distance, and for surpassing all the other mountains of this county in height and grandeur. The effect, produced by such an assemblage of objects, can hardly be conceived, and is impossible to be described. The mind filled and overborne by a prospect so various, so extended, and so sublime, sinks beneath its magnitude, and, feeling the utter incapability of adequate expression, rests upon the scene in silent and solemn admiration. The soul must be insensible indeed, which will not be moved by such a contemplation to adore the God of nature, from whom such mighty works proceed. Large as the ground of this great picture is, it comes within the scope of human sight, a circumstance, upon which the powerfulness of its impression materially depends. A greater extension of the parts, by throwing them far from view, would diminish their effect, and a reduction of their scale would lessen their grandeur. Much and justly as Killarney is celebrated for the varied beauty of its scenes, no single view it affords can vie with this in sublimity of character and greatness of effect.

But all pretensions to admiration do not rest upon the impression made by the whole, several of its parts being highly deserving of regard for their beauty or their singularity. In viewing a gigantic figure, the first and most powerful emotion is excited by its bulk; when the operations of wonder begin to subside, we desire to examine the proportions, and derive pleasure from the expression of features, and the symmetry of limbs. Among the tamer beauties of the scene, the island of Whiddy catches the spectator's eye, strikingly contrasted, as it is, with the barren wildness of the hills at either side. This island, the inhabitants of which are said to be remarkably well shaped, contains about 1000 acres; several of these are capable, in their state of natural fertility, of fattening the largest bullocks. It belongs to Lord Bantry, who, besides a deerpark, keeps some of it in his hands for pasture. Among the singularity of its circumstances one deserves to be mentioned, as a case without parallel, perhaps, in any other part of the kingdom. The inhabitants, to whom a lease is as yet unknown, have continued to hold their farms under his lordship's family, for sixty years, without any alteration of rent!

The second division of that great French armament, which threatened these shores in 1796, came to anchor on the north-west quarter of this island, and though they remained a long time in expectation of being joined by the rest, it is very remarkable that neither hostile nor curious motives induced them to set one foot upon the shore. Their boats too were often seen rowing about in the bay, probably for the purpose of taking its soundings. The station they occupied, and the course by which they entered, are commanded by the higher parts of the island, where the principal works for the defence of the bay have, in consequence, been constructed. . . .

The island, on which there are many inhabitants, and much tillage, is well watered, containing, besides springs, a pretty large fresh-water lake. There is one also of salt water, remarkable for eels of great size. A spaniel swimming there, in pursuit of water-fowl, is said to have suddenly disappeared, the prey, as it was supposed, of those voracious fishes. The fact of his being drowned is sufficiently established; the immediate cause of his death may admit of some question.

All the good soil of the district, however, is not confined to Whiddy, the lands adjoining the head of the bay being also distinguished for verdure and fertility. On the shore at Bantry are found several detached

Bantry House, home of the White family, including four Earls of Bantry, since 1739.

fragments of lime-stone, of dark colour and hard texture, not unlike some veins of the Duhallow quarries. A gravelly hill on the north side of the town appears to contain a good many of them, but the rock they belonged to has nowhere appeared. The roundness and attrition of these stones shew that they have been brought from some distance, torn from their native beds by tempest or deluge. The parent rock may possibly lie in some part of the bay, at too great a depth for present discovery. From the encroachments, known to have been made by the ocean on several parts of the coast, it is not unreasonable to suppose that some of our deep bays might have been originally vallies. One of the Skelig rocks on the Kerry coast is said to be composed of limestone, and might once have been connected with the land, from which at present it is very remote. There are in that county some calcareous tracts extending towards the sea, with one of which this rock might formerly have been joined. On the north side of Bantry bay is a calcareous shistus, similar from its description to that of the Leap in West Carbery. It produces a brown lime, and has been used for cement by Mr. Hutchins of Ballylickey. This is the only desideratum of limestone here, the coral sand supplying all its purposes as a manure.

But the place most celebrated for combining the softer graces of the waving wood with the wildest rudeness of mountain aspect is Glangarriffe (the rough glen) situated, on the north side of the bay, at the head of a small harbour or cove. The hills that inclose this romantic glen rise in great variety of rocky forms, their sides and hollows being covered profusely with trees and shrubs, among which the arbutus, rarely found to adorn our native woods, appears in a flourishing state. Here, as at Killarney, nature seems to have been at wanton variance with herself, and, after exciting a war between two rival powers, to have decided in favour of the weaker party. Among stones of immense size, thrown together in the wildest confusion, and apparently forbidding the possibility of useful produce; among bare and massive rocks that should seem destined to reign forever in barren desolation, arises a luxuriance of sylvan growth, which art would hardly hope for in the happiest situations. The extent of this woody region, which winds through the mountains for some miles, is very considerable. Iron was formerly smelted in this neighbourhood, when timber was more abundant and less valuable. A river, abounding with salmon and sea trout, runs through this glen, in dry weather, (as Johnson observes of a similar situation) 'fretting over the asperities of a rocky bottom,' when swollen with rains, rolling a torrent of frightful magnitude into the bay. It is passed by a good stone bridge, attributed to Cromwell, and still bearing his name, though it should seem that nothing to be gained on the west side of the river could have been worth the trouble of the undertaking. The usual mode of visiting Berehaven, even now, is by water, the voyage from Bantry, with a tolerable fair wind, being made in four or five hours. The distance by land along the old pass, which I have travelled, was thirty miles; but, expedition being impracticable from the ruggedness of the way, the time required to perform it, even for an active traveller, was from ten to twelve hours. The distance has been reduced, and the communication greatly facilitated of late, by a new line of road.

From Glangarriffe westward, some places excepted that skirt along the margin of the bay, to the furthest extremity of the Durzey islands, the ground is coarse, mountainous, and rocky beyond description. Population, however, even here has made great advances, and with it the tillage necessary to its wants. Rude as it is, the produce of the rents is now very considerable, which may, in some degree, be imputed to the influx of money arising from the labour of the new works. Some of the mountainous tracts are certainly capable of much improvement, and every arable spot within reach of the bay enjoys the advantage of sea manure. But a great proportion of this quarter seems doomed by nature to everlasting infertility, as far as culture is concerned, being incapable of any thing beyond a poor summer pasture for small and hardy animals.

The last of nature's uncommon and astonishing displays that remain to be mentioned is the water-fall or cataract of Hungry-hill, in comparison with which O'Sullivan's cascade at Killarney, and the water-fall at Powerscourt near Dublin, shrink into insignificance. The eye, accustomed to the various wonders of Alpine scenery, may doubtless view this stupendous fall with less emotion; but what will the lowland inhabitant think of a river, tumbled from the summit of a mountain, elevated more than 2000 feet above its base, and almost perpendicular in its ascent? In the first part of its progress, the side of the hill is so steep as to suffer the water to fall from a vast height, unimpeded by the rocky projections, which the spreading base of the mountain opposes to its descent in approaching the bottom. It thus assumes the double character of fall and cataract. At the back of this great mountain are several lakes, one of which supplies the water of the fall. This grand and singular spectacle, often to be plainly distinguished from the town of Bantry, fourteen miles distant, appears in full majesty only after heavy falls of rain, sufficiently frequent in this district to give the inhabitants numerous opportunities of seeing it in all its glory.

From a district of this description little will be expected for the catalogue of towns, fine seats, or cultivated country. The remote situation of Bantry, notwithstanding its proximity to such a bay, seems to preclude it from emerging above the obscurity of a little country town. The original cause of prosperity, and which would now be capable of conferring it in no ordinary degree, has long ceased. In the beginning of the last century, the bay abounded with pilchards, the catching and curing of which gave, even at that time, wealth and employment to numbers, as many remaining vestiges of the houses employed for this purpose sufficiently attest. Before Smith's time (1750) they had deserted the bay, but herrings and sprats remained in great profusion. These advantages, however, were not enjoyed exclusively by Bantry, for all the southern coast possessed a similar abundance. The gradual disappearance of all these kinds has at length left the coast destitute of anything deserving the name of a fishery. As the cause of their departure is inscrutable, it seems fruitless to speculate upon the possibility of their return.

The greater part of this district was once in the possession of the O'Sullivans, who had many seats and castles on the bay. There are still some very respectable descendants of this family, one of whom, settled in Spain, is said to derive a title from Bearhaven. The principal residents of the name live, I understand, on the Kerry side of the hills.

The chief seat of the district is Sea-court, Lord Bantry's residence, pleasantly situated near the town, on the south side of the bay. The plantations appear to thrive well about the house, which, though commanding a fine view of the bay, is low and well sheltered. The peculiarity of the soil on some parts of the demesne is deserving of notice. The higher parts, which from their steep and sloping form should appear to be very dry, are for the greater part of the year extremely wet and spewy, not in consequence of an impermeable rock approaching the surface, but from a deep substratum of yellow retentive clay. The productive soil, that forms its surface, is very shallow, and rarely dry even in summer, yet the quality of the pasture is remarkably kind, and, strange to tell, peculiarly favourable to the feeding and fattening of sheep. I know no instance of any thing similar, but this seems to be the region of wonders.

From *Statistical Survey of the County of Cork*

Anne Plumptre

1814

BORN IN 1760, ANNE PLUMPTRE was the daughter of Dr. Robert Plumptre, president of Queen's College, Cambridge. Well educated and skilled in foreign languages, she was the first to translate German plays for the London stage. Plumptre lived in France from 1802 to 1805 and wrote a book on her experiences there. Well known as an admirer of Napoleon, she claimed she would welcome him if he invaded England, as he would do away with the aristocracy. In 1814 and 1815 she visited Ireland; the book of her travels was published in 1817. Plumptre died at Norwich in 1818.

The town of Bantry, which stands almost at the head of the bay, is not large, but has one good street, with a very comfortable inn. Its ancient name was Ballygobbin; it was also for a while called the Old Town, another settlement having been made to the north of it, where, in the time of Oliver Cromwell, Ireton had fortifications erected: many people in consequence emigrated from the old to the new establishment. But afterwards, when the country was restored to tranquillity, these fortifications were neglected and suffered to fall into decay, and the Old Town was found to be more eligibly situated from its immediate vicinity to the bay, so that the New Town in its turn was deserted, and the old one has ever since flourished under its present name. Near it once stood a Franciscan abbey, founded in the fifteenth century by the O'Sullivans, a sept of great distinction in the country, but no trace of it now remains.

The bay is twenty-six miles in length, and in some places nine miles over; it is esteemed the finest bay in all Ireland; the depth of water in the midst is forty fathoms. About fifty or sixty years back the town of Bantry carried on a great trade in salted herrings and pilchards, from the immense quantities taken in the bay; they were principally exported to Spain, Portugal, and

Anne Plumptre.

Italy. It is a remarkable thing that in these hot countries, where the climate naturally produces a great propensity to thirst, the inhabitants seem particularly fond of strong thirst-creating kinds of food, such as the salted and dried herrings of our country, the cod of Newfoundland, and the anchovies and sardines of their own seas; not to mention their *caviare*, and *potargo* or *poutargue*, two of the very strongest species of food that can be imagined. We might also instance the excessive love of garlick and of high-spiced dishes in hot countries; one should have supposed these kind of foods more suited to cold northern climates, and such as are of a milder nature to southern latitudes. So great was the fishery formerly in Bantry Bay, that in the year 1749 a Mr. Mead obtained a premium from the Dublin Society for having caught and cured within the year 380,000 fish, reckoning six score to the hundred. Another person, about the same period, cured in one year 482,500 herrings and pilchards, and two hundred and thirty-four barrels of sprats. This immense swarm of fish ceased soon after; and for many years the numerous stages erected around the bay for curing them have been neglected and useless. The bay still yields fish in plenty of various kinds, but not in this extraordinary profusion. . . .

It is needless to remark how much this bay became the subject of public notice and eager attention in the year 1796, when a French fleet was for some time moored there. I must however observe upon the extreme inaccuracy with which this circumstance is mentioned in *The Traveller's Guide*. It says that the fleet was fitted out by the Consulate at the solicitation of the United Irishmen. Now at the time the Consulate was not established in France, the executive government was in the Directory. Again, it says that the fleet was dispersed in the Bay of Bantry; on the contrary, they had quitted the bay before their dispersion. Having waited there in vain for the arrival of the General, Hoche, who was to command the land forces, and who was to follow the fleet in a frigate, but owing to a storm was prevented joining them, they, after expecting him in vain as long as the admiral judged expedient, sailed off. It seems to have been a most ill-chosen spot for the success of their enterprise, since the immense rocks, which surround the bay every where, must have presented a natural obstacle, almost insurmountable, to a landing ever being effected. Since that time fortifications have been erected at different parts about the bay, particularly on some islands near the entrance; but the breadth of water is such that vessels might always, in sailing up, keep out of reach of the batteries; the difficulty of landing presents a much more powerful obstacle to invasion from this quarter than can be offered by any fortifications art could raise. There is no strand about the bay; the rocks rise in some places directly from the water, in others almost close to it.

From *Narrative of a Residence in Ireland*

Caesar Otway

1822

CAESAR OTWAY (1780–1842), who was born in County Tipperary, was educated at Trinity College, Dublin. Following ordination, he served as curate in a country parish for seventeen years, and later became a leading preacher at a Dublin chapel. In 1826 Otway co-founded the *Christian Examiner*, the first religious magazine associated with the Church of Ireland. He was the first to publish stories by William Carleton. An antiquary and an admirer of Irish scenery, Otway co-operated with George Petrie in the first volume of the *Dublin Penny Journal* under the pseudonym 'Terence O'Toole.'

On the following day my kind entertainers took an excursion towards the fall of Adrigoll, or Hungry Mountain. We passed between the sea-shore and the Sugar-loaf mountain, along a new road made to Bearhaven, on the McAdamized plan; and nothing could be finer than the road, or grander than the outline of the mountain scenery – to the left, the broad expanse of Bantry Bay, – to the right, the mountains. We had no longer in view the woods of Glengariff; no improvement, no cultivation. At length we came to where the continuous line of hills was interrupted, and room left for an open valley through which a stream descended and joined the sea. A pretty bridge, a sort of village, a church, and close to the sea-shore a comfortable parsonage house, and straight before us Hungry Mountain, with the bed of the waterfall, like a dark deep chasm, indented down its side. But the weather had already set in with peculiar dryness, and there was not a rill of water where in winter is a fearful cataracht.

'Did you ever see a dumb church?' said one of my companions.

'And pray what is a dumb church?'

'Why it is a church lately built and consecrated; but which has now no service in it, and is let go to neglect and ruin.'

'And how long is this church built, for it, at this distance, from its position, colour, and elevation, appears to be quite a modern structure?'

'It is not more than ten or twelve years erected; the present primate consecrated it.'

'Come, let us take a walk to see this first specimen that has come under my observation of a dumb church.'

Accordingly, the greater number of the party proceeded to take a view of the church. As we approached it, the desolation became more and more conspicuous; the windows all broken, sashes destroyed, shutters torn off their hinges, roof all stripped.

You might have supposed that the French when they came into Bantry bay thirty years ago, had landed here and made this their bivouac for the night, and left it in the morning, a specimen of what ruthless invaders could perpetrate: but it was no such thing; this place of worship was not thought of until twenty years after the French, by God's providence, were driven from our shores. Its ruin, then, was quite a native work; and there it stood a monument of desertion by Protestants, and of demolition by Romanists. We climbed in by one of the windows, a goat could have got in, and did get in, the same way; – and what desolation! – the pews torn to pieces, the floor ripped up, and nothing remaining entire but the pulpit, it seemed left in mockery of the ruin it overhangs. Into it I ascended, and was moved to address Him who heareth prayer, that he might put it into the hearts of those having authority to restore this desecrated structure, to repair the place where once his honour dwelt; and that in future times the truth of the Gospel and unsearchable riches of Christ should be preached with power and converting influence, from this now deserted pulpit. When we reached the entrance door of this degraded temple, it appeared that, for some years at least, no entrance had been made by this way; for long stalactites were hanging down from the door-way, formed by the slow combination of water with the lime of the damp wall; and there they hung like long white fingers, forbidding the door to open on its rusty hinges. Whatever was the cause of all this, my wish was that I could have the use of Aladdin's lamp, and by giving it a good scrubbing, induce the slave of the lamp to lift up that dumb church, and exhibit it for half an hour to the Lord Primate of Ireland.

But this is not explaining the matter; whence all this? what made the church dumb? where the parson? where the church-wardens, and the

While her companions climbed Hungry Hill in 1838, Georgiana Chatterton stayed at the foot sketching this scene.

Protestant parishioners? Good Mr. Reader, not so fast, it is easier to exhibit effects than to explain causes. I was but a stranger. I could only obtain hearsays, and perhaps prejudiced accounts. The parsonage house I saw about a mile off; it looked at that distance snug and comfortable; a nice green lawn; many trees; prettily, nay, beautifully situated on the shore of the sea, and surrounded by the sublime and various mountains. I heard stories, perhaps not true, how the greater part of the Protestants had turned Catholics; how even the clerk of the parish had shown the example, and in order to procure his salary, had actually torn up the pews of the church and sold the timber. I heard how, some years ago, perhaps a hundred, a clergyman, on being asked, whether in his ministration he had been successful in inducing the natives of his parish to renounce their Romish superstition! laughed outright, 'What, convert the Papists! No, no! On the contrary, all the Protestants somehow or other are turning Papists.'

This certainly would be so unlucky a confession from any Protestant minister, that I hope it never took place. But this is quite certain, that many Protestants in this district have within this half-century joined the Church of Rome; and the loyal and high-spirited yeomanry, that the piety and patriotism of the Boyles, &c. &c. had planted in these districts, has, under the neglect of careless parsons, and the discountenance of greedy landlords, in a great measure merged into the mass of the Romish population. Not far from the church was a little hut, with a potato-garden attached to it, surrounded by a stone wall, in which a woman was digging with all the muscular energy of a man, with an old hat on her head, without stockings, coarse clouted shoes, and a simple woollen gown, and short petticoat of the same texture. She exhibited one of the most succinct and robust figures I ever saw in the costume of a woman. As she was the only person to be seen in the vicinity of the deserted church, I called her from her work, which she seemed to leave reluctantly, and asked, 'What was the cause of that house of worship being in such a state?'

'Why then, in troth, sir, though it is now no longer the place I desire to go to, yet it is a shame, and grief to me often as I look out of my cabin door to see it in that state.'

'Why, what do you mean, my good woman, by saying that you go no longer to such a place? did you ever go to church?'

'Why, not all out to that place; but all my kiff and kin were Protestants; but I go, as all about go, to mass.'

'Ah, my dear good woman! how could you, if reared in the Protestant faith, condescend to degrade your understanding by giving up its reasonable service for the system you have adopted?'

'Why, it is easy for you gentlemen, as you are, to talk – but look at me, a desolate widow, without one on the living earth to protect me, or give me a meal's meat – look at that poor cabin – look at this little garden – I have robbed it from the rock – it was I that picked up all the stones out of it, and built these walls; it was I carried earth to it on my back; it was I dug it; it was I carried on my dripping head, weeds out of yonder sea to manure it; and here I am a lone and desolate crathur, not a living soul to lift his hand in my favour, and take my part. How could I continue a Protestant? I never knew the difference between the two persuasions – all about me tould me that the ould ancient faith was the safe and secure church, built up as that rock – a church no more to be moved than the mountain before us, and what better could I do than take the safe side for this world and the next? Oh! if I had, when my poor husband died, and God rest his soul – if I had remained a Protestant, not a herring would I have got to make kitchen for my pratie, nor a lock of wool from a Christian to make this camlet to cover my poor back.'

The woman spoke with a feeling, and an agitated anxiety to excuse herself, which convinced me that she was not quite satisfied in her mind that she was right. I asked whether she could read? She said she could.

'Do you ever read the Testament of our Lord Jesus?'

'That I do,' said she, 'and I am proud to own it to you, but would not like to confess it to another.' My companions had all deserted me, and were beckoning me to follow, yet still, I lingered beside poor Mary Blake, and before I parted, I directed her to passages in her Bible, exhibiting the need of one only, and all-sufficient Saviour, 'the way, the truth, and the life,' – only able to save – only competent to mediate – only sufficient to intercede – as man, touched with the feeling of our infirmities – as God, capable of hearing prayer; why fly to another? – why let go holding to this head, to trust to living priests or dead saints? I spoke with all my soul, and with all my strength. Oh, that I had spoken as forcibly as I felt, when seeking thus to turn a sinner from the error of her ways. There was a tear in the woman's eye as I departed, which convinced me, and yet I might be much mistaken, that though Mary Blake will continue all her life to go to mass, that living, she will continue to read the Gospel, and dying, she will rest alone on the all-sufficient merits of her crucified Redeemer.

In this neighbourhood was the mansion of Ross McOwen, and the place where it was situated was pointed to me, where dwelt one of the principal branches of the O'Sullivans of Cork, the two elder branches, those of McGillicuddy and McFineen Duff, being established in Kerry, and the lineal descendants of the O'Sullivan Bear being long settled and ennobled in Spain, where with the O'Donoghues, O'Donnells, and O'Higgins, they have cast some fresh blood, and some portion of Irish activity into the stagnant veins of the Castilian nobility. Of Murtough O'Sullivan's establishment at Ross McOwen, I have received the following curious and characteristic account, from a valuable and venerable correspondent:

'More than fifty years have elapsed since I first visited Bearhaven, and among other excursions, in company with a friend, walked to a place called Ross McOwen, where was an old mansion-house on the south-side of Hungry Hill, and at a small distance from the bay. This dwelling, though it might savour somewhat of the bleak and dreary from without, yet presented nothing of cold or dismal within: on the contrary, hospitality of the warmest kind was the order of every day, let who will be the comer or the visitant. There was a copse near it, the remains of a considerable oak-wood, that the hospitable expenses of O'Sullivan's table contributed to reduce to a very limited size – we had come to it for the purpose of shooting wood-cocks, and were soon joined by O'Sullivan's son, who carried a gun, but had no ammunition, with which, however, we supplied him. After continuing our sport for some time, a message arrived from the old gentleman, desiring the favour of our company at his house, an invitation which I would most gladly have declined, did civility permit it, conceiving from the 'Mount Dismal' appearance of the outside, that all within was correspondent, but I was agreeably disappointed. Murtough O'Sullivan's person and countenance were prepossessing, his manners and conversation those of a well-bred gentleman, whose youth had been passed in polite society, and who, '*mores hominum multorum vidit et urbes*.' It was evident that the rays of fortune which shone upon his youth, had

Scene from Sugarloaf Mountain, drawn by W.H. Bartlett.

been withdrawn in his old age, and that the style of his entertainment was at variance with his wishes. But he made no complaint of his altered state; offered no apologies for the plainness of his fare, and was as cheerful as if he had entertained with claret and venison. We remained longer than might seem prudent, considering that it was a winter's night, and that we had some miles to return over rock and bog, for, as to road, that was an accommodation then wholly unknown; but we were furnished with a sober guide, and two excellent ponies, as expert at climbing rocks as goats, and the only risk we ran was a chance slide into a bog-hole. This being a matter of common occurrence, was only a thing to be laughed at; and though the night was dark, I think I occasioned but one opportunity for mirth during the entire ride. My companion was not so fortunate.

'One circumstance concerning the old house of Ross McOwen I must not omit, as it is curious. It was not uncommon formerly to have water admitted into the kitchen, by means of an aperture in the wall, through which it was introduced by a wooden pipe, and let out again by another opening underneath. In this old house it was managed otherwise, a large stream being admitted near one of the angles, which flowing close to the wall, discharged itself at the opposite side; at the point of admission a strong iron grating was fixed, allowing passage to nothing but water, of which, a certain quantity was permitted to enter, the overflow during the rains being carried off by an external channel. It will be naturally asked, for what culinary purpose could such a stream be required? The answer, if not obvious, is very satisfactory, as a ready way, not only of supplying the cook with means of washing fish, which constituted a great part of the daily food, but also of catching it. Salmon and sea-trout abound in Bantry bay, and in their proper seasons, seek every stream of fresh water, in which to deposit their spawn – that they will ascend even smaller streams than that of Ross McOwen I know from actual experience; and the proximity of this stream to the bay, renders the fact extremely probable, that salmon and sea-trout were frequently taken as well as dressed in O'Sullivan's kitchen. A salmon, which made part of our dinner, we were assured, was so caught in the kitchen not three hours before.'

A respectable old gentleman who lived near Adrigoll for many years, relates many curious anecdotes of the awkward mixture of pride and pauperism, still operating amongst the fallen classes of the royal race of O'Sullivan. When the formation of roads became an object of public exertion in that quarter, he happened to pass by a small party of labourers just at their dinner hour – all were sitting sociably together, consuming their humble but warm meal, which their wives and families had brought – but one was sitting apart and alone disconsolate on a rock.

'How comes it, my honest fellow, that you are not as well provided as your neighbours, have you no wife to bring you your dinner?'

'Troth then, it is I that have a wife, and that's the case as why my dinner is not after coming.'

'Oh, poor woman! I suppose she is lying in, or she is sick?'

'Arra musha not at all, your honour; troth she is neither sick, nor sore, nor sorry – I'll be bound master, she is as big and as brave a body, as any man's wife from Bear to Bantry; but I'll tell you, master, what's the matter – she's a lady.'

'A lady – why, what do you mean by a lady?'

'Arra now don't you know – sure she's of the thick blood, she comes of the O'Sullivans.'

'Well, but lady as she is, the O'Sullivans must eat – she's not above dining – she has mouth and teeth like other people.'

'Oh! then it is she that has-ate-och, then let Biddy O'Sullivan alone for that, a better man than ever I was, she would ate out of house and home; and then, sir, she would break the bank in drinking tay. But though, sir, she will ate dinner with me, aye and after me – she is not the one to bring it to a poor body that's after working all the day – that would be bringing down her quality stomach too much your honour – by this pipe I hold in my fist, she would as soon carry Sugar Loaf on her head, or Hungry Hill in her hand, as bring me (and I have been a good man to her) my dinner.'

'This is a strange story, friend.'

'Strange is it? – why it's as true as you are there.'

'Well, but if she don't work or go abroad, she is surely a good wife at home – she knits your stockings, she mends, she makes for you.'

'Och, the sorrow one stitch – knit my stockings, wash, mend, make, for me! – May I never sit under Father Mahony's knee, or ever see mass, if one hole in my stockings she ever darned, or even one needlefull of thread did she ever fill in mending or making for me.'

'It would appear then, that you have a heavy bargain of this lady-wife of yours.'

'Why, what signifies complaining, sure she's mine, and it's the will of God, and that's enough. But harkee, your honour, (and here the poor fellow lowered his voice to a whisper, and inclined his head towards my ear, lest any of the royal O'Sullivans should overhear,) by the powers, if it were to be done over again, I'd sooner go on board a man-of-war, and live under a cat-o'-nine-tails, than be married to a LADY.'

From *Sketches in Ireland*

Thomas Crofton Croker

1824

CORK-BORN THOMAS CROFTON CROKER (1798–1854) travelled extensively in the west and south of Ireland, collecting folktales and songs, many of which he sent to Thomas Moore. His *Fairy Legends and Traditions of the South West of Ireland* (1825), which created a deep impression in England, was also translated into German by the brothers Grimm, and into French. Croker worked in London at the Admiralty. A member of various learned societies, he helped to found several others, including the British Archaeological Association. He also wrote *Researches in the South of Ireland*, *Legends of the Lakes*, *The Popular Songs of Ireland* and two popular humorous books, *Barney Mahoney* and *My Village Versus Our Village*.

At Beerhaven, near the mouth of the river Kenmare, on the county Cork side, a most gratifying sight presents itself in a large copper-mine at full work. This mine was discovered about nine years since by Mr.

Puxley, one of the proprietors of the property on which it is situated, who soon after sent to Cornwall for an experienced captain, and it has now been in successful operation for more than eight years, with every appearance of long continuing a prosperous work. A gentleman who visited it in 1822 informed me, that it was giving constant employment to about six hundred persons, of both sexes, and of all ages from ten years upwards. The monthly expenditure was from 900*l.* to 1000*l.*, and the mine produced from 150 to 200 tons of ore in the same time.

Besides paying the proprietors very handsomely, the blessing which this mine has been to the surrounding country can only be appreciated by those who have witnessed such a scene. The place where, but a few years since, the barren and rocky mountains could scarcely sustain the lives of a few half-starved sheep, is now the scene of busy and useful employment, dispensing competence and comfort to hundreds. The principal works are carried on about a mile and a half from the water, and the ground rises to a considerable elevation. The vein crosses the regular strata of the country, which is a hard rock of graywacke, at a small angle, taking a direction about two points to the south of east and the same to the north of west. The matrix of the vein is a white opaque quartz, in part of its course of the amazing width of sixty feet (which has been proved by cutting through it), but the ore has seldom exceeded three feet in breadth.

From *Researches in the South of Ireland*

Hermann von Pückler-Muskau

1828

PRINCE HERMANN VON PÜCKLER-MUSKAU (1785–1871) first visited England in 1815. He was so impressed with the gardens that he created an English-style park around his home in Muskau. The undertaking proved so expensive that he soon ran out of money and credit. Ever resourceful, he married Lucie, Countess Pappenheim, daughter of the Prussian Chancellor Hardenberg. Nine years his senior, Lucie's charms were her wise and witty company – and her potential fortune. But Hardenberg became disenchanted with Hermann and disinherited Lucie. With no source of income, the newlyweds arrived at an ingenious solution: they divorced, and Hermann travelled to England to look for a rich bride. Though he failed in his quest, he sent long descriptive letters to Lucie; however, they give no indication that he hoped to find a bride in the wilds of Beara.

Glengariff September 26th

To write to you to-day is really an effort which deserves reward, for I am excessively tired and have, like my father Napoleon, been obliged to drink coffee incessantly to keep me awake.

I left Killarney at nine o'clock in the morning in a car of the most wretched construction and followed the new road which leads along the upper and lower lake to the Bay of Kenmare. This road discloses more beauties than are seen from the lakes themselves, which have the great disadvantage of affording a picturesque view on one side only; – the other shore is quite flat.

Eight miles from Killarney we reached the highest point of the road, where stands a solitary inn. You look down upon the broad valley, in whose lap lies the greater part of the three lakes, so that you behold them all with one glance.

From this point the road descends, leading between naked mountains of bold forms to the sea. It was fair-time when I arrived in Kenmare and I could hardly penetrate through the bustling crowd with my one-horse vehicle, especially from the number of drunken men who would not – perhaps could not – get out of the way. One of them fell in consequence of an attempt to do so and knocked his head so violently on the pavement that he was carried away senseless – a thing of such common occurrence that it attracted no attention. The skulls of Irishmen appear to be universally of a more firm and massive construction than those of other people, probably because they are trained to receive shillelah blows. While I dined, I had another opportunity of observing several affrays. First a knot of people collect shouting and screaming; this rapidly thickens and all at once, in the twinkling of an eye, a hundred shillelahs whirr in the air and the thumps – which are generally applied to the head – bang and snap like the distant report of fire-arms, till one party has gained the victory. As I was now at the fountain-head, through the mediation of mine host I bought one of the finest specimens of this weapon, yet warm from the fight. It is as hard as iron and that it may be sure to do execution, it is also weighted at the end with lead.

The celebrated O'Connell is now residing about thirty miles from hence, in his solitary fortress in the most desert region of Ireland. As I had long wished to know him, I sent a messenger from this place and determined, while waiting for his answer, to make an excursion to Glengariff Bay, whither I accordingly set out as soon as I had dined.

Driving is now completely at an end; I can proceed only on a pony or on foot. I set out, a pony carrying my baggage and I and my guide

Prince von Pückler-Muskau.

walking by his side. If either of us was tired, the good little horse was to carry us too. The sun soon set, but the moon shone bright. The road was not uninteresting though horribly bad, often leading through bog and brook without bridge or stepping-stone. It became indescribably difficult after six or eight miles, where we had to climb a high and nearly perpendicular hill, treading only on loose and pointed stones, from which we slipped back at every step nearly as far as we went forward. The descent on the other side was still worse, especially when a mountain intercepted the moon's light. I was so weary that I could walk no further and seated myself on the pony. This little creature showed almost human intelligence. Going up-hill he helped himself with his nose and I think even with his teeth, as a fifth leg, and down-hill he wriggled with incessant twisting of his body like a spider. When he came to a boggy place, in which there was only here and there a stone thrown by way of step he crept as slowly as a sloth, always first trying with his foot whether the stone would bear him and his burthen. The whole scene was most singular. The night was so clear, that I could see around me to a great distance; but nothing met my eye save rocks ranged above rocks of every shape and kind, standing out gigantic, wild and sharp against the sky.

About an hour before you reach Glengariff Bay the landscape becomes as luxuriant and park-like as it had heretofere been dreary and barren. Here the rocks arise in the strangest forms out of Hesperian thickets of arbutus, Portugal laurel and other lovely and fragrant shrubs.

In the valley sparkled solitary lights and a gentle breeze waved the tops of the high oaks, ashes and birches, intermingled with beautiful holly, whose scarlet berries were visible even by moonlight. The magnificent bay now glittered under the web of moonbeams which lay upon it, and I really thought myself in Paradise when I reached its shore and alighted at the door of a pretty, cheerful inn.

Kenmare September 27

At six o'clock I was stirring and at seven in the magnificent park of Colonel White, brother of Lord Bantry, whose family possesses all the country around the bays of Bantry and Glengariff, perhaps the most beautiful part of Ireland.

Mr. White's park is certainly one of the most perfect creations of that kind and owes its existence entirely to his perseverance and good taste. It is true that he could nowhere have found a spot of earth more grateful for his labours.

The climate is the most favourable possible for vegetation, moist and so warm that not only azaleas, rhododendrons and all sorts of evergreens stand abroad through the winter, but even, in a favourable aspect, camellias. Dates, pomegranates, magnolias, lyriodendrons, &c. attain their fullest beauty, and the three last are not even covered. The situation affords extensive views, remarkable variety and yet a complete whole, inclosed within high mountains. Bantry and Glengariff bays are seas in miniature and supply to the eye the want of the ocean.

Such a work deserves a crown, and the excellent man who, with slender means, but with singular talent and perseverance, has accomplished it, ought to be held up as a model to those Irish proprietors who spend their money abroad. I heard with real satisfaction, that on his and Lord Bantry's estates party hate is unknown. Both are Protestants, all their 'tenants' are Catholics; nevertheless they render an obedience as boundless as it is voluntary and cordial.

You may be sure that I was eager to make the acquaintance of so admirable a man; I esteemed myself, therefore, highly favoured by fortune in meeting him in the park inspecting the operations of his workmen. I readily accepted his invitation to breakfast with him and his family, and found in his wife a lady with whom I had made a transient acquaintance in the whirl of London.

They urged me to stay some days, which was impossible for me, as I had already announced myself at O'Connell's, but I shall certainly avail myself of their invitation on my way to Cork.

From *Tour in England, Ireland and France in the Years 1826, 1827, 1828 & 1829*

Georgiana Chatterton

1838

HENRIETTA GEORGIANA IREMONGER, born in London in 1806, married Sir William Chatterton of Castle Mahon, County Cork, at the age of seventeen. Her first book, *Aunt Dorothy's Tales*, appeared anonymously, but the second, *Rambles in the South of Ireland*, proved to be one of the most successful nineteenth-century accounts of travels in Ireland, the first edition selling out within a week. She went on to write many tales, novels, poems and travel accounts. After the Famine the Chattertons retired to England. Following the death of Sir William, Lady Chatterton married Edward Dering. She became a convert to Roman Catholicism in the year before her death at Malvern Wells in 1876.

Lady Chatterton.

The following day we started by water for Castletown, which is a thriving little place, at the extremity of the western side of Bantry Bay. We intended to have gone by land, and secured, as we thought, two jaunting cars, to take us there early in the morning; but when the morning came, no cars were to be had; so the Inn-keeper at Glengariff persuaded us it would be both shorter, and more agreeable, to go in *his* six-oared boat. As the day was beautiful, and the sea smooth, I made no objection to the plan; though we had all some misgivings that it would prove a tedious business; and we were right. Three hours of hard pulling, and considerable tossing, round some of the rocky headlands which project into the bay, only brought us to Adrigoil, a little village just under Hungry Mountain and scarcely half-way to Castletown. The scenery, however, amply repaid us during the whole row. We passed near some curious caverns in the rocky cliff; but I am always so uncomfortable on the sea, that I could not perfectly enjoy anything. At Adrigoil, the gentlemen intended to ascend Hungry Mountain, which expedition, every one said, could not be accomplished under five hours: it would then be six o'clock before we could again embark.

When we landed at the beautiful little bay of Adrigoil, I felt so tired of the sea, and so apprehensive of another row to Castletown late in the evening, that I longed to find some conveyance by land. Except the pretty Glebe House, Adrigoil contains only a few scattered cabins, not one of which appeared big enough to shelter any animal larger than a pig. Ten miles, 'only ten Irish miles,' was stated to be the distance to Castletown; but rather than encounter my bitter enemy, the sea, in the dark, and in an open boat, I said I would walk. This was declared to be impossible. But, while we were all debating the subject, a woman came up and asked if we would come and rest ourselves a little at the clergyman's; she added, that he was unluckily from home, but that she knew he would be very happy to see any travellers at his house, all the same, and nothing would make him so well pleased as to hear that they had been comfortable there. We smiled at her good-natured bull, and still more good-natured face, but told her we were pressed for time.

'And is the lady going up the mountain too?' she enquired, with a face of alarm.

'Oh no,' said I, 'but I wish very much that I could get on to Castletown by land.'

'And sure why can't ye? Isn't it for the likes of you to do as is most plasin' to ye?'

I soon discovered that the clergyman's maidservant was one of those sort of people whom it is delightful to meet with when we are in a dilemma; a person who never thinks anything impossible, a character full of suggestions and comfortable expedients, and whose energy is sure to help one in any emergency.

In less than half an hour a cart and horse appeared; where they came from I never could learn; they seemed to spring out of the rocks at the behest of this most comforting woman. A *cart*, mind, not a car, nor anything half so convenient as the worst cart to be found in England, or on the Continent either. This primitive concern consisted of a few flat boards nailed together, laid on two long poles. Round this raft-like concern there were no rails, or ledge, to prevent my maid and myself, and our cloaks, from jolting off. On this we lay, for to sit was almost impossible; and off we went, amid the laughter of the whole party.

Variety is certainly pleasant, even when that variety is caused by the most dislocating of conveyances; and I enjoyed the journey extremely. In a totally new situation one loses most of that feeling of self-identity with all the cares and anxieties of life, which often depress our feelings. I seemed to catch the same spirit of happiness with those people who jolt along to market on such a vehicle, and I gave myself up to pleasant

People took to the roads in a variety of vehicles, like this one sketched by the Halls in 1842.

thoughts. There were few habitations along the side of the road, but we met some of the wildest-looking people I ever beheld – wild, I mean, in appearance, not manners – for I was particularly struck with the civil respectful way in which they all bowed to us, even though we travelled on the commonest vehicle. Many stopped to speak to our driver; perhaps to enquire by what chance he was driving such an unusual load as two bonneted females. But their curiosity was not obtrusive; and though they were evidently surprised, they did not stare at us disagreeably.

The appearance of the dwellings of the peasantry was more truly wretched than any I have ever seen. The people, particularly the children, were worse clothed. Some of the younger children, completely naked, were playing about before the miserable hovels. How strange that such rude habitations should send forth a people of such good and refined manners, 'who be,' as our driver said, 'the civilest-spoken folks in all Ireland, and have more good will to each other than is to be found in any other country on the face of the wide world.'

The amusing thoughts which my new position excited were only disturbed towards the end of our three hours' drive by the apprehension of finding a very bad inn, or, worse still (as I should be alone all the evening), no accommodation at all. My too active imagination was busy with expedients; though I had not much fear of finding a resting-place of some sort or other in a country where unkind looks or actions never meet the eye. So I only pictured to myself some interesting clergyman, and his good wife, or daughter, trying to make me comfortable; or an honest farmer, making the best of his humble dwelling, and turning everything topsy-turvy for my accommodation.

But then my entrance into Castletown on such a vehicle, covered with straw, in an old crumpled bonnet, and worn-out cloak, would not look at all respectable; and who would believe I was a 'real Lady?' These misgivings increased to such a degree, that as we drove jingling and creaking up to the inn door, my weary bones and exhausted mind did feel as if a very considerable portion of their future well-being depended on finding immediate accommodation and repose. I also inwardly hoped that the innkeeper might not look cross. The outside of the house appeared to promise well, but an old and ugly woman came to the door.

When the driver asked if there were rooms, she nodded her grey dishevelled locks, and I thought her beautiful. She helped me off the cart, and I hobbled upstairs, tired and stiff; but, oh! the joy and surprise of finding a large, well-furnished, and most comfortable sitting-room, with fresh flowers on the table, and beautiful geraniums in the windows! Everything was new and clean, and doubly delightful, as all this was unexpected. After the old woman had shewed me the nice bed-rooms, at the back of the house, looking out on the noble bay, I thought she was by no means so ugly, and I could have kissed her furrowed cheek.

My quarters, however, really needed not the fatigue of such a journey as I had just accomplished, nor the fear of finding no resting-place, to make them appear most excellent. The inn, indeed, proved to be such a one as would be considered good even at an English watering-place; which is very surprising, as the town is at the extremity of a long peninsula which leads to nothing, nor is there a road to or from it, except by Glengariff.

In the joy of removed apprehension, and the thought of what delight my fellow travellers would feel at finding me in such agreeable quarters after their hard day's work, I flew from room to room, sketched some picturesque figures from the window, and made a panoramic outline of the bay and its majestic mountains, from my bed-room. After thus occupying myself for some time, I felt so much rested that I was quite equal to a walk; and about half an hour before sunset I started off from the inn of Castletown, with my maid, on an exploring expedition.

We left the town by a road which I found led to the Copper Mines of Allihies; along which we proceeded until we met a sort of procession of men and boys on horseback, with branches of oak in their hands, and accompanied by women running alongside, uttering joyful shouts and acclamations. Not willing to encounter this merry but somewhat boisterous party, we retreated before their advance, and I enquired of a quiet, pretty-looking girl the reason of these doings. She said, while her fine eyes beamed with delight, that it was the O'Sullivan, the lord o' the soil, who had gained his cause. We afterwards heard that he was a descendant of the ancient family of O'Sullivan, who were the ancient lords of the soil, and that he had that day taken possession of a property near the town, about which there had been a long law suit.

Soon after we had met this gay procession, we heard shouts of joy in another direction; and as we were turning the corner of a street, a number of little boys ran up against us, and nearly overthrew my maid in their hurry and zeal to push forwards a large tar-barrel. We took refuge from the madcap glee of these boys in the doorway of a house where a woman was standing with her child in her arms. She seemed fully to participate in the general feeling of joy, and yet with true motherly fondness she looked every instant in her child's face, and smiled with more intense delight as she saw it clap its little hands, and crow at the unwonted noise and confusion.

Where a mother trusts herself with a loved child one feels safe: and I therefore remained by her side, watching the proceedings of the clamorous little group which surrounded the great tar-barrel. The boys placed it at the side of a gate which, I was told, was the entrance to Mr. O'Sullivan's place; and filling the barrel with hay and straw, set fire to it, and it was soon in a blaze. As the brilliant flames ascended, the clamours and huzzas became louder than before. Other tar-barrels in different parts of the town also began to blaze, and the dim twilight around now looked dark.

When I moved away from these demonstration of rejoicing, I felt myself obliged to hasten my steps, from seeing, alas! some men in a state of intoxication reeling (meandering, as some would say) along the street. But, notwithstanding, I took a last look at the fond and exulting mother, who instinctively clasped her child nearer to her bosom as these horrible men approached, and she called to another child, about two years old, who was standing outside, to come in.

Was it fear I saw then depicted on her hitherto happy countenance, or a natural horror of a vice she must every day see, or a presentiment of the dreadful event which soon plunged her in grief?

The next morning we heard that, about twelve o'clock that night, some drunken men upset the flaming tar-barrel. Its burning contents ran down and entered the door of the very cottage in which I had taken refuge, and which was thus set on fire. The woman was downstairs, but her children were asleep in the room above. Of course the anxiety of a mother was more powerful than self-preservation. She did not attempt to escape herself from the house, which was in flames in a moment, but ran upstairs and clung to the bed which contained her darling children. A gentleman who happened to be passing by, with that instinctive quickness which distinguishes superior minds, dashed into the burning cottage, and hearing the poor woman's cries above, regardless of the danger, hurried up. He there found the wretched mother straining convulsively her eldest child to her bosom. He tried to drag her away, but she was so paralyzed and bewildered with terror that she could scarcely move. The flames began to ascend the staircase – already the bed, to which she clung with the energy of despair, was enveloped in smoke. The clothes caught fire, when with a desperate effort, Mr. Davy, the gentleman whom I have mentioned, succeeded in carrying her off. He dashed again through the flames, and the woman, with her eldest child, were placed by him in safety in the street. The poor little child had suffered most; it was much scorched, and its little head was in a sad state, but the mother scarcely noticed this, so anxious was she to obtain the attention of the people. 'My child – my child – my little darling baby!' she exclaimed, with frantic despair, pointing up towards the window of the room which she had just left. No one understood her meaning except Mr. Davy, who immediately imagined that there was yet another human being exposed to the devouring fire. With wonderful presence of mind, he soon procured a ladder, and again entered the burning room. The mother stood in breathless agony gazing towards the window. Everyone had now become interested both for the mother and her heroical preserver – all stood in an agony of suspense – no sound was heard but the fearful cracking of the flames and fall of the burning rafters. Suddenly arose a thrilling shout from all assembled. 'Hurra, hurra!' was repeated, as Mr. Davy descended the ladder with the little infant in his arms. The mother saw it was her child, and she pressed it to her heart with a feeling not to be told. Poor woman! In that moment of intense joy, of unmixed delight and gratitude towards the preserver of her baby, she did not for one blissful moment perceive that the poor child's features were blackened – that it scarcely breathed; but Mr. Davy saw it all; and with the delicate perception which belongs to bold and noble minds, knew in an instant what the mother's feelings must be, and judged that it might deprive her entirely of reason if she knew that probably her little darling could not survive. With gentle firmness he took the baby from her, almost contriving that she should not see its horrible state; said he would carry it to his kind friend, the Doctor, who would attend to the burns, and directed her attention to her other child, who, he perceived, was not dangerously injured. The woman passed that night at a neighbour's house, occupied in attending her elder child. So completely shaken, however, had her mind been, that she became alarmingly ill, and raved towards morning in a fearful manner: the next day she sank into a deep sleep. As for the poor baby, it lingered only a few hours. When we left Castletown, the following day, no one had ventured to tell the unfortunate mother that her youngest child was dead.

This was not the only misfortune which occurred that night, but the other seemed almost a just retribution for the misery caused by those drunken men who had upset the tar-barrel. Soon after this deplorable occurrence one of them fought with his companions, and received a blow which fractured his skull. In a state of intoxication, and with his mind agitated by bad passions, the wretched man was hurried into the presence of his Maker! . . .

Friday. About half-past twelve we started for the Copper Mines of Allihies, and on our way passed near Dunboy, a castle celebrated in history as the last hold of the Irish under O'Sullivan, in the reign of Elizabeth. It is now a pleasant residence, belonging to the Puxley family; and a castellated addition is now making to the house. The ascent of the Knockoura mountain is very steep – even a light jaunting car can with difficulty be drawn up. I could not help applying the poetaster's rhymes on the achievement of General Wolfe to ourselves:

What was very bold, nay very particular,
We climbed up rocks that were perpendicular.

The view as we ascended was very fine, including the bay and headlands, and much of the mountain scenery which was now familiar to the gentlemen from their visit yesterday to Hungry Hill.

After we passed the highest point of the ascent, we had a magnificent view over that part of the Atlantic of which the mountaineers were deprived yesterday by the fog. Dursey Island and Blackball Point, which has a tower upon it, form one side, and Sheep's-head the other, of the entrance to Bantry Bay. The Skilligs (with which we were destined to become better acquainted afterwards) made their appearance in the extreme distance. They are two remarkable rocks, which seem to be nearly similar in shape, and stand about ten or twelve miles out to sea. Before us were the Hogs, two rocky islands apparently lying just at the mouth of the Kenmare river; beyond was Darrynane Bay, with its lofty mountains. Then, nearer, Cooleagh Bay, which is the summer harbour of the mines. On the side of the rocky eminence before us were the works of the mines – the engines and cottages of the miners scattered irregularly about. Of this extended view, which gives a map-like idea of the south-west of Ireland, the annexed sketch will convey some, but, I fear, an imperfect

The Allihies Copper Mines sketched from the top of Knockoura in 1838 by Georgiana Chatterton.

notion. We had a note of introduction to the Protestant chaplain of the mines, and we found him most civil and attentive to us.

The mines are now far from being so productive as formerly. The Company by which they are worked is at present going to great expense in a search, hitherto unavailing, after a new vein, and if the assertion of one of the captains is correct, they are now losing money. This account, however, is at variance with the stated produce: formerly it amounted to 600 tons a month; now it averages 350 tons. Copper ore is worth £9 a ton, but the purchasers always take off 2 1/2 per cent. a ton to cover their risk: consequently the real price is £7. 10s. 0d. a ton; this, at the former rate of production, would give £54,300 a year; and at the reduced rate of supply would still give £31,500 a year. An eighth goes amongst the owners of the fee, four, I think, in number; formerly the principal one received £4,000 a year. The company's shares amount to 64 which are divided, I was told, between five proprietors, of whom Mr. Puxley, whose place we passed today, is the chief.

The works, it is said, employ one thousand people. Girls, who attend the washing of the ore, get 3 1/2 d. a day; boys, 6d.; men, from a shilling to 1s. 4d. Miners work by task-work; a gang undertakes a piece of work at so much per ton, the price being fixed by a master, the ore to produce 10 per cent., to ascertain which an assay office is established. There are four captains. The men are paid monthly, and the calculation is made so as to give the men who handle powder about 1s. 4d. a day, the others about 1s. Many Cornish miners and their families are established here, and the English and Irish, notwithstanding a difference of religion, agree perfectly well together. It is said that for ten years there has not been a quarrel among the workmen, owing to a rule, which is strictly enforced, that whoever quarrels is immediately dismissed. We visited the school, where the children looked very comfortable; the girls with their hair very coquettishly braided and arranged. As we ascended afterwards we met two little Cornish children, one of whom answered 'Tolerably well' to every question . . .

The mine is now about 110 fathoms deep, and they are working it deeper, the vein occupying a narrow space. Five steam engines are employed; the first we visited works the crushing machine and the pounders. Over the pounded ore water is passed, the ore is then sifted, and, after a number of successive washings, the dross is separated. The situation of the head Captain, as the principal miner is termed, is worth about £300 a year, which includes his house and perquisites. Our reverend guide was extremely polite, but I though rather too fond of steam-engines, of the construction of which I must confess myself very ignorant, although I cannot help seeing the revolution they are effecting everywhere and in every thing. After having inspected the first works, we ascended to another engine, which is much higher up the mountain: and on our way we saw some curious clefts in the rock, which had been made by former excavations, and travelled over heaps of ore, the refuse of former works. The Captain observed that as far as his experience went, in Irish mines the richest part of the vein is near the surface.

The upper engine is used for pumping water out of the excavation; near it is the vent for the escape of the smoke from another engine, which is at work in the mine, about 160 feet below the surface. To pay this engine a visit, and thus to see something of the interior, was our next object; for which purpose we re-ascended. The passage by which we entered has a rail for bringing out the ore, and it also serves as a channel for the exit of the water pumped up. We had a wet and dirty walk. Stooping low, and creeping along the side, to avoid the water, we advanced to the steam-engine; we then diverged into a side gallery, to see the men at work. By means of ladders, the lower levels are attained; but as we were not properly equipped, none of my party attempted to descend. On our return, we visited some of the cottages, and with all my partiality for Irish peasants, I could not but see the striking superiority in point of cleanliness of the cottages belonging to the English miners.

After leaving the mines, we proceeded by a short cut to the top of the pass, as the road was too steep to allow of our remaining in the carriage: we were accompanied by a poor fellow, who just before our arrival had lost his thumb, from an accident with a steam engine; he however will receive pay until he is able to return to his work: this is done by an arrangement, under which a small deduction is made from the pay of those employed. At the top of the pass, we joined the carriage, but the rapidity of the descent made us all pedestrians again, and we reached Castletown after a very agreeable excursion, just before dark. Dr. A.* came to us in the evening, and we arranged a water expedition to see some caves near the mouth of Berehaven harbour, before our departure tomorrow. . . .

We crossed Berehaven to see some caves, which were said to be curious, and we lay to, as sailors term it, in a heavy swell, to make sketches of them. Afterwards we stood out to sea, so as, in nautical phraseology, to open the Three Castle-head and Mizen-head; we saw the rock from which Dr. A. had taken two eaglets this year, now the noble birds which are chained before the house at Dunboy. It is strange that the old birds offered no opposition, but sat quietly on an adjoining rock, looking on, while their offspring were captured.

Our next movement was across the bay to see the group of curious rocks called the Pipers; then we landed in the grounds of Dunboy, which are pretty; the house is to be castellated, and the workmen are now occupied in erecting a lofty tower, which is to have two companions. There is a nice little harbour at Dunboy, where the copper ore, from the mines of Allihies, is shipped in winter. We landed about half-past eleven at Castletown, and immediately afterwards left our landlady – the old flaxen-wigged waiter, who on Sundays enacts the character of priest's clerk – the old woman of all-work, and our comfortable quarters, with something approaching to a sincere feeling of regret. Our drive however served to dispel this sentiment. It was very agreeable, and we had a delightful day. Hungry Hill in all its glory. The gentlemen looked proudly up towards it, exulting that they had been on its summit. Beyond Adrigoil, as we passed the Goile mountain, the guides pointed to a large stone which appeared some way above us, and told us that it had served as a gallows for a robber who was executed there some years ago. The gentlemen said that they had heard this story on their ascent of Hungry Hill. The stone, as far as we could judge, was one of those huge upright stones, which are believed to have been reared in pagan times.

The scenery here delighting us, we dismounted from our jingling vehicles, to make sketches. A copy of that which I took is placed at the

* Dr. Philip Armstrong

commencement of the present volume. The huge mountain is the Sugar-Loaf, the scene of the legend of Shanagown and the unlucky crab, which caused the death of her wicked husband by a fit of indigestion.

From *Rambles in the South of Ireland during the Year 1838*

John Windele

1839

THROUGHOUT HIS LIFE CORK-BORN John Windele (1801–1865) was fascinated by the archaeology and literature of ancient Ireland. With fellow antiquarians he undertook many archaeological expeditions, where he examined and sketched sites and ruins. Ogham inscriptions were a special interest of his, and he saved many stones from destruction by creating a 'megalithic library', now at Cork University. Windele also studied old Irish-language manuscripts, and his extensive collection is now in the possession of the Royal Irish Academy.

There are two routs from Bantry to Glengariff, one by water, the other by land; each abounding in beauty and variety, but puzzling enough as to choice. In truth both ought to be seen, and for that purpose the tourist should take to the road on his outset from Bantry, and return by water.

A new road, in progress of construction, from Bantry to Glengarriff, will link that fairy district more closely with the town. In addition to the advantage of a level, and running along a picturesque coast, it will shorten the distance by two miles. The measurement of the present road is about ten miles.

The first object to be visited on the way is the *Assig*, or fall of Dunamark, one mile from Bantry. Immediately before reaching the bay, which is here full in view, the *Mialloch*, (i.e. the murmuring river,) is crossed by a small bridge, and, a little below it, the water is precipitated from a height of between thirty and forty feet, over a ledge of rock, worn into the most singular forms. The appearance of the fall, when the river is swollen by rains, is highly striking and beautiful. In the dry season, it is less impressive; whilst the vicinity of the mill and brewery of J. Murphy, Esq. in diverting a portion of the water, further diminishes the volume and effect. The neighbouring peasantry say, that salmon occasionally shoot up this fall, although others, less credulous, relate that only two have been known to effect the feat within the last hundred years. *Dun-na-mbarc*, which signifies the fortress of boats or barks, is remarkable in Irish history, as the landing place, according to a legend quoted in Keating, of *Ladhra*, the first mortal that ever trod upon the island. He was one of the companions of *Cesarea*, who, *forty days before the flood*, sought the Irish shore. Downengmarc, the Nards, Coureloume, &c. were granted (9th James 1st.) to Richard Lord Delvin, to hold for ever in common soccage. The Mialloch has its rise at the foot of *Knuckhoena*, a mountain within three miles of Dunmanway, remarkable for a cave, whose sides are inscribed with various characters.

From Dunnamark to *Reendonegan*, the distance is about a mile and a half. The lake of Reendonegan, (i.e. O'Donegan's head-land,) is a long sheet of water, apparently about half a mile in length, and separated from the head of Bantry bay by a narrow neck of land. The adjoining grounds are planted, and have a pleasing effect. *Gurteen-roe*, (i.e. the little red garden,) adjoining, is the seat of Shea Lalor, Esq. and 'Reendonegan house' of Daniel O'Sullivan, Esq., a brother in law of O'Connell.

Upon the Ouvane, are *Bally-lickey* (the ford of flags or slates,) the seat of A. Hutchins, Esq. and *Reendesart*, of Mrs. Warner. The river is crossed by a bridge of five arches. The woods in the vicinity belong to Lord Kenmare. *Reendesart*, which stands at the north side of the river, is an old fashioned house, with steep gables, massive chimnies, and abundance of ivy; a portion of the building is ruinous. An original structure, which preceded this, was one of the strong holds of Sir Owen O'Sullivan Beare, (Temp. Elizabeth,) but it was taken and demolished by Ireton, during the great Rebellion. In the bay without, Rabbit and Hogg islands are in view. . . .

The town of Kenmare, seventeen miles from Glengariff and thirty from Bantry, is situated at the north side of the *Roughty*, in a fertile limestone vale, nine miles long, and nearly a mile broad. It was, until recently, better known, and is still called in Irish, by the name of *Neddeen*, or more correctly *Nad Fion*, i.e. the cave or nest of Fion or Fingal; a cave near the town being still pointed out as the retreat of that redoubtable hero. Its environs bear a cheerful aspect of improvement, which contrasts agreeably with the dreary barrenness and desolation of the mountain tracts lately passed in the approach to it. The town contains 170 houses, and a population, according to the last census, of 1072 souls. It was first established, in 1670, by Sir William Petty, who introduced an English colony there; but until a recent period, it remained little better than a miserable village. In 1780, Arthur Young found Neddeen to contain but three or four good houses. It is at this day, a thriving and increasing town; and, considering the brief space of time within which the change that has led to this condition has been in operation, its growth has been of very great rapidity. For this, it is mainly indebted to its noble proprietor, the

Donemark Falls, near Bantry, one of the waterfalls that attracted lovers of the picturesque to Beara.

Marquis of Landsdown, the descendant of Petty. Under his fosterage and encouragement, the town has been, in a great measure, erected, and new approaches, – the efficient cause indeed of its prosperity, – constructed. The facility thus given to communication, and the conveyance of agricultural produce, having removed the main obstacles to its improvement and advancement. The completion of the great Landsdown suspension-bridge across the *Sound*, the foundation stone of which, was laid, in 1838, by the Marquis of Landsdown, and which is the first of the kind attempted in Ireland, will greatly encrease the advantages of its natural position. It will connect the two branches of the great road between Bantry and Killarney, and its cost will be defrayed jointly, by the Marquis of Landsdown and by the Board of Works. Already the erection of a Pier, for the use of shipping and the fishery, has been found not the least of the many useful improvements originally contemplated. The town consists of one principal street, and a lesser one, which stretches to the 'Sound,' as that part of the bay, near the town, is called, from its great contraction. It possesses a news-room, a hotel, and excellent lodgings for the conveyance of sea bathers, a Constabulary station, a Bridewell, Petty Sessions house, and

Market house; the latter built at the cost of its noble proprietor. The petty sessions are held on every Monday. The Church, rebuilt in 1814, is situated on a gentle eminence, about half a mile to the east of Kenmare, near the junction of the *Sheen* and *Roughty*, and facing the old cemetery of the locality on the opposite shore. The Chapel, a modern erection, stands near the eastern extremity of the town. Kenmare, also, possesses a small Wesleyan Meeting house.

The Kenmare river, on whose northern shore the town is situated, as already stated, is a fine estuary of the river Roughty (or red river). Its greatest length is about thirty miles, and in breadth, it varies from a few hundred yards to upwards of seven miles. Ptolemy, in the second century, notices this bay under the name of Jernus, or as some copies have it, *Ibernus*; and, in the circumjacent territories he places the *Velabri* or *Velibori*, – the Irish *Siol-Eibhir* (Silures), manifestly the Iberi or Illiberi of Spain, who gave the name to the *Ebro* of that country.

From *Historical and Descriptive Notices of the City of Cork*

Anna Maria & Samuel Carter Hall

1840

ANNA MARIA FIELDING (1800–1881) was born in Dublin and grew up in County Wexford. Samuel Carter Hall (1800–1889), a London journalist, was the son of Colonel Hall who had played a key role in the development of the Allihies copper mines. In 1824 they married. Mrs. Hall's *Sketches of Irish Character* was an immediate success and her subsequent books on Irish subjects were highly regarded. *Ireland: Its Scenery, Character, etc.*, written in collaboration with her husband, is one of the most comprehensive travel books of nineteenth-century Ireland.

The far-famed Bay of Bantry is, perhaps, unsurpassed by any harbour of the kingdom for natural beauties combined with natural advantages. As we approach it, along the dreary road from Skibbereen, a sudden turn, at the base of a rugged hill, brings us suddenly within view of the most striking objects which make up the glorious scene. Far and away, in the distant background, tower, and meet the clouds, the lofty Mangerton and Macgillicuddy's Reeks; nearer, rises Hungry Hill, the Sugar Loaf, and a long range – the Caha Mountains – among which it is said, and said on good authority, there are no fewer than three hundred and sixty-five lakes – the number having, of course, suggested a legend, that some holy saint prayed effectually for one to supply water for each day of the year. Little flat and fertile islands lie at the feet of the spectator; and, nearly facing the town, Whiddy Island, with its fierce-looking fortifications, and its fields rich with the promised harvest. It is impossible to do justice to the exceeding grandeur and surpassing loveliness of the scene; the whole of it is taken in by the eye at once; we are not called upon to turn from side to side for new objects to admire – we gaze upon it all; and he must be indeed dead to nature, who does not drink in as delicious a draught as Nature, in the fullness of her beauty, ever presented.

Anna Maria Hall.

The road into the town – a town that has been too truly described as 'a seaport without trade, a harbour without shipping, and a coast with a failing fishery' – runs immediately under the fine demesne of the Earl of Bantry – and all the way it is one continued line of beauty; we never for a moment lose sight of the distant mountains, or the foreground of green islands; while the ear is gladdened by the mingled harmony of the rippling waves, and the birds that sing among the foliage of the thickly and gracefully wooded plantations.

There are not many islands in this vast expanse of water – 'Whiddy' is the largest; and there are besides Hog, Horse, Coney, and Chapel Islands, flung into the glorious bay – land-locked, as we have said, by gigantic abrupt headlands, beyond which the Killarney mountains seem to tower into the clouds. . . .

To visit Glengariff, the tourist may proceed either by land, or by water across the bay; – it is obvious that the best mode will be to go by one way and return by the other, both offering strong temptations to the lover of the picturesque. Those, however, who take it in their route to Killarney, and do not design to make any stay at Bantry, had better continue the road; for the bay may be seen fully from the hills above either Bantry or Glengariff; or, at all events, by taking a boat a mile or two from the shore of either. . . . After passing three or four miles of good road, and comparatively cultivated land, we entered a rude and rugged district; barren hills

The Halls were not the only visitors to remark on the makeshift dwellings of some inhabitants.

towering over us at either side; and among them rapid streams rushing over gigantic stones down into the valleys. We left to the right an interesting object – a little chapel nestling among the barren hills; and a short way farther on we passed one of those singular dwelling places, by no means rare in this wild part of the country; we were startled by a human form issuing from a mass of huge rocks; and, upon inquiry, learned that a family actually lived in a hole which the rocks protected and sheltered. They had evidently fallen, ages ago, in the position they retained, enclosing and covering a natural chamber. On entering, we found a woman with three children; – the man was at work in the adjacent 'garden'; – here they contrived to exist during the summer months; for we ascertained that, in winter, they quitted it for some neighbouring town, where they worked or begged, according to circumstances. The woman replied to our few questions with cheerfulness and civility; and to an expression approaching to condolence as to the misery of her lot, replied 'It's bad enough to be sure, yer honour; but there's many have worse places to lay their four bones in.' While conversing with her, we observed a singular character watching our movements; it was one of the Kerry peasants, mounted on a small active pony, sitting in front of a pair of hampers, in which he had conveyed his tubs of butter to the market of Cork, from which he was now returning. The hampers were fastened to the horse by a rope of hay; and his bridle, which was merely twisted round the nose of the animal, was made of the same material. In this primitive style he galloped up and down hills as

Kerry Dragoon.

fearlessly, and far more safely, than a steed fully caparisoned for the chase. We learned that he was one of the class known in cities and towns by the cognomen of 'Kerry Dragoons.' We made a sketch of him, and introduce him to our readers. He was a fine handsome fellow, with keen grey eyes, white teeth, and a complexion bronzed by healthy exercise; by no means communicative, however, for to our questions he had but one answer – 'Nein English.' As we drew near Glengariff, we had a foretaste of the rich treat we were about to enjoy; for, long before we had again a glimpse of the bay, the scenery assumed a rich and luxuriant character, strongly contrasting with the dreary solitude we were leaving.

Language utterly fails to convey even a limited idea of the exceeding beauty of Glengariff – 'the rough glen' – which merits, to the full, the enthusiastic praise that has been lavished upon it by every traveller by whom it has been visited. It is a deep alpine valley, enclosed by precipitous hills, about three miles in length, and seldom exceeding a quarter of a mile in breadth. Black and savage rocks embosom, as it were, a scene of surpassing loveliness – endowed by nature with the richest gifts of wood and water; for the trees are graceful in form, luxuriant in foliage, and varied in character; and the rippling stream, the strong river, and the foaming cataract, are supplied from a thousand rills collected in the mountains. Beyond all, is the magnificent bay, with its numerous islands, – by one of which it is so guarded and sheltered as to receive the aspect of a serene lake. The artist cannot do it justice; and the pen must be laid aside in despair! Our memories, indeed, recall every portion of the magic spot – but only to convince us how weak and inefficient must be our efforts to describe it. We are again wandering through the glen – among majestic trees, fantastic rocks, and bubbling rivulets, which every now and then rush by huge masses of stone, and, finding a declivity, roar along their rapid way, until, encountering some new obstruction, they creep awhile, and anon force a passage onwards, breaking into masses of foam – forth ere the mountain torrents crawl or gallop to mingle with the broad Atlantic. The song of birds is either hushed or unheard; and but for the ripple or the roar of the waters, there is no sound to disturb a solitude perfect and profound. We look up to the mountains; they are of all forms, altitudes, and outlines. The most prominent among them is the Sugar-loaf, Slieve-na-goil, 'the mountain of the wild people', with its conical head, soaring into the clouds; and to the rear, but at a considerable distance, Hungry Hill, with its naked and meagre sides, down which runs a stream from the lake upon its summit, until, gathering as it goes, it breaks in a tremendous cataract of eight hundred feet, expanding as it falls, and flinging a spray around it, that seems to cover with a thick mist a third part of the hill:

Now a blue wat'ry sheet: anon dispersed
A hoary mist; then gathered in again,
A darted stream along the hollow rock,
This way and that tormented, dashing thick.
From steep to steep with wild refracted course,
And restless roaring to the humble vale.

We turn from the mountains but a step, and gaze over the broad bay; the foreground is composed of islands of various shapes and sizes; and we stand in the midst of cultivation, as if nature had resolved upon mingling as much grandeur and beauty as the eye could take in at once. We turn again and look inland; enormous rocks are scattered in all directions, without order or arrangement, but graceful from their very confusion; seeming as if the giants of old had done battle here, and fought with huge masses they had wrenched from the adjacent mountains.

From every part of the glen some attractive object may be discovered; but the best view, perhaps, is to be obtained from a small hill – small in comparison with its stupendous neighbours – in the immediate vicinity of a chapel west of the village; it places the spectator in the very centre of a glorious panorama, absolutely bewildering from its profusion of beauties. There will be a gush of enjoyment from the heart the instant this hillock is ascended. But it is from the road to Kenmare that the surpassing loveliness of the valley, and the full glory of the bay, will be seen to perfection. For three or four miles the traveller winds round the side of a mountain – a steep and weary road, so barren of interest that he has ample leisure to ponder over, and fix in his mind, the marvels he has seen. Suddenly he arrives on the brow of the hill. He is over the glen, many thousand feet above the ocean, which he beholds stretching out into space, while the islands appear as dots upon it; the river that runs through the valley has dwindled to a white thread; the trees have gathered into masses, and the hill upon which he stood a while ago seems no bigger than a fairy mound. Midway down are scattered cottages, the pale smoke from which alone distinguishes them from mole-heaps. Thin and narrow streams, like snow-wreaths, are running from the mountains; and every now and then his eye falls upon the lakes that send them forth to fertilise the valley. The whole scene is within his ken – its sublime beauty and its transcendent grandeur – ocean, mountain, glen, and river. He is in the midst of solitude; the clouds are on a level with him; at times, they hide for a moment every object from his sight. There is no song of bird to break the perfect loneliness; but if he looks upward he will see the eagle winging his way homewards in solitary grandeur. We were startled by the scream of one of them flying over our heads, so near to us that we could almost count the feathers in his wing. Our feeling was that he had seen enough of the sublime and beautiful in Nature, and need go no further in search of either.

On the summit of the mountain an incident occurred to us, which we may not omit to notice in this record of the most gratifying and interesting portion of our journey:

We had been gazing so earnestly upon the scene below and around us, that we had not noted the sudden appearance of a lad, upon a bank, a little to the left of the place on which we stood; but our attention was attracted by his clapping his hands together, and laughing, or rather shouting loudly, in evident delight at the scene. There was nothing in his appearance different from that of many young goatherds we had passed, and who hardly raised their heads from the purple heath to gaze at our progress. His sun-burnt limbs were bare below the knees; but his long brown hair had been cared for, and flowed beneath a wide-leafed hat, that was garnished, not untastefully, by a couple of wreaths of spreading fern. His garments were in sufficient disorder to satisfy the most enthusiastic admirer of 'the picturesque'; and although we called to him repeatedly, it was not until a sudden diffusion of cloud had interfered between him and the sunset, so as to diminish the light, and of course lessen the effect of the shadows, that he noticed us in the least; indeed, it was evident he would not have done so at all, but for the unexpected appearance of another 'child of the mist,' in the person of a little bright-eyed girl – literally one mass of tatters – who sprang to where the boy stood, and seizing his hand, pointed silently to us. He descended immediately, followed by the girl, and after removing his hat, stood by the side of our carriage, into which he peered with genuine Irish curiosity.

To our question of 'Where do you live?' the mountain maid replied 'Nein English.' We then addressed ourselves to the boy, when the girl placed her hands on her lips, then to her ears, and finally shook her head. 'Deaf and dumb?' I asked. Upon which she replied, 'Ay, ay, deaf, dumb – deaf, dumb.' The little creature having so said, regarded him with one of those quick looks so eloquent of childish love; and seizing his hand, raised her rosy face to be kissed. He patted her head impatiently, but was too closely occupied examining the contents of our carriage to heed her affectionate request. His eye glanced over our packages without much interest, until they rested on a small black portfolio; and then he leaped, and clapped his hands, making us understand he wanted to inspect it. His little companion had evidently some idea that this was an intrusion, and intimated so to the boy; but he pushed her from him, determined to have his own way. Nothing could exceed his delight while turning over a few sketches and some engravings. He gave us clearly to understand that he comprehended their intent – looking from our puny outlines to the magnificent mountains by which we were surrounded, and smiling thereat in a way that our self-love could not construe into a compliment.

While he was thus occupied, his little companion, struck by some sudden thought, bounded up the almost perpendicular mountain with the grace and agility of a true-born Kerry maiden, until she disappeared; but she soon returned, springing from rock to rock, and holding the remnants of her tattered apron together with evident care. When she descended, she displayed its contents, which interested us greatly; for they were her brother's sketches, five or six in number, made on the torn-out leaves of an old copy-book in pale ink, or with a still paler pencil. Two were tinged with colour extracted from plants that grew upon the mountain; and though rude, they bore evidence of talent. The lad could have had no instruction; the copy-book was the property of his eldest brother, and he had abducted the leaves to record upon them his silent observations on the magnificence of Nature, whose power had elevated and instructed his mind. We should not have read even this line of his simple history, but for the opportune passing of another 'Kerry Dragoon' – a wild, brigand-looking young fellow, mounted between his market-panniers on his rough pony – who proved to be the lad's brother, although he did not at first tell us so.

'We all,' he said, 'live up high in de mountain; but I can't trust him to look after de goats by himself. His whole delight is puttin' down upon a bit of paper or a slate whatever he sees. I'd ha' broke him off it long agone; but he was his mother's darlin', and she's wid de blessed Vargin these seven years, so I don't like to cross his fancy; besides, de Lord's hand has been heavy on him already, and it does him no harm, no more than himself, except when any of de childer brake what he do be doing; den he goes mad intirely; and strays I dunna where; though, to be sure, de Almighty has his eye over him, for he's sure to come back well and quiet.'

The lad at last closed our portfolio with a heavy sigh, and did not perceive, until he had done so, that his little sister had spread out his own productions on the heather, which grew so abundantly by the road-side. He pointed to them with something of the exultation of spirit so natural to us all when we think our exertions are about to be appreciated; and he bent over them as a mother would over a cherished child. His triumph, however, was but momentary – it was evident that his having seen better things rendered him dissatisfied with his own, for, while gathering them hastily together, he burst into tears. We gave him some pencils and paper, and a few engravings; and as the evening was approaching, bade him a hasty farewell; as he stood, his little sister clinging to his side, waving his hat on a promontory, while we were rapidly descending into the valley.

The village of Glengariff consists of but a few houses; there is a little inn, happily situated at the head of the bay; and the glen is divided between two proprietors – Lord Bantry and the widow of his brother, Colonel White. His lordship has a small lodge, where he generally resides, in a valley away from a view of the sea; but the other seat skirts the left of the bay, is cultivated to the water's edge, and commands a view of the principal island, on which is built a Martello Tower – as if for the express purpose of giving interest and value to the demesne.

The old bridge, now a picturesque ruin, which, in ancient time, was on the high road to Berehaven, is called 'Cromwell's Bridge.' History being silent as to the origin of the name, we must have recourse to tradition. When Oliver was passing through the glen to visit the O'Sullivans, he had so much trouble in getting across the narrow but rushing river, that he told the inhabitants, if they did not build him a bridge by the time he returned, he would hang up a man for every hour's delay he met with. 'So the bridge was ready agin he come back,' quoth our informant; 'for they knew the ould villain to be a man of his word.'

From *Ireland: Its Scenery, Character, etc.*

William Makepeace Thackeray

1842

Now best-known as the author of *Vanity Fair*, William Makepeace Thackeray (1811–1863) was born in Calcutta and educated in England. His first book, *The Paris Sketch Book*, was published in 1840. That same year he visited Ireland and again in 1842, under contract to produce *The Irish Sketch Book*, for which he also drew the illustrations. Thackeray once described novel-writing as 'a dreadful trade', and, had the financial returns been the same, would have much preferred to write history. Among his other novels are *Barry Lyndon, Pendennis* and *The Newcomes.* Thackeray also wrote for *Punch* and later edited the *Cornhill Magazine.*

W.M. Thackeray.

A smart two-horse car takes the traveller thrice a week from Bantry to Killarney, by way of Glengariff and Kenmare. Unluckily, the rain was pouring down furiously as we passed to the first-named places, and we had only opportunity to see a part of the astonishing beauty of the country. What sends picturesque tourists to the Rhine and Saxon Switzerland? within five miles round the pretty inn of Glengariff there is a country of the magnificence of which no pen can give an idea. I would like to be a great prince, and bring a train of painters over to make, if they could, and according to their several capabilities, a set of pictures of the place. Mr. Creswick would find such rivulets and waterfalls, surrounded by a luxuriance of foliage and verdure that only his pencil can imitate. As for Mr. Cattermole, a red-shanked Irishman should carry his sketching-book to all sorts of wild noble heights, and vast, rocky valleys, where he might please himself by piling crag upon crag, and by introducing, if he had a mind, some of the wild figures which peopled this country in old days. There is the Eagle's Nest, for instance, regarding which the Guide-book gives a pretty legend. The Prince of Bantry being conquered by the English soldiers, fled away, leaving his princess and children to the care of a certain faithful follower of his, who was to provide them with refuge and food. But the whole country was overrun by the conquerors; all the flocks driven away by them, all the houses ransacked, and the crops burnt off the ground, and the faithful servitor did not know where he should find a meal or a resting-place for the unhappy Princess O'Donovan.

He made, however, a sort of a shed by the side of a mountain, composing it of sods and stones so artfully that no one could tell but that it was a part of the hill itself; and here, having speared or otherwise obtained a salmon, he fed their Highnesses for the first day; trusting to heaven for a meal when the salmon should be ended.

The Princess O'Donovan and her princely family soon came to an end of the fish; and cried out for something more.

So the faithful servitor, taking with him a rope and his little son Shamus, mounted up to the peak where the eagles rested; and, from the spot to which he climbed, saw their nest, and the young eaglets in it, in a cleft below the precipice.

'Now,' said he, 'Shamus my son, you must take these thongs with you, and I will let you down by the rope' (it was a straw-rope, which he had made himself, and though it might be considered a dangerous thread to hang by in other countries, you'll see plenty of such contrivances in Ireland to the present day).

'I will let you down by the rope, and you must tie the thongs round the necks of the eaglets, not so as to choke them, but to prevent them from swallowing much.' So Shamus went down and did as his father bade him, and came up again when the eaglets were doctored.

Presently the eagles came home: one bringing a rabbit and the other a grouse. These they dropped into the nest for the young ones; and soon after went away in quest of other adventures.

Then Shamus went down into the eagles' nest again, gutted the grouse and rabbit, and left the garbage to the eaglets (as was their right), and brought away the rest. And so the Princess and Princes had game that night for their supper. How long they lived in this way, the Guide-book does not say; but let us trust that the Prince, if he did not come to his own again, was at least restored to his family, and decently mediatized: and, for my part, I have very little doubt but that Shamus, the gallant young eagle-robber, created a favourable impression upon one of the young Princesses, and (after many adventures in which he distinguished himself,) was accepted by her Highness for a husband, and her princely parents for a gallant son-in-law.

And here, while we are travelling to Glengariff, and ordering painters about with such princely liberality (by the way, Mr. Stanfield should have a boat in the bay, and paint both rock and sea at his ease), let me mention a wonderful, awful incident of real life which occurred on the road. About four miles from Bantry, at a beautiful wooded place, hard by a mill and waterfall, up rides a gentleman to the car with his luggage, going to Killarney races. The luggage consisted of a small carpet-bag and a pistol-case. About two miles farther on, a fellow stops the car: 'Joe,' says he, 'my master is going to ride to Killarney, so you please to take his luggage.' The luggage consisted of a small carpet-bag, and – a pistol-case as before. Is this a gentleman's usual travelling baggage in Ireland?

As there is more rain in this country than in any other, and as, therefore, naturally the inhabitants should be inured to the weather, and made to despise an inconvenience which they cannot avoid, the travelling-conveyances are arranged so that you may get as much practice in being wet as possible. The traveller's baggage is stowed in a place between the two rows of seats, and which is not inaptly called the well, as in a rainy season you might possibly get a bucketful of water out of that orifice. And I confess I saw, with a horrid satisfaction, the pair of pistol-cases lying in this moist aperture, with water pouring above them and lying below them; nay, prayed that all such weapons might one day be consigned to the same fate. But as the waiter at Bantry, in his excessive zeal to serve me, had sent my portmanteau back to Cork by the coach, instead of allowing me to carry it with me to Killarney, and as the rain had long since begun to insinuate itself under the seat-cushion and through the waterproof apron of the car, I dropped off at Glengariff, and dried the only suit of clothes I had by the kitchen-fire. The inn is very pretty: some thorn-trees stand before it, where many bare-legged people were lolling, in spite of the weather. A beautiful bay stretches out before the house, the full tide washing the thorn-trees; mountains rise on either side of the little bay, and there is an island, with a castle in it, in the midst, near which a yacht was moored. But the mountains were hardly visible for the mist, and the yacht, island, and castle looked as if they had been washed against the flat gray sky in Indian-ink.

The day did not clear up sufficiently to allow me to make any long excursion about the place, or indeed to see a very wide prospect round about it: at a few hundred yards, most of the objects were enveloped in mist; but even this, for a lover of the picturesque, had its beautiful effect, for you saw the hills in the foreground pretty clear, and covered with their wonderful green, while immediately behind them rose an immense blue mass of mist and mountain that served to relieve (to use the painter's phrase) the nearer objects. Annexed to the hotel is a flourishing garden, where the vegetation is so great that the landlord told me it was all he could do to check the trees from growing: round about the bay, in several places, they come clustering down to the water's edge, nor does the salt-water interfere with them.

Winding up a hill to the right, as you quit the inn, is the beautiful road to the cottage and park of Lord Bantry. One or two parties on pleasure bent went so far as the house, and were partially consoled for the dreadful rain which presently poured down upon them, by wine, whisky and refreshments which the liberal owner of the house sent out to them. I myself had only got a few hundred yards when the rain overtook me, and sent me for refuge into a shed, where a blacksmith had arranged a rude furnace and bellows, and where he was at work, with a rough gilly to help him, and of course a lounger or two to look on.

The scene was exceedingly wild and picturesque, and I took out a sketch-book and began to draw. The blacksmith was at first very suspicious of the operation which I had commenced, nor did the poor

Originally a thatched roadhouse, the Eccles Hotel was renovated in the latter half of the 19th century with such comforts as a library and picture gallery.

fellow's sternness at all yield until I made him a present of a shilling to buy tobacco – when he, his friend, and his son became good-humoured, and said their little say. This was the first shilling he had earned these three years: he was a small farmer, but was starved out, and set up a forge here, and was trying to get a few pence. What struck me was the great number of people about the place. We had at least twenty visits while the sketch was being made; cars and single and double horsemen were continually passing; between the intervals of the shower a couple of ragged old women would creep out from some hole and display baskets of green apples for sale: wet or not, men and women were lounging up and down the road. You would have thought it was a fair, and yet there was not even a village at this place, only the inn and post-house, by which the cars to Tralee pass thrice a week.

The weather, instead of mending, on the second day was worse than ever. All the view had disappeared now under a rushing rain, of which I never saw anything like the violence. We were visited by five maritime –

nay, buccaneering-looking gentlemen in moustaches, with fierce caps and jackets, just landed from a yacht: and then the car brought us three Englishmen wet to the skin and thirsting for whisky-and-water.

And with these three Englishmen a great scene occurred, such as we read of in Smollett's and Fielding's inns. One was a fat old gentleman from Cambridge – who, I was informed, was a Fellow of a college in that university, but whom I shrewdly suspect to be butler or steward of the same. The younger men, burly, manly, good-humoured fellows of seventeen stone, were the nephews of the elder – who, says one, 'could draw a cheque for his thousand pounds.'

Two-and-twenty years before, on landing at the Pigeon-House at Dublin, the old gentleman had been cheated by a carman, and his firm opinion seemed to be that all carmen – nay, all Irishmen – were cheats.

And a sad proof of this depravity speedily showed itself: for having hired a three-horse car at Killarney, which was to carry them to Bantry, the Englishmen saw, with immense indignation, after they had drunk a series of glasses of whisky, that the three-horse car had been removed, a one-horse vehicle standing in its stead.

Their wrath no pen can describe. 'I tell you they are all so!' shouted the elder. 'When I landed at the Pigeon-House . . . ' 'Bring me a postchaise!' roars the second. 'Waiter, get some more whisky!' exclaims the third. 'If they don't send us on with three horses, I'll stop here for a week.' Then issuing, with his two young friends, into the passage, to harangue the populace assembled there, the elder Englishman began a speech about dishonesty, 'd——d rogues and thieves, Pigeon-House: he was a gentleman, and wouldn't be done, d——n his eyes and everybody's eyes.' Upon the affrighted landlord, who came to interpose, they all fell with great ferocity: the elder man swearing, especially, that he 'would write to Lord Lansdowne regarding his conduct, likewise to Lord Bandon, also to Lord Bantry: he was a gentleman; he'd been cheated in the year 1815, on his first landing at the Pigeon-House: and, d——n the Irish, they were all alike.' After roaring and cursing for half an hour, a gentleman at the door, seeing the meek bearing of the landlord – who stood quite lost and powerless in the whirlwind of rage that had been excited about his luckless ears – said, 'If men cursed and swore in that way in his house, he would know how to put them out.'

'Put *me* out!' says one of the young men, placing himself before the fat old blasphemer his relative. 'Put *me* out, my fine fellow!' But it was evident the Irishman did not like his customer. 'Put *me* out!' roars the old gentleman, from behind his young protector. '—— my eyes, who are *you*, sir? who *are* you, sir? I insist on knowing who you are.'

'And who are you?' asks the Irishman.

This crowded touring car, drawn by Thackeray, was typical of those that served the Bantry-Kenmare route.

'Sir, I'm a gentleman, and *pay my way*! and as soon as I get into Bantry, I swear I'll write a letter to Lord Bandon Bantry, and complain of the treatment I have received here.'

Now, as the unhappy landlord had not said one single word, and as, on the contrary, to the annoyance of the whole house, the stout old gentleman from Cambridge had been shouting, raging, and cursing for two hours, I could not help, like a great ass as I was, coming forward and (thinking the landlord might be a tenant of Lord Bantry's) saying, 'Well, sir, if you write and say the landlord has behaved ill, I will write to say that he has acted with extraordinary forbearance and civility.'

O fool! to interfere in disputes where one set of the disputants have drunk half-a-dozen glasses of whisky in the middle of the day! No sooner had I said this than the other young man came and fell upon me, and in the course of a few minutes found leisure to tell me 'that I was no gentleman; that I was ashamed to give my name, or say where I lived; that I was a liar, and didn't live in London, and couldn't mention the name of a single respectable person there; that he was a merchant and tradesman, and hid his quality from no one;' and, finally, 'that though bigger than himself, there was nothing he would like better than that I should come out on the green and stand to him like a man.'

This invitation, although repeated several times, I refused with as much dignity as I could assume; partly because I was sober and cool, while the other was furious and drunk; also because I felt a strong suspicion that in about ten minutes the man would manage to give me a tremendous beating, which I did not merit in the least; thirdly, because a victory over him would not have been productive of the least pleasure to me; and lastly, because there was something really honest and gallant in the fellow coming out to defend his old relative. Both of the younger men would have fought like tigers for this disreputable old gentleman, and desired no better sport. The last I heard of the three was that they and the driver made their appearance before a magistrate in Bantry: and a pretty story will the old man have to tell to his club at the 'Hoop,' or the 'Red Lion,' of those swindling Irish, and the ill-treatment he met with in their country.

As for the landlord, the incident will be a blessed theme of conversation to him for a long time to come. I heard him discoursing of it in the passage during the rest of the day; and next morning when I opened my window and saw with much delight the bay clear and bright as silver – except where the green hills were reflected in it, the blue sky above, and the purple mountains round about with only a few clouds veiling their peaks – the first thing I heard was the voice of Mr. Eccles repeating the story to a new customer.

'I thought thim couldn't be gintlemin,' was the appropriate remark of Mr. Tom the waiter, 'from the way in which they took their whisky – raw with cold wather, widout *mixing or inything*.' Could an Irish waiter give a more excellent definition of the ungenteel?

At nine o'clock in the morning of the next day, the unlucky car which had carried the Englishmen to Bantry came back to Glengariff, and as the morning was very fine, I was glad to take advantage of it, and travel some five-and-thirty English miles to Killarney.

The Irish car seems accommodated for any number of persons: it appeared to be full when we left Glengariff, for a traveller from Bearhaven, and the five gentlemen from the yacht, took seats upon it with myself, and we fancied it was impossible more than seven should travel by such a conveyance; but the driver showed the capabilities of his vehicle presently. The journey from Glengariff to Kenmare is one of astonishing beauty; and I have seen Killarney since, and am sure that Glengariff loses nothing by comparison with this most famous of lakes. Rock, wood, and sea stretch around the traveller – a thousand delightful pictures: the landscape is at first wild without being fierce, immense woods and plantations enriching the valleys – beautiful streams to be seen everywhere.

Here again I was surprised at the great population along the road; for one saw but few cabins, and there is no village between Glengariff and Kenmare. But men and women were on banks and in fields; children, as usual, came trooping up to the car; and the jovial men of the yacht had great conversations with most of the persons whom we met on the road. A merrier set of fellows it were hard to meet. 'Should you like anything to drink, sir?' says one, commencing the acquaintance. 'We have the best whisky in the world, and plenty of porter in the basket.' Therewith the jolly seamen produced a long bottle of grog, which was passed round from one to another; and then began singing, shouting, laughing, roaring for the whole journey. 'British sailors have a knack, pull away – ho boys!' 'Hurroo, my fine fellow! does your mother know you're out?' 'Hurroo, Tim Herlihy! you're a *fluke*, Tim Herlihy.' One man sang on the roof, one *hurroo'd* to the echo, another apostrophized the aforesaid Herlihy as he passed grinning on a car; a third had a pocket-handkerchief flaunting from a pole, with which he performed exercises in the face of any horseman whom we met; and great were their yells as the ponies shied off at the salutation and the riders swerved in their saddles. In the midst of this rattling chorus we went along; gradually the country grew wilder and more desolate, and we passed through a grim mountain region, bleak and bare, the road winding round some of the innumerable hills, and once or twice by means of a tunnel rushing boldly through them. One of these tunnels, they say, is a couple of hundred yards long; and a pretty howling, I need not say, was made through that pipe of rock by the jolly yacht's crew. 'We saw you sketching in the blacksmith's shed at Glengariff,' says one, 'and we wished we had you on board. Such a jolly life we led of it.' They roved about the coast, they said, in their vessel; they feasted off the best of fish, mutton, and whisky; they had Gamble's turtle-soup on board, and fun from morning to night, and vice versa. Gradually it came out that there was not, owing to the tremendous rains, a dry corner in their ship: that they slung two in a huge hammock in the cabin, and that one of their crew had been ill, and shirked off. What a wonderful thing pleasure is! To be wet all day and night; to be scorched and blistered by the sun and rain; to beat in and out of little harbours, and to exceed diurnally upon whisky-punch – 'faith, London, and an arm-chair at the club, are more to the tastes of some men.

After much mountain-work of ascending and descending (in which latter operation, and by the side of precipices that make passing cockneys rather squeamish, the carman drove like mad to the whooping and screeching of the red-rovers), we at length came to Kenmare, of which all that I know is that it lies prettily in a bay or arm of the sea; that it is approached by a little hanging-bridge, which seems to be a wonder in these parts; that it is a miserable little place when you enter it; and that, finally, a splendid luncheon of all sorts of meat and excellent cold salmon may sometimes be had for a shilling at the hotel of the place. It is a great vacant house, like the rest of them, and would frighten people in England; but after a few days one grows used to the Castle Rackrent style. I am not sure that there is not a certain sort of comfort to be had in these rambling rooms, and among these bustling, blundering waiters, which one does not always meet with in an orderly English house of entertainment.

After discussing the luncheon, we found the car with fresh horses, beggars, idlers, policemen, &c., standing round of course; and now the miraculous vehicle, which had held hitherto seven with some difficulty, was called upon to accommodate thirteen.

From *The Irish Sketch Book*

Johann Georg Kohl

1842

BORN IN BREMEN, JOHANN GEORG KOHL (1808–1878) studied at the universities of Heidelberg and Munich. He journeyed widely throughout the world and was a prolific travel writer: Hungary, Russia, the Ukraine, Canada, the United States, Great Britain and Ireland were among the countries he visited. His books *Travels in Canada, Russia and the Russians* and *Austria* were as popular in their English translations as they were in German.

At Kenmare we found a suspension bridge, the only one in Ireland. The peninsula on the opposite side of the river was, however, just as barren and desolate as the one we had just left. Some of the mountains scattered over it are called the Glanerought mountains, and one is styled the Hungry Hill, an appellation extremely suitable to all the hills of Kerry. On the map are here laid down several rivers, which, although it was not the time of the year when they were likely to be dry, I could not discover. Not even one of the little brooks was to be seen, in which our wood-covered German hills are so abounding. The deposits of moisture from the atmosphere remain mostly in the morasses and bogs above described, and the hills and mountains may be regarded as huge sponges, which suck

Opened in 1841, the bridge connecting the Beara and Iveragh peninsulas was the first suspension bridge in Ireland.

up the humidity at some seasons and at others become again dry and withered. They contain very few perennial springs.

The plant which flourishes most here is the furze, whose yellow blossoms frequently enliven the dark valleys, and burst from the chinks and crevices of the rocks.

These wild regions have never been better cultivated, or more thickly peopled, than they are at present, nor will probably be so for many years to come. . . .

Ireland may indeed have formerly had much more wood than it has at present, and the large trunks of trees found in the bogs prove this; but I protest only against the notion that this rocky desert was ever covered by the endless beautiful groves I have heard spoken of. Besides the patches of potatoes before mentioned, the landscape was here adorned by a not less pleasing feature, namely, the new school buildings which rose on the waste. Even the road here is entirely new, not having been completed above a year and a half. Extraordinary difficulties opposed themselves to its formation; in many places rocks had to be blasted, and at the highest point a tunnel had to be cut through a mountain; and yet this is by no means the only undertaking of the kind completed within these few years in Ireland.

I had hitherto occupied the entire cushioned bench of the mail car, and I rejoiced when, as we were crossing a mountain, a woman jumped up and placed herself beside me. She was a Sullivan, – a name as common in Kerry as that of O'Brien in Clare, or Blennerhasset in Tralee. The lower members of the clan are called by the simple name, but the more distinguished mark their superior rank by the addition of O, – as O'Sullivan. Another family most widely extended in Kerry is that of the McCarthys, and I was informed that there were few people in the county who did not belong to one or other of the two clans.

The woman was smoking, and had a lighted piece of turf in her hand, which she said she was going to carry to her husband, who was at work at a little potato field up among the rocks. As I looked at her once or twice, she took her pipe from her mouth and offered it to me, but sorry as I was, I felt compelled to decline the courtesy. Strange, that all the world over so much politeness should be connected with this stinking weed. From the wigwam of the savage to the luxurious apartment of the Turk, or the elegant saloon of Paris, tobacco, in some form or other, meets us everywhere as a token of civility, and the snuff-box handed to a stranger has just the same signification in civilized Europe as the pipe of peace in the hut of the Indian.

At the top of the mountain Mrs. Sullivan got down from the car, and began to climb up the rocks with her lighted piece of turf in her hand, by the smoke of which we long distinguished her path. Wherever an Irishman is found there we are also sure to find potatoes and a smoking turf fire.

Through broken and blasted rocks we reached at length the point where the road-makers seem to have wearied of winding in a zigzag direction up the mountain, and to have resolved boldly to cut their way through it.

After entering the tunnel we turned our backs upon Kerry, and issuing forth at its southern extremity, we beheld the county of Cork lying before us lit by the rays of a brilliant sun. . . .

At the very entrance to the county of Cork we come to another celebrated little Paradise, – the mountainous district of Glengariff. Here we meet with innumerable cars laden with sea-sand proceeding into the interior. It is found very useful to mix with the cold clay and the acrid bog earth; as the Irish say, 'the sea-sand cuts up the clay,' and without it much of the land now under cultivation would be entirely useless. The fine new roads make the transport of this article much easier than it was formerly, and contribute, therefore, not a little to the improvement of the agriculture of the country. The sand from Bantry Bay, called 'coral sand,' is thought especially advantageous. It consists, in great measure, of broken shells and chalk.

The valleys of Glengariff are richly wooded and sprinkled with many pretty country houses, and the bay on which the village lies is as full of islands as the lakes of Killarney.

This is the renowned Bantry bay, so spacious, so deep, so tranquil, and so well sheltered on all sides, that it is said all the fleets in the world might safely anchor in it. It was in this bay that, towards the close of the last century, the French attempted a landing; here that, according to Thomas Moore, the colonists from Spain landed above a thousand years ago; and here, too, in all probability, the Phoenicians first set foot in Ireland, at some unknown period.

The prospect from the mountains over these waters is truly charming, and just as much so the road running round the bay, into which several little rivers pour their waters, while several inlets of the sea run far into the land. We crossed them by bridges overgrown by rich draperies of ivy, and several small islands were connected with the main land in a similar way. The steep headlands running out into the sea were often covered with potatoes to their farthest points, and sometimes with turf. In one of the little creeks we found a boat laden with oysters, generally very abundant on the western coasts of Ireland. For sixpence we bought such a quantity that some of our company overeat themselves, and had to remain behind, indisposed, at Bantry. Apropos of oysters, whenever I eat them in Ireland, somebody was sure to tell me a certain story of a man, who, having been advised to eat oysters by way of exciting an appetite, complained to his doctor that though he eat a hundred every day before dinner he had not noticed that his appetite was a bit better than it used to be. As this anecdote never failed to be told me on such occasions, I suppose I must set it down as a national Irish oyster anecdote. . . .

The town of Bantry, lying on a little elegantly formed bay, curving from the great one, is a very pretty place, and so I have generally found the towns lying immediately on the coast of Ireland. Idleness, disorder, poverty, dirt, decay, and ruin exist to a far greater extent in the interior. There is in the very nature of the sea something essentially fresh, healthy, and animating, that acts, perhaps, with a beneficent influence on those who dwell along its shores.

The fisheries of Bantry bay were formerly celebrated, but now, as of so many other European fisheries, we hear that they are no longer so productive as they were, either because the fish has greatly diminished in quantity, or that it has taken another direction. If this branch of industry has declined, however, another kind or fishing, that for sea-sand, is much on the advance. Formerly there were but few vessels employed in it, but now the number has so much increased that it has been deemed advisable to build a separate quay for them, along which I saw them lying in a long row. The greater activity manifested of late in the improvement and extension of Irish agriculture has given the great impulse to this branch of trade.

Even in this comparatively flourishing place, however, there are beggars and rags enough, as we found to our cost when we entered the fish market, which is a court surrounded by walls. Scarcely had I and my companions entered this place than we were surrounded by twenty or thirty beggars, who closed the iron gates behind us and declared they would not let us out again till we had purchased our freedom. As we hesitated about complying with a demand made in this style, the fishwomen came to the rescue and drove away the beggars, but only to plant themselves before the door and declare that the tribute to be paid belonged of right to them.

The town belongs to the Earl of Bantry, whose son, Lord Berehaven, takes his title from an island lying in the bay. Both these noblemen were absent, although they do not belong to the class of absentees, but usually reside here on their charming domains.

We paid a visit to their castle, which lies on the sea shore at the distance of an agreeable walk, but the housekeeper made at first some difficulty about showing it, as 'my lord' was 'very particular, and the castle was *all papered up*.' The idea of an entire castle wrapped in paper certainly excited my curiosity, and having found means to overcome the scruples of the housekeeper, we entered, and found, as it had been described, every thing from top to bottom of the house wrapped in paper – that is, in the great sheets of the Cork Constitutional, the paper of the largest circulation in this part of Ireland. The chairs and tables, the chandeliers, the walls, the bannisters, the door handles, the doors themselves, all were confided to the protection of the Cork Constitutional, to preserve them from dust or injury in the absence of the family. Even a metal figure of St. Patrick, and some antique metal dishes, hanging on the wall near it, were carefully wrapped up. The latter were said to be Spanish, but I could find nothing about them to indicate such an origin.

The entire mansion, though of great antiquity, wanted nothing of modern elegance and comfort; the English alone understand how to make themselves really comfortable in one of these old castles. . . .

As my friend was rather fatigued, he retired early, and I went out alone to take a walk late in the evening on the sea-shore, and soon perceived a something, I could not make out what, moving before me. As it passed a house some rays of light from a window discovered to me a strange kind of head gear decorated with flowers, which I recollected to have been worn by a beggar woman who I had seen in the fish-market. She was one of the mob who had closed the gates behind us, and in the wildness and eagerness of her gesticulations had suggested to me some doubts of her sanity, a suspicion somewhat confirmed by the fantastic character of her attire. She wore a yellow petticoat, the tattered remains of a large red shawl, which she trailed behind her in the dust like a train, and a man's round hat, with a broad brim decorated with a garland of artificial flowers. In her hand she carried a stout stick, by the aid of which she moved swiftly along. Altogether she reminded me of a character in one of Walter Scott's novels, as these half insane oddly decorated beggars always do, for she was by no means the only one of the class I had seen in Ireland.

Mary Sullivan, for that was her name, was now proceeding in a very quiet orderly manner along the shore of Bantry bay; at last I approached and bade her good evening, and she made a perfectly civil reply. It appeared that her business for the day was over, and, although she still wore the costume of her part, she had left the stage, and was on the point of returning to her private abode. As she said it was situated not far from the town, on the shores of the bay, I offered to accompany her to it, for I had a wish to see the dwelling of an Irish beggar at night.

We crossed some broken rocky ground, and at last, as it seemed to me, turned quite out of the beaten path, but Mary Sullivan said there was no other way, so on we went. She said if I would give her my hand she would lead me in safety to the hut, which it appeared belonged, not to her, but to her sister. These poor people generally prefer a wild looking place to live in; they seem to think they are more independent if their abodes are not very accessible, and the benefits of the great undertakings of the English in road making, are by no means so universally acknowledged by the Irish as we might suppose. We reached at last the hut of the Sullivans, which stood on a naked rocky ground, washed by the waters of Bantry bay, and crept in. The Irish are a very religious people, and have all kinds of pretty pious salutations always at hand. If they pass people at work in a field the regular form is 'God bless your work,' and the answer 'Save you too.' If one praises a person or even a thing, or more especially a child, one must never forget to add 'God bless it,' for praise always seems suspicious to an Irishman, and, unless accompanied by an invocation of God's blessing, it appears to him to indicate a desire either to possess it oneself or to destroy it by calling towards it the attention of fairies and bad spirits, who are always on the look out for what is beautiful. An Irish mother would rather hear a stranger say, 'What a nasty screaming, disagreeable brat your child is' than 'What a charming little angel you've got there,' unless he instantly warned off the bad spirits by adding 'God bless him.' As they never forget to ask a blessing, they are also most diligent in returning thanks. 'Thanks to the great God,' is a phrase often in their

The road connecting Kenmare and Glengarriff was completed in 1839, with tunnels cutting through Esk Mountain.

mouths, and certainly I believe in their hearts also. They often utter this thanksgiving even when speaking of a misfortune, as 'I've lost my poor dear little child, thanks to the great God,' a phrase that always reminded me of the Russian '*slawa bogu*,' which generally closes every story.

We crept into the hut of the Sullivans with the usual salutation of 'God save you all,' and heard the response 'God save you kindly' from the sister of Mary Sullivan and her half-grown daughter, who were crouching over a turf fire boiling potatoes. A little girl and boy were lying on the ground in company with some pigs, and gnawing a halfraw potato which they had taken from the pot.

The hut was lighted partly by the fire, and partly by a dim lamp, that hung from a rafter. The lamp was a large sea shell, filled with fish oil, in which was burning a rush wick.

The father was not at home, having been for some days upon the water, helping to collect coral sand, but another strangely sounding voice came from the corner of the hovel, which had taken no part in the pious salutation. I asked who was moaning there. 'It is my eldest son, your honour,' was the reply, 'he's an idiot – thank the great God – and he often moans so the whole day long.' By the feeble glimmer of the lamp I now recognised a poor creature, who seemed to me more miserable and helpless than almost any I had ever beheld. It was a young man about twenty years of age, lying in a sort of box, representing a bed, and which was indeed the best bed the hut contained. He had under him straw and rags, and a pillow for his head, but he lay sobbing and trembling all over. His mother showed me some parts of his miserable frame. His arms and legs were like those of a skeleton, and several of his fingers had grown together. As we touched him he lifted up his head, and gazed at us with a vacant look.

'He has been so from his birth, your honour,' said the mother. 'For twenty years we have been obliged to feed him so, without his being able to do the least thing for us.'

'And yet you love him?' said I to the poor mother, thinking perhaps that an unfortunate creature like this could hardly be attended to in the midst of such poverty.

'Love him? to be sure, your honour. Isn't he my own son, God bless him. Eh, Mavourneen, look up then,' she added, raising him carefully up, and laying his head on her arm, while she stroked his crippled hand. 'I'm the only one, sir, that understands his language. He never asks after any body but me. I give him every morning his potatoes, and, when I've got any, milk and porridge. You see he's got a better bed than any of us. Don't sob so, darling.'

Mary Sullivan, the old aunt of the idiot, had, in the meantime, hung upon a peg her flower-adorned hat, and the other parts of her costume, and had taken from her pocket some potatoes and a fish, which had probably been given to her. The potatoes she laid at the corner of the fire which she seemed to consider as her own, hung the fish up by a wire over it to roast, and then took out her pipe and began to smoke. She told me, in answer to my question, that she spent about a halfpenny a-day in tobacco, that is fifteen shillings a-year, which, for a beggar, appeared to me to be no inconsiderable sum. For a halfpenny one can buy, in Ireland, a large piece of bread; and I could not help wishing that some second Father Mathew might arise, to preach a total abstinence from tobacco, and induce the poor Irish women to expend what it costs them in wholesome food for themselves or their children.

Tenderness and hospitality are the universal characteristics of the Irish. They have also a certain easy politeness of manner towards strangers, which, in the higher classes, somewhat resembles that of the Parisians, but is met with just as often in the huts of the poorest beggars. In many countries, the stranger who enters the hut of a poor family, is stared at in dumb astonishment by the inmates, till they become familiar with him.

Not so in Ireland. Dirty and ragged as they are, they offer what they have, without embarrassment, to the most fashionably-dressed visitor; and although they never forget the respectful address, 'your honour,' yet they always appear to consider him what he really is – their guest and equal.

When I parted from the Sullivans, I was accompanied to the door by many a warm 'God speed ye,' and by the most cordial thanks for the honour I had done them by my visit, and for the sympathy I had expressed for the unfortunate son and brother. The two little ones had, in the meantime, lighted a couple of dry fagots, by way of torches, and accompanied me out over their irregular mountain path. When at last I drove them back, and bade them farewell, I saw them for some time standing together on the hill-top, throwing the light of their torches before me on my path, while their clear, sharp, childish voices echoed around, as they shouted, 'Take care, your honour! take care. God speed ye!'

From *Ireland, Scotland, and England*

Asenath Nicholson

1845

ASENATH NICHOLSON *née* Hatch (1792–1855) first thought of visiting Ireland when she worked among poor Irish emigrants in New York. In 1844, recently widowed, she set off for Ireland with two bags of Bibles in Irish. She must have presented a quixotic figure in her polka-dot coat, bonnet and rubber boots as she tramped the countryside. But though her success with the Bibles was limited, Nicholson made a contribution to Famine relief. In 1847, she started a one-woman relief operation, distributing food from her own resources. She spent time in Cork with Temperance campaigner Father Theobald Mathew before returning to America in 1852.

When about leaving Cork for Killarney I intended taking the shortest and cheapest route; but Father Mathew said, 'If you wish to seek out the poor, go to Bantry.' I took his advice, went to Bantry, and there found a wild dirty seaport, with cabins built upon the rocks and hills, having the most antiquated and forlorn appearance of any town I had seen; and the people in rags and tatters such as no country but Ireland could hang out.

The night was dark and rainy when I reached the town, and a comfortable parlour and cheerful fire hid the appalling desolation that brooded without. The morning opened my eyes. I made my way upon the rocks, found upon the sides of them some deplorable cabins, where smoke was issuing from the doors, and looking into one, the sight was appalling. Like an African kraal, the door was so low as to admit only a child of ten or twelve, and at the entrance a woman put out her head, with a dirty cloth about it; a stout pig was taking its breakfast within, and a lesser one stood waiting at a distance. The woman crouched over the busy swine with her feet in mud, and asked what I wanted.

Asenath Nicholson.

I told her my errand was to see how they do in Ireland, among the poor. 'An' faith, you see enough on 'em here.' Looking in, I saw a pile of dirty broken straw, which served for a bed for both family and pigs, not a chair, table, or pane of glass, and no spot to sit except upon the straw in one corner, without sitting in mud and manure. I ascended the rock a little higher, and entered a second. On the left hand of the door was a bank on which lay a young man upon straw; and upon a couple of stools sat the master and mistress, waiting the cooking of a pot of potatoes for breakfast. 'Is anyone sick?' 'No, no, idle, idle,' answered the mother; 'nothin' to do, and so he lies in bed. The old man here has no airn'd but a shillin' since St. John's.' 'And how do you live?' 'We gets our potatoes when we can, ma'am; and that's all, ye see.' 'So you live, because you can't die?' 'Just so, lady; because the Almighty God don't see fit to take us away, an' we must be content with what He sends us; but sure, may we ask, what brought ye here among these wild rocks?' 'To see the poor of Ireland; and I hope to go through the country, and see them all.' 'And ye'll have a long purse when ye return.' Supposing she alluded to money, I told her, 'Not a pound, perhaps.' 'But ye'll have the whole chart of Ireland, ma'am.'

I looked at this woman, and at the appurtenances that surrounded her. 'The whole chart of Ireland,' from her lips that could neither read English nor Irish! She had a noble forehead, an intelligent eye, and a good share of common sense; she had breathed the air of this wild mountainous coast all her sad pilgrimage, and scarcely, she said, had a 'dacent garment covered her, or a wholesome male of mate crassed her lips, save at Christmas, since the day she left the parents that rared her.' Telling them I wished someone to carry my carpet-bag to Glengariff, the old man said he had a son as honest as any lad in Bantry, and he should take it for a shilling; the bargain was quickly concluded. A lofty, well-finished poor-house was behind these abodes of misery, and the old lady showed me up the slippery pathway to the gate. This was closed, and no admittance; the keeper was not there, and not a person in it, and never had been, though all things had been ready for a year; the farmers stood out, and would not pay the taxes. It is a pity that the money laid out to build, and pay a keeper for sitting alone in the mansion, had not been expended in giving work to the starving poor, who might then have had no occasion for any house but a comfortable cottage.

I left an Irish Testament where the man of the family could read Irish well, and where no Bible had ever been. The peasants in this part of the country are not so afraid of the Scriptures if they speak Irish, because they attach a kind of sanctity to this language.

The next morning looked a little propitious, and I hurried to Wigwam Row, to apprise the boy that he must be ready for the journey.

This Wigwam Row is entitled to a little explanation. It consists of a row of cabins, built literally upon a rock, upon the sloping side of a hill, where not a vestige of grass can grow, the rock being a continued flat piece like slate. The favoured ones who dwell there pay no rent, having been allowed in the season of the cholera to go up and build these miserable huts, as the air upon the hill was more healthy. And there, like moss, to the rocks have they clung, getting their job when and where they can.

After much beating and battering at the crazy door, the old man peeped out, calling, 'Who's there? and won't it do as well for me to go?' 'I have no choice,' replied I. 'In an hour,' said the old man, 'I will be with ye.' The hour had not expired when the old man was at the door, with 'We had better take the airly part of the day.'

We soon left sight of Bantry, and hurried on through the mud to the amazement of the multitudes we met on their way to town for market. But the Bay of Bantry – the bay of all bays – stretched out on our left with its islands, and what with gaping on either hand, and looking now and then how to avoid the mud, my gallant John would be far before me. He would often sit down upon a wall, till I was within speaking distance, then, giving the wallet a further hitch upon his shoulder, would rise and hasten on, thus not leaving me a moment for rest. At last I contrived to lighten my burden, by taking my huge black muff, which was quite the gaze of men and women, as well as the fright of all the children in mountain and glen, and drawing it up closely at one end, so that the Irish Testaments that were in it could ride safely. I begged my guide to allow me to fasten the muff to his wallet, as the day was getting warm, and it quite impeded my travelling. Hanging at one end, and being large and made of the fur of the black bear of the American forest, it made John an object of still greater interest to the wondering peasantry, who all seemed to be acquainted with him. 'And what is this, John? and what sort may the cratur be that's hanging at your back?'

On a sudden, a terrible crash was heard, and lo! the handle of the basket had given way. Out tumbled books, Wicklow pebbles, etc., and a complete overturning of all the contents of the wallet took place. With strings and pins, matters were again adjusted in a tolerably good way; but John, in fastening all together, had the shrewdness so to manage that the muff was again turned over to me.

Before the filthy door of my lodging-house were horses, men, and asses in thick array. John with his wallet squeezed through, and I followed before the passage was closed. 'This is the way, ma'am,' leading me up a dark whisky deposit, entered by a hole a few feet high. In this place stood a dirty woman pouring muddy coffee into bowls, and sending it to a mass of ragged countrymen, who were drinking it without milk. She was occasionally interrupted by a call for hot punch; 'Going, going,' was the answer, and going they were in very deed. This lodging was the height and depth of all that I had seen in depravity. 'Can I have some boiling water?' 'When the men are sarved, ma'am.' John had seated himself upon a bench, quietly smoking, past all hurry, though in the greatest haste for the last three hours. Saying to him, as he was in fear of night, he had better take a loaf of bread, and not wait for the kettle. 'Aw,' he said, 'I'll wait for the kettle, plaise God.' The kettle came, a bowl of cocoa and a loaf of bread were soon dispatched. 'Take care of yourself and your things, ma'am, or ye'll not have a ha'p'orth belonging to ye,' he whispered as he went out.

When John was sitting upon the wall, eating a piece of bread, I asked, 'Do you expect to go to heaven?' 'No, ma'am, I shall never go to heaven. The poor, ma'am, are great sinners, and must not expect to go there.' 'The poor will certainly go to heaven, if they repent.' He still insisted, 'The poor are very wicked, and must not expect to go there. No, no, ma'am, I shall not get there.' As he was departing, I said, 'John, I shall see you no more, and I beg you to go to Christ, and be saved.' He paused, resting on his stick; then giving me a piercing glance of desponding bitterness, he shook his head, and answered emphatically, 'That can never be for me.' What had so firmly fixed this opinion, I could not nor can I imagine, for it seems to be the prevailing consolatory belief of the peasantry in Ireland, that the poor are in a much better way for heaven than the rich.

I stepped back into the room, and for a few moments gave the gaping multitude full scope for curiosity. They stood before me, they sat down by my side, they minutely examined my dress, they asked all sorts of questions

A 19th century engraving of the Bay of Glengarriff with Garinish (Ilnacullin) Island and Cromwell's Bridge.

concerning America – 'An' maybe ye didn't know Mick Flanagan, or Pat Dogherty? An', by dad, she'd a dacent body, and she never come the long way without a good bit in her purse,' etc. When the wonder began to flag, I put my luggage into the care of the hostess, and went out to wander in the glen, and by chance came upon an old decayed bridge, which is said to have been constructed by Cromwell to march his army over, when he wasted Ireland. The name of Cromwell is hated by every peasant in Ireland, and scarcely a decayed castle, bridge, or abbey, but what the stranger is told, 'This is the doin' of the blackguard Cromwell.'

Ascending a rock overlooking the road, I saw beneath me a group of all ages, from 'the man of grey hairs' to the nursling at the mother's breast. Not an individual, man, woman, or child, had on a whole garment, and many of them, like 'Joseph's coat,' were variegated with 'many colours': patches of all shades, with threads of all hues, adorned the limbs of these rustics, who had heard of my arrival, and had come out to see 'the wonderful body' that had left her 'country and kin to say the poor Irish.' They were God's creatures made in His image, and bound to the same tribunal with me. Singing a hymn, in which all instinctively joined, if not devoutly,

I said a few words on the subject of temperance, and the regret I felt that I should find this glen given to the immorality of drinking, when a great part of Ireland had become so sober. They murmured a response – 'By dad, she's right,' and slowly walked on, while I descended to enter the lodging. They came nearer, urged me to 'smoke a blast' or to 'take a drap' (notwithstanding my lecture), talked of my coat and bonnet; came bracing themselves against the wall, some sitting close by my side, and others squatting upon the ground at my feet. Fortunately for me, the organ of fear is not so largely developed as in some of more flexible texture, and my greatest suffering arose from pity and disgust.

My room was up a broken staircase, leading from the kitchen. A dilapidated door with a broken latch, like an inn among the far western wilds of America; a floor of loose boards, gaping wide between joints into the kitchen below; and all sorts of lumber, from the three-legged chair, broken chest, and crazy table, to the ploughshare, with the worn-out gear of the ass, and basket for peat and manure. As my door was past all fastening, a company at whisky and cards, at every pause in the whisky or play, would in turn push it a little wider, and look in. This continued till one o'clock, when I, still sitting, knew by the 'God bless you's' and 'Ye'll be late for the night,' that the company were retiring. In the kitchen early on Sunday morning a goodly number were in waiting, and in ten minutes from my landing at the bottom of the stairs, not less than a score had arranged themselves in positions where the most favourable gape at me could be secured. Nor had one wasted a precious moment too long at the toilet. Some stood with hair erect, some with an apology for a shirt, and some with remnants of coats; some with waistbands sufficiently strong to support desperate trowser-legs held with a deadly grasp by a tatter here and there; some with dresses turned over their heads, and some pinned about their waists; some with cloaks, and some with caps, and all with naked feet. They were all quietly fixed, when I gathered up my effects, put them in charge of the girl, and hurried into the glen, stopping neither to warn nor rebuke – a morning long to be remembered.

Being told there was no church held in the place, and that Lord Bantry was a Protestant, lord or no lord I determined to venture to his house, and if possible spend the day with him. 'He's a convairsable body, and he'll make ye right welcome,' I was told. At the gate-house the cleanly woman met me at the door, and kindly invited me in to take breakfast. The neat little cottage, and cleanly-spread table, were such a contrast to the den I had just left, that I felt that I was still within the reach of something human.

I sent my card in to the noble lord; and he returned it by the hunched-back girl in attendance, who civilly said his lordship, being ill, was sorry he could not see me, but would send a boy to show me the curiosities of the glen. The gamekeeper's wife invited me into a neat little parlour, and showed me everything of interest about the mountain. She was English, and quite unreconciled to stop in Ireland. When I reached the lodge, the hospitality was repeated by the generous offer of a room and board without any charges. What could be kinder, and what could be cheaper?

Two days' rain kept me in the house, only giving opportunity for a call at the Saturday night's lodging place to take my luggage. The man was a pledge-breaker, and a besotted drunkard, and his wife a professed teetotaler, only taking her hot punch when going to bed. When I told them why I left the house, she left her bowl of tea and went away. He hastily arose, and took down a large Douay Bible from a dirty shelf, over the kegs of whisky, and wanted to 'discoorse me' to show both his knowledge of Scripture, and the lawfulness of his employment. This wicked house had been, I was told, the ruin of the glen. It had been five years before baptised by Father Mathew, but he then gave pledges for a stated period, when requested, and, when the time expired, many rushed headlong into the fatal vortex. 'They are too much for me,' said the poor priest, 'since that publican's house has been opened.'

On our route we passed a couple of rocks, celebrated for having been the abode of a family of seven for three years and a half. Lord Bantry at last built them a cabin, and turned them into it. This novel habitation is composed of two rocks, meeting overhead, like the roof of a house, and so wide at the bottom that there was room for a bedstead. The upper end of the rocks are so snugly joined, that they could be closed with leaves and brush, as the occupants might choose.

On my return, a little girl was ready to accompany me up the glen to the 'Eagle's Nest.' We had a river to cross without a bridge, and the late rains had so swollen it, that the stepping-stones were covered. I made my way over rocks, bogs, and hillocks in despair, till a ragged peasant, driving a horse with two baskets of lime across his back, called out to the child, in Irish, 'I'll go and lift her across.' He was old, and I did not think it safe; but he rolled up his pantaloons, waded the river, and proffered his services in Irish. As I declined, he found a place where, taking me by the hand, he helped me, at considerable peril, over the slimy rocks; and, ascending the precipitous bank, he braced his feet, pulled me up the steep, and set me on terra firma.

In half an hour we reached the slated house under the mountain. The entrance was blockaded by an old worn-out horse, with two baskets of lime on his back. We crawled under the straw bridle of the horse, and entered a room where manure stood in isolated hillocks, and a calf and a pig were leisurely walking between them.

'Do you read Irish?' I asked the woman. With a pause of astonishment she looked upon me, and, with a child-like laugh, said, 'I read! The like of me read! Not a ha'p'orth of Irish or English.' Her daughters were in like condition, and as much diverted at my strange question as the mother. Speaking of the goodness and mercy of God, they sobered at once; and after talking a few moments, we left without presenting any books, as they could not read.

Children from the thickly-clustered cabins now crowded forth, and one bawled out, 'A penny for a crass, ma'am.' This means, translated, a ribbon crossed upon the arm, to be worn on St. Patrick's Day, which was near at hand.

The 'Eagle's Nest' was the last wonder, deriving its name from an eagle having made its nest in a fissure of the rock towards the top of the mountain. And you are told that a man named Sullivan supported a family of six, as he testified, by going to the nest daily, and taking the flesh of lambs, hares, and deer, which were left for the young ones. This tremendous mountain has a hideous, grand, and awful appearance, looking down upon these wretched abodes smoking beneath.

Getting home across the river was the next question. My guide said we should 'be destroyed' getting through the bog and rushes on the other side. Engrossed in my thoughts, I heeded neither the admonitions of the child nor the peril in my path. I stepped upon the rocks, and soon found myself in a perilous situation; the rocks slippery and far asunder, the water deep and turbid, and I could neither take off my India-rubber shoes nor maintain my position with them on except with a great effort. I saw my folly, and directed the child to take a horizontal direction up the bank, and watched till at last she stood on the steep bank over my head. To retrace my own steps or stay where I was, looked alike impossible, and to try to ascend the bank would be almost madness. There was no alternative but onward. I clasped a bunch of hanging twigs; they loosened the earth, and I felt myself sliding. The presence of mind of the child saved me; she caught the twigs in an almost supernatural grasp and said, 'Take hold at the top, lady, and I will hold fast at the bottom so that you can't pull them up.' It was done; I was on the bank, and not till I looked down the precipitous steep did I realise the presumptuous step I had taken.

I took another ramble later to the head of the glen, a distance of nearly three miles. Following a path leading from the main road, I saw a broken cart, and then upon my left an aperture into what I thought might be a cave or mountain den. There I found a pig nestled in some straw, and a voice from within called out, 'Maybe ye'd like to come in and take a hait by the fire.'

Thackeray sketched these pipe-smoking women – a common sight in 19th century Beara.

Had this invitation proceeded from a sepulchre, it could not have been much more surprising – and not half so unnatural for the abode of the dead as the living. I stooped down, stepped over the obstinate pig, and entered.

Against a huge rock – for there was no chimney – there burned a few little twigs of wood. Three sisters – the eldest seventeen, the second twelve, and the third two, all nestled in straw; neither bed nor table encumbered the room.

'Where do you sleep?' I asked.

'Poor folks must do as they can, ma'am – we lie here,' pointing to a pile of straw on the left.

'How do you live?'

'As we can, ma'am.' I then spoke of Jesus Christ. 'I don't understand ye,' said she. 'Do you not know whom I mean by Jesus Christ?' I asked.

She could not comprehend me, and the second sister said, 'We don't go to church or chapel, ma'am.' I inquired how long they had lived there. 'One year, ma'am.' They had no father, and the mother had gone from home, begging, I supposed.

This day finished my tour in the glen, and it had been the most peculiar of any I had had in Ireland. I had found that man, left to instinct alone, will not make himself as comfortable as the beasts of the field, or birds of the air. Here were literally exemplified the words of Job, when he said of the poor – 'They embraced the rock for a shelter.'

And here I would add, if any one thinks that man has anything to boast since the fall, let him explore the mountains, the glens, the caves, and even the towns of Ireland; and, lest he should find a loophole for his pride, let him go to the places where the Bible is known, and if the grace of God have not changed the heart, he will find the same degradation in morals as in those places where it has not been read.

Saturday morning, 7th March. Though this glen, in point of filth and whisky-drinking, stands pre-eminent, yet they suffered the plainest rebuke without a retort. They received tracts, and thanked me after reading them, for giving them such kind advice; and the priest, who lived some miles from the glen, sent a message by his clerk, thanking me for the advice I had given, and the tracts I had distributed. A right spirit and a right manner have much to do in the success of introducing any principles clashing with long-cherished ones of our opponents.

If a sanctimonious monk, full of zeal for his church, with crucifix and rosary in his hand, should come into our houses and tell us we are all going to perdition, because we did not say his prayers, and embrace his faith, and insist that we should assemble our household to hear the truth from his lips, would we do it? Should he rail on our clergy, and denounce our Sabbath Schools, think you he would get a patient hearing?

Let us reverse this picture – let us allow our brethren of the human family the same prepossession, however absurd they may be, till, by a course of Christian charity, we show them that the religion we profess is indeed what we call it, a religion of love, and calculated to do the most permanent good.

Our path lay over brambles amid rivulets and walls, up one of the tallest mountains in the glen, from the summit of which is one of the most picturesque views in all Glengariff.

It was a long and difficult ascent, but courage kept me steady. I was told that there are in this glen, and upon the mountains, three hundred and sixty-five lakes. This I am not prepared to prove or dispute, yet I think it may not be improbable. The hill ascended, we reached the newly-walled road made upon the top of a narrow ridge of mountain, with a glen on each hand at our feet, a precipitous steep of many yards leading to these ravines, which in most places made a dizzy and fearful sight to the traveller. At length the tunnel, hewn through a rock like the arch of a bridge, met our eyes. Here was the wonder of wonders. For the distance of eighty perches a hole is cut sufficiently wide and high for coaches to pass, and the only light admitted is from the entrance at each end, and one little aperture in the top. The water was percolating through the rock, and darkness made it a prison not inviting for a long tarry. Giving full scope to my voice in singing, the echo was tremendous. After walking some miles we came to the house of the priest of the glen. He had gone, 'but,' said his housekeeper, 'ye'll meet him on the way, and ye'll know him by the sign of the white horse he rides.' Within three miles of Kenmare we saw the sign of the 'white horse' and I introduced myself. He thanked me kindly for lecturing his people at the glen, and said he had got discouraged. Five years before, Father Mathew had made them all temperate, but that publican's house had upset the whole work. I begged him to visit their cabins and lecture them on their filth. 'I have done so, but they heeded nothing I could say.' He lived seven miles from them, had another parish in charge, and he knew not how to remedy these evils; 'but to-morrow I have been thinking of making a trial from the altar, and I would take the liberty of using your name.' Poor man! if indeed he felt the necessity of using me as a scarecrow, certainly I should not object, but I doubted the efficacy of the remedy.

While talking to the priest, who directed me to the best lodgings in town in his name, a ragged young man, with a cart and high railing about it, filled with turf baskets, drawn by a miserable-looking pony, passed us. They assisted in adjusting me and my luggage. My young driver talked fluently of America, and said he should go there but for the little gal he had married, who would be lonesome without him.

'The little gal you have married! you are not yet twenty!'

'That I ain't, and the gal is but thirteen or fourteen.'

'Nonsense, nonsense. What can you do with a wife?'

'And maybe I don't know; why, work, and take care of her.'

'And how much do you have a day?'

'Sometimes the sixpence, and when I gits a job with the pony, it's a shilling or fifteenpence.'

'And with this you expect to support a wife?'

'With the turn she can git now and then from a lady.'

He was a sharp-nosed stinted boy, not in appearance more than sixteen, yet he had as high hopes of aggrandisement as though a candidate for parliament. Enviable content! Happy misery!

From *The Bible in Ireland*

Anthony Trollope

1845

ANTHONY TROLLOPE (1815–1882) joined the Post Office in London in 1834 and spent most of the years 1841 to 1859 in Ireland, retiring in 1867. He was responsible for the introduction of the pillar-box in Great Britain. A prodigious writer, Trollope is especially renowned for his Barchester series of novels, with their ecclesiastical setting, and the Palliser novels, which have a political background. Other literary work includes plays, travel-writing, short stories, biographies and literary sketches. Trollope spent several family holidays in Glengarriff. The following letter was written years later to a recipient whose identity is not recorded.

Anthony Trollope.

Waltham House, Waltham Cross — Nov. 18, 1864

My dear Sir,

I very well remember the occurrence at Glengarriff to which you allude, & I shall bear the marks of it with me to the grave. I also remember taking you and Mr. Royle down to O'Sullivan's waterfall and having a great scramble up to the road, where the car and your father had been waiting for us about an hour. All that happened as I think in 1845 –

and was therefore as you say nearly 20 years ago. I cannot run now as fast as we ran over the bog; though I am just as fond of waterfalls, and of broken bridges by moonlight. I still have, hanging in my room, a sketch by you of Cromwell's bridge and another by Mr. Royle, which you two were kind enough to send me as memorials of the accident.

I have enquired after you once or twice since, and had heard that you were a painter, but could never quite trace you. Your name has been rather prolific in artists. Whenever you find yourself in London I shall be very happy to shake your hand again. I am most often to be found at 193 Piccadilly or at the Garrick Club.

Very faithfully yours,
Anthony Trollope

From *The Letters of Anthony Trollope*

Frederick Fitzwilliam Trench

1847

THE REVEREND FREDERICK FITZWILLIAM TRENCH (1799–1869), who held the post of perpetual curate at Cloughjordan in County Tipperary, visited West Cork during the Famine, and described in a series of letters the dreadful conditions he had seen. The extract quoted was written from Cloughjordan on 22 March 1847.

In the districts which are now being depopulated by starvation, coffins are only used for the more wealthy. In every village the manufacture was remarkable at the doors of the carpenters' houses, and in the country parts I often met coffins carried on the backs of women, and boards for making coffins. At Glengarriff, strange to say, the Roman Catholic Chapel is turned into a place for making coffins. Seeing two men at work there, I went in, in company with Rev. Mr. Morgan, the curate of the parish. I said to one of the carpenters, 'What are you making, boys?' 'Coffins and wheelbarrows, sir'; and I saw the planks marked out for the sawyer to the length of coffins. At Bantry, I saw lying at the corner of one of the streets, two coffins for the use of the poor; they call them 'trap coffins'; the bottom is supported by hinges at one side, and a hook and eye at the other. In these coffins the poor are carried to the grave, or rather to a large pit, which I saw at a little distance from the road, and the bodies are dropped into it. On my return to the spot where I first saw these two coffins, I found them occupied with corpses, and placed on a car about to be drawn by a horse to the grave. Another coffin of the same kind had been sent in another direction for another body; but I was told in this district the majority were taken to the grave without any coffin, and buried in their rags: in some instances even the rags are taken from the corpse to cover some still living body.

From *Realities of Irish Life*

Alfred Tennyson

1848

ALFRED TENNYSON (1809–1892), who enjoyed the greatest popularity ever accorded to an English poet during his lifetime, visited the famous Hungry Hill waterfall in 1848. The jarvey who drove him there declared a close kinship with the families of MacCarthy Mór and O'Sullivan Beare: as proof he displayed an old seal with their quartered arms, and stated that by rights he should be reigning in these parts. Together they sought shelter from torrential rainfall in a roadside cottage occupied by a poor woman and her young son. In 1878, during his last visit to Ireland, the poet laureate told the story to Alfred Perceval Graves, who later included it in his memoirs. In the retelling Graves incorporated Hallam Tennyson's quotation of his father's words, which, however, contained an error: the jarvey would not have claimed to be the king of *Connaught*.

The 'king of Connaught' dried my stockings and went to sleep on a bench. The woman drew me up a stool to the turf fire with the courtly air of a queen. While he was asleep I heard the mother say to the boy 'Johnny' several times (she didn't speak a word of English). The King awoke, and, as we were going out, I said 'Johnny', and the little boy with a protuberant paunch (protuberant, I suppose, from eating potatoes) ran forward and I gave him a sixpence. The woman, with her black hair over her shoulders and her eyes streaming with tears, passionately closed her hands over the boy's hand in which was the sixpence. When the King and I climbed into the car, I, in

Alfred Tennyson.

my stupid Saxon way, thinking it was the beggarly sixpence that had made the woman grateful, expressed my astonishment at such gratitude. 'It was not the sixpence, your honour,' he said, 'it was the stranger's gift.'

From *Irish Literary and Musical Studies*

Rose Trollope

1849

WITH HER HUSBAND ANTHONY, Rose Trollope *née* Heseltine visited the southwest of Ireland several times on family holidays. In 1849 the couple accompanied Anthony's mother on a walking tour. A famous writer in her time, Fanny Trollope (1780-1863) was the author of 115 volumes and is now best known for the controversial *Domestic Manners of the Americans*. Rose left us the following account of her mother-in-law's reactions to Glengarriff and Bantry.

We took her to Killarney, with which she was enchanted. Lord Kenmare's park especially delighted her. She walked through the gap of Dunloe as easily as if she had been twenty-nine instead of sixty-nine! . . .

One day we put her on one of Bianconi's cars running to Glengariff, after much protest on her part against the ramshackle-looking machine. Presently, however, after a few jerks, and a dozen 'Niver fear, yer honour!' from Mick the driver, she almost persuaded herself that she would rather travel through Ireland in that way than any other!

Glengariff was not a success. She was tired with her journey; the tea was rubbish; the food detestable; the bedrooms pokey; turf fires disagreeable, and so on. And now looking back on it all, I feel that she had grounds for complaint; and I should vote it – nasty. However, the next day was better, when we drove through the Bantry demesne.

From *Frances Trollope: Her Life and Literary Work from George III to Victoria*

Charles Kingsley

1860

CHARLES KINGSLEY (1819–1875), clergyman, novelist and poet, is chiefly remembered for *The Water Babies*. He was rector of Eversley in Hampshire for many years, later professor of modern history at Cambridge and a canon of Westminster. In outlook Kingsley was a Christian Socialist, influenced by the teachings of John Ruskin: thus his works *Yeast* and *Alton Locke* highlight the plight of the poor in the midst of Victorian prosperity. Of his historical novels, *Westward Ho!*, which chronicled the defeat of the Spanish Armada, was the most successful.

Letter to his wife Frances:

The Falls of Kenmare July 15, 1860

Charles Kingsley.

Very happy here. There is no fishing, but there will be tomorrow, for the water is coming down again, and we are off early to a famous lake . . . Henry was showing us his Turkish and Crimean journal last night. He is a splendid fellow; full of good sense and humour, and as honest as the day. I think him a most valuable, liberal, right-minded man, who has made good use of his eyes . . . I shall be glad to stay another week, especially as I have not caught a salmon for nine days, and there is finer fishing than Sligo awaiting at my feet when the water comes down, which it is beginning to do. I saw a mighty seal close here the other day, rolling about, with a black head as big as a calf, salmon-hunting. There are whales here and grampuses, but we have seen none. We have plenty of sea-boating and yachting, but I don't care for that since I have caught salmon; I can think of nothing else . . .

Writing to Rev. F. D. Maurice:
Derreen, Kenmare August 8, 1869

Your letter followed me hither, whither I and Rose [his daughter] have wandered to see the Froudes, and pretend to catch salmon which will not be caught, amid such a neglected paradise of mountain, sea, river, lake, island, as makes my heart sad. Justice to Ireland is indeed wanted. But the justice would be, to live among the people, civilize them, give them leases, let them vote for Satan if they liked; only bring personal love and care to bear on them. Treat them as peasantry are treated in England, and all would be well. If the system which I see in Ireland of actually preventing civilization and wealth, for fear of increasing population, goes on fifty or twenty-five years more, the Irish landlords will have to alter considerably.

From *Charles Kingsley, His Letters and Memories of His Life*

James Anthony Froude

1866

JAMES ANTHONY FROUDE (1818–1894), the literary executor and biographer of Thomas Carlyle, wrote a 12-volume history of England and some British colonial histories. He often visited the Killarney and Kenmare areas from 1863. Between 1867 and 1872 he several times rented Derreen House at Lauragh from the Marquis of Lansdowne. Here Froude worked on the controversial *The English in Ireland in the Eighteenth Century*, and also collected material for his novel *The Two Chiefs of Dunboy*, which was loosely based on two eighteenth-century Beara men, Morty Oge O'Sullivan and John Puxley. With the death of his wife, the family holidays at Derreen ended.

J.A. Froude.

An exquisite drive of three hours brought me to Kenmare, a town at the head of one of the long fiords running up from the Atlantic, which readers of Macaulay will remember as the scene of a brilliant defence made by a small body of Protestant settlers against the Irish insurgents. It was not my first visit to the place. Thirty years before I had passed through it from Glengariff in a long vacation holiday. The Lansdowne Arms was still in its old place; but the generation which frequented it had passed away. The 'boy' who was then driving me called my attention, as I remember, to a group of gentlemen at the door. There were two

O'Connells, cousins of the Liberator, at that time in the zenith of his glory. There was Morty O'Sullivan* and another whose name I forget. The point about them was that each had killed his man in a duel, and Morty had killed two. He was one of the old fire-eaters, a spare well-dressed refined-looking person, a descendant of the old chiefs of Berehaven, ruling the wreck of his inheritance with an authority scarcely less despotic as far as it extended; like his ancestors, in perpetual feud with his neighbours, and settling his quarrels with them in the field or in the law courts. He had lived – I should say 'reigned', for that is still the word – at Derreen itself. He had screwed his tenants, drunk whisky enough daily for ten degenerate mortals, such as now we know them, turned his house into a pigstye, and been loved and honoured throughout the valley. Morty the Good he was called, the king of the golden age of Kerry, and unhappy only in the incapacity of one of his sons, whom he never could teach to handle a pistol like a gentleman. The young O'Sullivan took kindly to the ways of the family; quarrelled with a companion before he was out of his teens, and went out to settle the dispute in legitimate fashion. But Morty augured ill for the result. He ordered the wake beforehand, and was disappointed, it was to be hoped agreeably, when the object of his care was brought home only shot through the foot.

Morty had been now long in his grave. Litigation had crippled his fortune and the famine finished it. His boys were scattered over the world and his place knew him no more. Morty was gone, and the fighting squirearchy to which he belonged was gone also, extinct like the dodo; and in the place of the group which I remembered, one or two harmless clerks belonging to the town stores were lounging at the porch in the summer gloaming comparing salmon flies, or talking about the cricket club which had been set on foot there by some neighbouring gentlemen.

Besides these were a couple of smart-looking boatmen, one of whom, after ascertaining who I was, informed me that my friend had sent up his yacht, a smart cutter of twenty tons, and that if I preferred a sail to a longer drive they were ready to take charge of me. The wind was from the east, light but fair, and they believed that it would not drop till midnight. But we had still seventeen miles to go. I inquired what would happen if it did drop, and as the answer was vague I determined to stick to my car, and to lose no time, for it was growing dark. My driver declined a change of horses. The small well-bred Irish car horse does his forty miles a day through the season with only an occasional rest, and seems little the worse

* Froude's alias for Peter McSwiney

for it. Away we went again after a halt of three quarters of an hour, and three minutes brought us to the suspension bridge crossing the head of the fiord, one end of which rests on the peninsula where the Protestants were besieged. That, too, with its traditions was a thing of the past, and might have furnished a text at any other time for its appropriate meditations. But the scene was too beautiful for moralising. The pink evening light had faded off the mountains, but the tints which lingered in the western sky were reflected faintly on the glimmering water. The cutter was clearing out of the harbour with her big gaff topsail set and her balloon jib, and as she slid away the men tauntingly hailed my driver and promised to tell my friends that we were coming.

The mare received an intimation that she must put her best foot forward; we struck off to the right on crossing the bridge and entered a long fir wood which skirts the river, catching glimpses at intervals of the shining water through gaps in the trees.

By-and-by we emerged into open ground. The road was level, following the line of the bay for eight or nine miles, and crossing the mouths of valley after valley where the streams which drain the hills run into the sea. It was now dark, so far as a summer night is ever dark. The cutter still kept ahead of us, shimmering ghost-like in the uncertain light. Sometimes we seemed to be gaining on her – then, as a fresh puff of air overtook her, she stole away. At last our ways parted; she held on towards a headland far down the bay which she was obliged to round before she could enter Kilmakilloge, the harbour on which Derreen is situated. The road, to avoid a long circuit, strikes upwards over a pass in the hills, to descend on the other side into the head of the valley.

The ascent now became tedious; we had lost the cutter, and were climbing the broken side of an utterly barren mountain. The distant view was hidden by the darkness, and the forms immediately round us had nothing striking about them, beyond a solitary peak which shot up black and gloomy-looking into the sky. Two miles of walking ground made me impatient to be at my journey's end, and I was unprepared for the scene which was immediately about to break upon me.

We reached the crest at last – rounded a corner of rock, and were at once in another world. The moon had risen, though concealed by the hill which we had been ascending, and burst upon us broad and full as we turned to descend. Below us was a long deep valley losing itself to the left in the shadows in the Glengariff mountains; opening to the right in the harbour of Kilmakilloge, which lay out like a looking-glass in the midst of the hills in which it is landlocked. Across, immediately before us, was a gorge, black and narrow, the sides of which, in the imperfect light, appeared to fall precipitously two thousand feet. Beyond, at the head of the harbour, was a second group of mountains shaped in still wilder variety, while the bottom of the valley was traversed by a river divided into long shining pools suggestive of salmon and sea trout, and broken at intervals with cascades, the roar of which swayed up fitfully in the night air.

These glens and precipices had been the retreat of the last Earl of Desmond in the closing summer of his life. The long peninsula shut in between the fiords of Bantry and Kenmare was then covered from end to end with forest, inaccessible except by water, or penetrated by a few scarce discoverable horsetracks; inhabited by wolves, and by men who were almost as wild, and were human only in the ineffable fidelity with which they concealed and shielded their hunted chief. The enormous trees which lie in the bogs, or the trunks which break on all sides out of the ground, prove that once these hills were as thickly wooded as those which have escaped the spoiler, and in their summer livery delight the tourist at Killarney. Now, the single fault of the landscape is its desolation. Sir William Petty, who obtained the assignment of the principality of Kerry, on terms as easy as those on which the Colonial Office squandered millions of the best acres in Canada, considered the supply of fuel to be practically as inexhaustible as we now consider our coal measures. He set up refining works on the shore of the harbour, and tin and copper ore was brought over there, till the last available stick had been cut down to smelt it. Nature still struggles to repair the ruin, and young oaks and birches sprout of themselves, year after year, out of the soil, but the cattle browse off them as they appear; and the wolves being destroyed which once scared the sheep out of the covers, and gave them time to renew their natural waste, civilisation itself continues the work of the destroyer, and dooms the district to perpetual barrenness. Of the forests of oak and arbutus and yew which once clothed the whole of Kerry, the woods at Killarney have alone escaped; those and some few other scattered spots, which for some special reason were spared in the general havoc.

At one of these, the 'domain' as it is called of Derreen, I have by this time arrived. Two miles of descent balanced the climb on the other side. We are again in the midst of trees. Level meadows beside the river are dotted with sleeping cattle, we have passed a farmhouse or two, and now a chapel handsome and new, at a meeting of cross roads. We turn into a gate, a gravel drive leads us to where lights are shining behind overhanging branches. The harbour is close below us; a four-oared boat is going out for a night's fishing; the cutter is at this very moment picking up her moorings; we have not beaten her, but we are not disgraced ourselves. In another minute we are in the broad walk which leads to the house. The night was hot, my friend's

Carriages outside the Lansdowne Arms, Main Street, Kenmare, around the turn of the 20th century.

party were on the lawn; some of them had been dining on board a yacht, the lights of which were visible as she lay at anchor, a mile from the windows. They had come on shore in the yacht's gig, and were standing about reluctant to go indoors from the unusual loveliness of the evening.

They proposed a stroll round the grounds, to which I was delighted to consent. The house stood in the middle of a lawn, shut in on all sides by woods, through which, however, openings had been cut in various places, letting in the view of the water. The original building, which had been the residence of Morty and his sons, was little more than a cottage. It had been enlarged by a straggling wing better suited to the habits of modern times. Morty, who cared little for beauty, had let the trees grow close to the door. He might have shot woodcocks from his window, and I dare say he did; while the close cover had served to shelter and conceal his considerable operations in the smuggling line. This more practical aspect of things had been superseded by the sentimental, and by lopping and clearing, full justice had been done to the beauty – I may say, the splendour – of the situation. The harbour of Kilmakilloge forms a branch of the Kenmare River, from three to four miles deep, and pierced on both sides by long creeks, divided by wooded promontories. On the largest of these, some ninety acres in extent, the house had been placed. Two acres had been cleared to make a garden. Four or five more formed a field running down to the sea. The rest was as Nature made it, the primeval forest, untouched save for the laurels and rhododendrons which were scattered under the trees where the ground was dry enough to let them grow. Two rivers fell into the harbour at the upper end, one of them that along which I had just been driving, the other, the larger, emerging out of a broad valley under a bridge which, with the water behind, showed clear and distinct in the moonlight. All round us rose the wall of mountains, the broken outline being the more striking, because at night the surface details are lost and only the large forms are visible. The sky line on three sides was from two to six miles distant. On the fourth side, towards the mouth of the harbour, it was more remote; but here, too, the rim of mountains continued to the eye unbroken. The ocean was shut off by the huge backbone of hills which stretches from Macgillicuddy's Reeks to the Atlantic. To all appearance Derreen was cut off from the world as effectually as the valley of Rasselas; and, but for the intrusion of the postman, made evident by my friend's inquiries as to the last division and the white-bait dinner, but for the croquet wires which I stumbled over on the lawn, we might have seemed divided as utterly from all connection with the world and its concerns. We wandered through the woods and along the walks which followed the shore. The wind was gone: the last breath of it had brought the yacht to her moorings. The water was like a sheet of pale gold, lighted in the shadows by phosphorescent flashes where a seal was chasing a mullet for his supper. Far off we heard the cries of the fishermen as they were laying out their mackerel nets, a heron or two flew screaming out of some large trees beside the boathouse, resentful at the intrusion on their night's rest; and from overhead came a rush of wings and the long wild whistle of the curlew. . . .

A glance out of the window in the morning showed that I had not overrated the general charm of the situation. The colours were unlike those of any mountain scenery to which I was accustomed elsewhere. The temperature is many degrees higher than that of the Scotch highlands. The Gulf Stream impinges full upon the mouths of its long bays. Every tide carries the flood of warm water forty miles inland, and the vegetation consequently is rarely or never checked by frost even two thousand feet above the sea-level. Thus the mountains have a greenness altogether peculiar, stretches of grass as rich as water-meadows reaching between the crags and precipices to the very summits. The rock, chiefly Old Red Sandstone, is purple. The heather, of which there are enormous masses, is in many places waist deep.

The sky was cloudless, and catching the chance of performing my morning's ablutions in salt water, I slipped into the few indispensable garments, and hurried down to the front door. My host's youngest boy, a brown-cheeked creature of six, who was playing with the dogs on the steps, undertook to pilot me to the bathing-place, a move not wholly disinterested on his part, as the banks on either side of the walks were covered with wild strawberries and whortleberries. Away we went through the woods again, among the gnarled and moss-clothed trunks of oaks hundreds of years old, and between huge boulders draped with ferns and London pride, which here grows luxuriantly wild. The walk ended at a jutting promontory of rock, where steps had been cut, leading to the water at a soft spot where a dike of slate had pierced a fault in the sandstone. The water itself was stainless as the Atlantic. I jumped in carefully, expecting to touch the bottom, yet I could scarcely reach it by diving. I tried to persuade my companion to take a swim upon my back, but he was too wary to be tempted. He was a philosopher, and was speculating on making a fortune out of the copper veins which were shining in the interstices of the slate. Our friend the seal, whom we had seen at supper, seemed disposed to join me. A shiny black head popped up from under the surface thirty yards off, and looked me over to see if I was one of his relations; but after a careful scrutiny he disliked the looks of me, dropped under, and disappeared. The seals once swarmed upon this coast under shelter of popular superstition. 'The sowls of thim that were drowned at the flood' were supposed to be enchanted in their bodies, undergoing water purgatory. At times they were allowed to drop their skins, and play in human form upon the shore, and the mortal who was bold enough to steal the robe of some fish-maiden whom he could surprise, might win her and keep her for his bride. They are yielding slowly before what is called education and civilisation, and the last of them will soon be a thing of history like the last wolf; but the restriction upon firearms in Ireland still acts as a protection, and a few yet loiter about the quiet nooks where they find themselves unmolested.

Before I was dressed we heard a sound of oars; a boat came round the corner, rowed by the men belonging to the cutter. They had been out early to take up the fluke nets and overhaul the lobster pots, and were bringing in what they had caught to the house. A dozen plaice, two or three pairs of large soles, and a turbot twelve pounds weight, made up rather more than an average night's haul, obtained by the rudest of methods. The nets are of fine twine with a large mesh. They are from fifty to a hundred fathoms long, five feet deep, and held perpendicularly on the sand at the bottom, by a line of leads, just sufficient to sink them, and a line of small corks to keep them in an upright position. In these the flat fish entangle

A fisherman and his assistant.

themselves – such of them as are stupid enough to persevere in endeavouring to push through, and are without the strength, like the conger and dog-fish, to break the net, and tear a way for themselves. Huge rents showed where creatures of this kind had escaped capture; but the holes are easily mended, and so many fish can be taken with so much ease, that the people do not care to improve on their traditionary ways. The Pat of Kerry is either unlike his kindred in the rest of the island, or they are a calumniated race altogether. On Kilmakilloge he makes his own boats, he makes his own nets, he twists his own ropes and cables out of the fibre of the bog pine which he digs out of the peat. He wants but a market to change his skiff into a trawler, and to establish a second Brixham at the splendid bay of Ballinskelligs.

Half a dozen skate were lying on the bottom boards among the nobler fish, here used only to be cut up for bait; these, and a monster called an angel shark, begotten long ago, it would appear, from some unlawful concubinage between a dog-fish and a ray. There were three enormous lobsters besides, better in my experience to look at than to eat. On these coasts it seems as if the young vigorous lobsters kill their own prey without trouble in finding it, and the bait in the wicker pots tempts only the overgrown and aged, whose active powers are failing them.

I was to make the best use of my time, and at breakfast we talked over our plans for the day. Picnics, mountain walks, antiquarianising expeditions, fishing, salt or fresh, were alternately proposed. The weather luckily came to the assistance of our irresolution. It was still intensely hot. The rivers were low and clear as crystal, so it was vain to think of the salmon. The boatmen reported that the easterly wind was still blowing, but that from the look of the sky, and the breaking of the swell outside the harbour, they expected a shift in the evening, so we agreed to run down the bay in the yacht as long as the land breeze held, and trust to the promised change to bring us back. The ladies declined to accompany us, the ocean roll and a hot sun being a trying combination even to seasoned stomachs. So my friend and I started alone with the boys, with a packed hamper to be prepared against emergencies. The cutter was large enough for its purpose, and not too large. Though we did not intend to court bad weather, we could encounter it without alarm if it overtook us. We had a main cabin, with two sofas and a swing table; a small inner cabin with a single berth, with a kitchen forward, where the men slung their hammocks. We slipped our moorings and ran out of the harbour, passing the Cowes schooner, which lay lazily at anchor. Her owner and his party were scattered in her various boats, some had gone up to Kenmare marketing, some were pollock fishing, others were engaged in the so-called amusement of shooting the guillemots and the puffins, which, unused to firearms, sat confidingly on the water to be destroyed – beautiful in their living motion, worse than useless when dead. We flung our half-uttered maledictions at the idiots, who were bringing dishonour on the name of sportsmen. For a week after the bay was covered with wounded birds, which were dying slowly from being unable to procure food.

Before we turned into the main river we passed an island on which was a singular bank of earth, wasting year by year by the action of the tide, and almost gone to nothing: it was the last remains of a moraine, deposited who can guess when, by a glacier which has left its scorings everywhere on the hillsides. The people call it Spanish Island, and have a legend that one of the ships of the Armada was wrecked there. It is an unlikely story. No galleon which had doubled the Blaskets would have turned out of its course into the Kenmare river, nor if it had wandered into such a place could easily have been wrecked there. More likely it was a fishing station at a time when Newfoundland was undiscovered, and fleets came annually to these seas from Coruña and Bilboa, for their bacalao – their Lenten cod and ling. As many as two hundred Spanish smacks were then sometimes seen together in the harbour at Valentia.

The breeze freshened as we cleared out of Kilmakilloge. The main bay is here four miles broad, and widens rapidly as it approaches the mouth.

We saw the open Atlantic twenty miles from us, and we met the swell with which we had been threatened, but so long and easy that we rose over the waves, scarcely conscious of motion, and rattled along with a three-quarter breeze and every sail drawing, seven knots through the water . . . Thousands of sea birds wheeling and screaming over the water showed that the great shoals of small fish which frequent these bays in the autumn had already begun to appear. Gannets, towering like falcons, shot down three hundred feet sheer, disappeared a moment, and rose with tiny sprats struggling in their beaks. Half a dozen herring hogs were having a pleasant time of it, and besides these, two enormous grampuses were showing their sharp black fins at intervals, one thirty feet long, the other evidently larger, how much we could not tell, for he never showed his full length, though he rolled near us, and we could judge his dimensions only from the width across the shoulders. The sprats were in cruel case. The whales and porpoises hunted them up out of the deep water. The gurnet caught them midway. The sea birds swooped on them as they splashed in terror on the surface. They too had doubtless fattened in their turn on smaller victims. Our boys avenged the shades of some of them on one set at least of their persecutors. They threw over their fishing lines, and six or seven big gurnet were flapping in the basket before we had cleared the edge of the shoal. . . .

Anyhow I had had enough of salmon fishing for the day. We gave the rod and the basket to Pat to carry home, the big fish which he was too proud to conceal flapping on his back. Jack and I ate our luncheon and smoked our pipes beside the fall, and Jack, before we went home, undertook to show me the lake. The river followed the bend of the valley. We took a shorter cut over a desolate and bare piece of mountain, and as we crossed the ridge we found ourselves suddenly in the luxuriant softness of a miniature Killarney. The lake was scarcely a mile in length, but either the woodcutters had been less busy there, or nature had repaired the havoc that they had made. Half a dozen small islands were scattered on it, covered with arbutus and holly. The rocks on either side fell in grand precipices to the water. At the end was the opening of Glanmore valley, with its masses of forest, its emerald meadows and cooing wood-pigeons, and bright, limpid river reaches. For its size there is no more lovely spot in the south of Ireland than Glanmore. It winds among the mountains for six miles beyond the lake, closed in at the extremity with the huge mass of Hungry Hill, from the top of which you look down upon Berehaven. Here too the idea of sport pursued us – stray deer wandered over now and then from Glengariff – and my companion had stories of mighty bags of woodcocks made sometimes there when the snow was on the hills. My eye, however, was rather caught by a singular ruin of modern, unvenerable kind on the largest of the islands. Some chieftain's castle had once stood there, as we could see from the remains of massive walls on the water line; but this had been long destroyed, and in the place of it there had been a cottage of some pretensions, which in turn was now roofless. . . .

My space has run out. My tale is still half told. The next day was Sunday. The day following was August 20, when Irish grouse-shooting begins. If the reader's patience is unexhausted he shall hear of the scratch-bag we made in a scramble of thirty miles; of the weird woman that we saw among the cliffs; of the 'crass bull' that we fell in with, and the double murder in Coommeengeera. I have to tell him too how the grandson of Macfinnan Dhu was caught red-handed spearing salmon, and how the bloody Saxon had to stand between him and eviction. How we held a land court in the hall at Derreen, and settled a disputed inheritance. How we went to the Holy Lake and saw pilgrims from America there, and how when mass was over they made a night of it with the whisky booths and the card-sharpers. How we had another sail upon the river, how we attended a tenant-right meeting at the board of guardians of Kenmare, and how the chairman floored the middle-man there to the delight of his audience – the chairman, the brightest of companions, the most charming of men of business, the hero of the seal fight in Mr. Trench's *Realities of Irish Life*.

From *A Fortnight in Kerry*

Richard Turrell McMullen

1869

RICHARD TURRELL MCMULLEN was born about 1830 and became a member of the London Stock Exchange in 1853. He lived mainly at Greenhithe in Kent. He loved the sea and yachting and wrote a book of sailing memoirs, *Down Channel*, in which he recounts his voyage to Bantry Bay in 1869 on the 19-ton yacht *Orion*. He once described flying as 'an art which some have rashly essayed, but which there is no probability will ever triumph over the art of sailing to windward at sea.' McMullen died in 1891 while sailing solo across the English Channel to France.

August 19th. Noon, sailed from Doon Point for the Dursey Head, off which lie two remarkable rocks exposed to the whole drift of the Atlantic, called the Cow and the Bull. The former, distant from the head a mile and a half, is very fantastic in appearance. It is 203 feet high, has an arch on one side, and on the other a large gaping rent with a piece of rock jammed in, which seems to prevent the enormous slab from tumbling in upon the main rock. The latter, a mile farther seaward, is a very bold-looking rock 290 feet high, with a conspicuous tunnel through the centre.

Between the Head (which is rent into chasms, like most headlands on this coast, by the Atlantic storms) and the rocks are 35 fathoms water, with strong tides, and such a heavy sea that they are seldom approachable. Being much struck in 1861 with their very curious appearance, I resolved, if the opportunity presented itself during the cruise of 1869, to pay them a special visit, and if possible examine them from the boat. It was reported to me that boats could pass through the Bull, and even that a vessel might sail through; but I failed to meet with any person who could speak upon better authority than hearsay.

The wind being light from the S.S.W., with a swell from the west, it was late in the afternoon when we came up with the Cow, and got becalmed in the eddy tide so close to it that it was necessary to use the sweeps (long oars) to keep out of danger.

After clearing the Cow a quarter of a mile, I got into the boat with one of the men, and returned to examine it; but being on the wrong side, and not having time to pull round to leeward, I was compelled to sheer off on account of the swell, which looked very formidable from the boat, and turn my attention to the Bull, which we approached with great caution on the lee side. The height of the swell was frequently measured during the day, and ascertained to vary from 5 feet to 7 feet, the length of the higher waves being about twice that of the lower ones.

Although a swell of this height is considered smooth water on the Irish coast, it certainly would not be so considered at Margate if launched against their pier on a fine day. Being a long ocean swell, it represents a large and heavy moving body of water, which travels with great rapidity, and rushes upon an obstruction with such sustained weight that, viewed from the sea, it rises to about twice its height in green water before breaking into foam. Harmless enough in the deep water, you are soon made to know that it is terribly powerful if you venture within its influence when it begins to feel bottom. When we were in the trough, after pulling one or two seas clear of the *Orion*, she was out of our sight to the height of half the mainsail, and we were lost to their view altogether for long intervals, being in fact visible to them only when we both happened to be on the top of the sea at the same time. If I had not carefully measured the sea from the vessel, I should certainly have estimated the height considerably above 7 feet.

Opening the tunnel on the N.E. side, we lay to for a while at a respectful distance, and took a careful survey of it to see if the swell showed any disposition to break, which would be a sure sign of rocks near the surface. As it looked all fair, we pulled in between the points of entrance (projecting rocks), upon which the sea broke with considerable violence, but left a space of dark water sufficiently wide for the boat to pass between the surf.

The interior, which is about 50 feet high from the surface of the water, 40 feet wide, and 500 feet through, is like a grand hall with an undulating floor. A sounding taken in the middle, 7 1/4 fathoms half tide, showed the height of the cavern, from the bottom to the roof, to be about 100 feet. The roof is horizontal, but rugged; the sides are perpendicular and very smooth, lined a few feet below high-water mark with little mussels, in such myriads that the rock looks as if it were covered with black velvet.

Fine as the entrance looked on the N.E. side, it was not to be compared for grandeur to that of the S.W., upon which the sun shone, lighting up the huge blocks, and giving it the appearance of an immense castle gateway, swarmed to the top with thousands of gannets (solan geese) and gulls. Besides those at rest, there were thousands on the wing, all talking at once.

The scene was altogether so lively and enchanting that I was delighted, and turned the boat's head with great reluctance to pass through the cavern again to the *Orion*, which at that moment happened to be in a line with the centre of the arch, about half a mile off, looking, with the sun upon her, like a framed picture.

As the swell entered both ends at once, there was no 'run' to drive the boat backwards and forwards as in an ordinary cavern, but simply a vertical rise and fall of a few feet.

6.30 p.m., made for the land. 10 p.m., anchored in Garinish Bay, which in its safest and most protected part is so confined by a dangerous little reef, that I went ahead in the boat, and examined that side of the anchorage by rowing from Garinish Island to the reef, from the reef to the mainland at a right angle, and then diagonally to the spot where the anchor was to be let go. The night being moonlight and calm, I was able to do this, otherwise we must have anchored in a more exposed berth, or have kept the sea until daylight. . . .

For the information of anyone who wishes to know something of the general character of the south-west coast of Ireland, I may say that it is very wild and pretty, with many fine natural harbours. The scenery in some of them is magnificent, especially in Glengarriff, Ardgroom and Kilmakilloge – the former in Bantry Bay, the two latter in Kenmare river. Fish of all sorts is very plentiful, and can be bought for little money if you are too idle, or, as in my case, have not time, to catch it,

The climate is mild, humid, and much subject to haze, particularly in wet weather, when the coast is so densely shrouded in mist that navigation is extremely dangerous. According to the book of sailing directions, all the harbours are easily distinguished by certain features of the landscape or conspicuous old towers and beacons; but to render the instructions complete there should be added 'weather permitting,' for as a rule in wet weather the leading marks are in the clouds.

To sail this coast with any comfort, the largest-scale Admiralty Charts are indispensable, as the rocks are numerous, and buoys and beacons very scarce.

On all the rocks in Kenmare river there is only one small beacon.

In choosing open anchorages on this coast in stormy weather from the south and west, it is important to bear in mind that the wind often veers suddenly to the northward, and blows frightfully.

I will close these remarks by saying that provisions are good and abundant at the chief towns, and the people generally so civil and obliging that it is pleasant to deal with them.

From *Down Channel*

John Skelton

1870

SIR JOHN SKELTON (1831–1897) was a Scottish advocate and man of letters, chiefly in essays and biography. A frequent contributor to *Fraser's Magazine* and *Blackwood's Magazine*, he often wrote under the pseudonym 'Shirley'. In several works he espoused the cause of Mary, Queen of Scots. For thirty years Sir John served on boards for the administration of poor and public health law, and contributed to the official literature of the subject. A long-time friend of J.A. Froude, he recorded his memories of a family holiday spent with the Froudes at Derreen House in September 1870.

We were on our way to visit a friend whose name has long been, and long will be, illustrious in English literature; and the week which we spent with him on the bay of Killmackillog will not be quickly forgotten. The 'harbour' on which the house stands is surrounded on all sides by lofty mountains, which shut off the profane world. Their sides are bare of timber, but around the lawn forest-trees and rare shrubs, hollies, laurels, hedges of fuchsias, the pampas grass, the hydrangea, the myrtle, and the arbutus flourish luxuriantly. The woods are carpeted with ferns in autumn, and the loveliest wild-flowers imaginable are found in spring. Great dragon-flies sweep across the heather, and the curious

Post Office, with typically dressed people, illustrated by John Leech.

humming-bird moth flutters among the roses and geraniums. Nor are more material attractions wanting – the land flows, so to speak, with milk and honey. There are real Scotch grouse on the mountain-tops, where they find it cooler than in the valleys. There are hares and rabbits and wild-duck; salmon lying by the score in the long still reaches of the river; an oyster-bed on the beach; plaice, soles, turbot, lobster in the bay. There are water-birds, moreover, of various kinds; but no one cares to meddle with them; so that, at twilight, you hear close at hand the wild plaint of the curlew, and the next morning, when you go down to bathe, the cormorants gaze at you with utmost composure. . . .

The Catholic chapel and its vicinity on that day [Sunday] present a curious scene. The people assemble on the highroad and in the neighbouring fields. The donkeys and ponies are taken out of the carts and tethered to the bushes. Through the birch-trees that bend over the stream one sees young women, who have walked without shoes eight or ten or twelve miles, washing their feet in the running water. (They don't wear shoes in rainy Ireland, on the principle that it is *dryer* to wet their feet only, than their feet *plus* shoes and stockings.) Men and women and children are sitting about everywhere, a profusion of bright reds blazing through the green. Within the unfinished and unfurnished chapel the service is conducted in the most primitive fashion. The hum of voices comes in with the autumn sunshine until the host is raised, when for a few seconds there is deep stillness both within and without. Then the congregation leave the chapel – gathering into groups as at a fair – eating, drinking, buying, selling, winding up with a dance on the green. If you are looking on, some pretty, swift-footed Kerry girl will insist on your dancing with her – it is the custom of the country – and you must submit with the best grace you can. Then, late in the afternoon, the inhabitants of each district leave together in a body, and the loneliest glens are startled at dusk by the sounds of what always seemed to me in Southern Ireland a harsh and discordant merriment.

From *The Table-Talk of Shirley*

Marie-Anne de Bovet

1889

MARIE-ANNE DE BOVET was born at Metz in 1860. She first worked as a translator, and wrote several travel books, on Poland, Algeria and Ireland. Under the pseudonym 'Mab' she contributed to many French and English newspapers and periodicals. However, it is as a novelist that de Bovet was most prolific. Her works include *Contre L'Impossible, Confessions d'une fille de trente, Court Folie, Marionnettes, Ballons Rouges* and *La Terre Refleurira.*

The cars which convey tourists between Bantry and Killarney are large brakes, with parallel seats fixed high above the wheels, which hold twenty-three passengers, and are always full, the natives being much given to excursions. Beneath and behind is stowed the luggage, and four horses drag the heavy machine; add on days when it threatens rain, that is to say six days out of seven, a bundle of straw under each seat to keep the feet dry and a leathern apron for the knees. One wonders at first why in this rainy climate there is no such thing as a covered public conveyance. To that the Irish reply – Why do you travel if not to see the country? After all, they are quite right. Who has any business to do? Not we, assuredly, who are here solely for pleasure.

Rounding the bay by a wood that winds among terraced heights, we reach Glengariff. It is not a village, but a site. The name comes from a ravine, down which a stream precipitates itself into the bay. The old ruined bridge is a memorial of Cromwell. . . . In a little amphitheatre formed by the lowest spurs of the hills at the foot of Cob Dhur, an oasis of luxuriant verdure lies sheltered from every wind. Two rival hotels, two rival churches, some boatmen's houses, and two or three modest private dwellings have been built in this favoured spot.

But I despair of describing a place of which the picturesque grace and the penetrating charm take possession of one's being, melting the soul into a delicious torpor. Glengariff has something to gratify every taste. Botanists collect many rare varieties of fern; anglers find excellent trout-fishing; artists have an embarrassing choice of subjects; consumptives come in search of health, or at least of alleviation of their troubles to this sheltered corner where they breathe the salt air without exposure to the wind. Everyone finds at Glengariff endless artistic delights, together with a satisfying repose. Why leave it on pretext that we have the tour of Ireland to make? We shall see nothing more lovely: why not stay? That is what we asked ourselves in the evening, standing in the porch of the hotel looking at the bay silvered by the moon. To soften our regrets, we promised ourselves a renewal of the visit. But even whilst we thus solaced ourselves, a cloud darkened the heavens, the wind freshened, and almost immediately the first drops of a shower compelled us to seek shelter. In the morning it rained in torrents; should we go or should we not? Seeing the natives preparing without hesitation for departure, we suppose that they have reasons for expecting the weather to clear, and we take our places in the car, which presently fills so completely that they turn out a second. Wrapped in their mackintoshes and rugs, and tightly packed together, the twenty-three tourists open their twenty-three umbrellas, and wait patiently while the driver makes his final preparations. He does not hurry: but why should he, when everyone is there to amuse himself? He would only shorten the pleasure. 'Take your time, ladies and gentlemen,' say the natives, gently, to those nervous travellers who dance about devoured by the fever of departure, whenever a pause occurs. The habit is one to be got rid of in Ireland by anyone who wishes to survive a three months' tour. At first one frets and growls and storms. After three weeks one learns patience, and after all, the journey always gets done somehow.

To go from Glengariff to Kenmare, situated at the head of the bay of the same name, a long inlet parallel to Bantry Bay, we have to cross the mountains of Caha, rising to as much as 2,200 feet, and bearing unpronounceable names. How did these frowning and sterile wastes support the chiefs who held their barbarous courts in the still imposing fortresses of Dunkerron, Dunboy, and Cappanacuss? Destructive as the Irish hold the English conquests to have been to their prosperity, they cannot pretend that these mountains have ever produced anything but ferns and heather, offering the scantiest of pasturage. In the twenty-one miles between Glengariff and Kenmare one does not see a score of dwellings.

Gazing at the car.

How do the inhabitants of these wretched huts make a living? During the season they live by the mendicity of their children. You cannot go half a mile without an escort of both sexes and all ages, indescribably ragged, trotting barefoot in the mud around the vehicle, and offering you bouquets of heather, bunches of moss, and sprays of bog-myrtle. This goes on the whole way. For a quarter of an hour there may be a respite, then a new band emerges from some ditch, and you are thus handed over from brigade to brigade until you reach your destination. It may be guessed that this persecution detracts greatly from the pleasure of the journey. But how is it to be avoided? To give, encourages them; to refuse, does not drive them away, and one hardly likes to abuse them. There is nothing for it but to put up with the nuisance, as one does with the rain. The worst of it is that a moment comes when you have to laugh, and then you are disarmed and despoiled of your last coppers. After all, one can afford to laugh when it is only an affair of children; but steel the heart as one may, it is distressing to see an old woman – wrinkled and shrivelled like an Easter apple, wan, emaciated, and nearly blind, covered with rags that a *chiffonnier* would not put in his basket – running behind the vehicle, with swollen and bleeding feet wrapped in filthy linen. What can a few pence avail against such degradation? The penny, by the way, is throughout Ireland the monetary standard of the begging fraternity; they will take a half-penny, but with a grimace, and you will never pass for a 'real gentleman' or a 'great lady' if you are stingy to this degree.

The Irish are wise not to allow the weather to interfere with their movements. It is no paradox to say that it is much less disagreeable to be out in the rain than to watch it fall from behind the window of an inn. At least there is the scenery to divert one, though it is not seen at its best; and when one is obliged to make the best of things, the mountains and the sea are not wanting in interest under the alternation of sun and shower. As soon as the rain ceases the twenty-three umbrellas are closed, and the owners congratulate one another. The umbrella is a barbarous invention; with good waterproofs it is useless, and indeed troublesome. In this climate one learns to appreciate the tam-o'-shanter, the Scotch cap so generally worn by English tourists of both sexes. The climate of Ireland is vexatious rather than absolutely bad, and it has consolations the more delightful because they come unexpectedly. Thus, arriving at the top of the pass, where a tunnel two hundred yards long pierces the rock at the confines of the counties of Cork and Kerry, a puff of wind suddenly clears the sky, and a wonderful view extorts a cry of admiration from the least enthusiastic. The eye ranges over the whole Caha chain with its numerous lakes, which, lit up by a gleam of sun, look like masses of molten silver. In all directions streams great and small, swollen with the rain, rush down the granite crags, and wind foaming through the deep ravines at our feet. The new-bathed vegetation brightens the savage landscape with the infinite variety of its tones, from the gray green of the lichens to the sombre hues of the stunted firs which cling in the fissures of the rocks. To right and left are the two bays of Bantry and Kenmare, outlined with sand, and in front roll the blue waves of the broad Atlantic.

From *Three Months Tour in Ireland*

David McArdle

1893

IN MAY 1893 the Royal Irish Academy Flora and Fauna Committee organised its first excursion to the extreme southwest of Ireland. As part of the effort, David McArdle's main objectives were to examine the moss and liverwort flora, and to obtain specimens for the herbarium at the Botanic Gardens in Glasnevin, Dublin. McArdle (1849–1934), a plant collector and clerical employee at the Botanic Gardens, subsequently wrote a report of the excursion.

From Bantry there are two routes to Castletown-berehaven, where we were to stay, one by water, and the other by land. One of the party went in a small steam-boat, taking luggage, &c., while the remainder continued the journey by car, not a 'Bianconi', on which most of us at some period or other have made long journeys, but a comfortable omnibus, from the outside of which one can enjoy the scenery, and we soon made considerable progress through a most interesting country, the road being flanked on either side by wild rocky glens clothed with verdure. The harbour of Glengariff soon appeared in view, then the village, where we remained for a short time to change horses, and on again for Castletown-berehaven. We got an excellent view of the Sugar-loaf and Caha Mountains. The 'Deadhe', or Hungry-hill is conspicuous above all the others from its towering height; on its summit is a small lake that bears the reputation of harbouring something 'uncanny' beneath its dark waves, and two of our party, when collecting there, were warned in a solemn strain by a kindly native not to go near it. We passed the famous waterfall at Adrigole, and although only a slight stream was then falling we could form an idea of its grandeur after a heavy rainfall. We soon arrived at our destination, and were comfortably settled in Mrs. Murphy's Hotel.

The following day (Sunday) was quiet, and with the exception of an afternoon stroll about Dunboy, we did no actual work. On the 29th we carefully examined the bogs and lakes about Castletown-bere, and on to Pulleen. On the river bank *Rosa mollissima* was in bloom, and partly submerged *Littorella lacustris* was in fine form. On the rocks at the mouth of the river at Pulleen Cove we gathered Templeton's pretty *Enthostodon*, and a rare liverwort, *Fossombronia angulosa*, Dicks., which was growing abundantly in the crevices of the rocks forming the bed of the stream. On the 30th, Dr. McWeeney and I crossed to Bere Island, noted the more common plants, and took specimens of any rare or interesting ones, amongst which was *Cicendia filiformis*, of which Dr. McWeeney detected a few plants near the end of the island, not far from Piper's Point. This was the most interesting find amongst the flowering plants. We also gathered *Nasturtium amphibium*, Br., *Rosa pimpinellifolia*, L., *Myosotis collina*, Hoffm., and a few plants of *Pinguicula lusitanica*, L. Amongst the mosses I gathered *Campylopus longipilus*, Bridel., and *C. setifolius*, Wils., and the following rare liverworts: *Frullania germana*, Taylor, *Cephalozia denudata*, Spruce (Lindberg), previously known to grow in only two localities in Ireland; C. *divaricata* var. *Starkii*, Spruce (= *J. Starkii*, Funck), *Kantia arguta*, Nees., *Nardia hyalina*, Lyell., *Fossombronia pusilla*, L., *F. angulosa*, Dicks. The early part of the day only was favourable for our work, as in the afternoon it rained heavily, which, however, did not prevent us from covering a large portion of the island, and gathering many plants. A week might be spent collecting on the island with good results. On the 31st, Dunboy Wood and adjacent bogs were carefully examined. *Saxifraga umbrosa* and *Euphorbia hiberna* were in fine form; amongst the liverworts, *Lejeunea flava*, Swartz, the typical plant, not differing in form or luxuriance from specimens gathered by Dr. Spruce in the Amazon Valley in South America, and seven other species of the genus were gathered in more or less abundance in this moist, warm, shaded wood, including *Harpa-Lejeunea ovata*, Taylor (Spruce). I also detected *Kantia arguta*, Nees., *Nardia hyalina*, Lyell., and *Metzgeria conjugata*, Dill., and doubtless other varieties would reward a careful search. On the bogs, *Drosera rotundifolia* and *D. intermedia* were abundant and vigorous in the bright sunshine. A plant of the latter species had enfolded a Dragonfly with its glandular tentacles.

On June 1st, at 6 a.m., we all boarded the steamship *Tearaght* in Bantry Bay, commanded by Captain McCombie, who was much interested in our work, and promised to land us on Dursey Island, which he was passing. We had a good view of the rocky coast, Pulleen Harbour, Ballydonegan Bay, &c.; a sumptuous breakfast with our kind host concluded this little sea trip, which is not likely to be forgotten by us. The island we found scanty in vegetation on account of its exposed position and the dry season. *Senebiera Coronopus* was plentiful near the sea where we landed. *Anthyllis vulneraria* was abundant in bloom everywhere, and isolated patches of *Rosa spinosissima* were met with in several places. *Asplenium marinum* and *Crithmum maritimum* were plentiful amongst the rocks near the sea. Amongst the mosses *Campylopus longipilus*, Bridel., was plentiful in damp places, and on the rocks *Grimmia trichophylla*, Greville, and *G. leucophoea*, Greville, were gathered. The rarest amongst the liverworts collected were *Frullania germana*, Taylor, *Cephalozia divaricata* var. *Starkii*, Spruce, *Nardia obovata*, Nees (Carrington), very scarce; this is the true plant, with ascending stems and purple rootlets. *N. hyalina*, Lyell, *Fossombronia angulosa*, Dicks., plentiful amongst rocks near the sea. We collected carefully up to the highest point of the island, from which the view of the Kerry mountains compensated in some degree for the scantiness of the vegetation.

From *A Visit to Castletown-Berehaven*

Francis Joseph Bigger

1898

BELFAST-BORN FRANCIS JOSEPH BIGGER (1863–1926), author and antiquary, was a solicitor by profession. He encouraged Irish language, literature, music and sports through his involvement with the literary revival and language movement. Bigger edited the *Ulster Journal of Archaeology* for twenty years, and contributed to many periodicals in Ireland, England and the USA. At his own expense he restored churches and castles, and rescued gravestones and high crosses from damage and destruction. A friend of Roger Casement, his home in Belfast was a well-known meeting place for nationalists.

Last July, during the Conference of the Irish Field Club Union in Kenmare, I found opportunities to visit the interesting pre-Christian and Christian remains at Kilmakilloge and Feaghna in the ancient kingdom of Kerry. The former is situated in a townland of the same name close to the little harbour of Bunaw, on the Kenmare river, in the parish of Tuosist, the latter in the parish of Garranes in the adjacent parish of Kilcaskan, and both in the barony of Glanarought.

Francis Joseph Bigger.

I visited Kilmakilloge on Friday, the 8th July, the second day of the Patron held there, and was well rewarded for my visit. I have ridden over many of the roads in Ireland, but for beauty and variety of scenery I have travelled none to surpass in grandeur the road from Kenmare to Bunaw, along the coast of the Kenmare river. Not far from Kenmare, between the road and the sea, I noted a small stone circle, then a little further, on a height above the shore, the ruins of Ardea Castle, once a stronghold of the O'Sullivans. Part of the extensive keep has tumbled into the sea, being undermined by the action of the waves. The numerous islands enhance the variety of the scene, and upon this hot summer day the blueness of the water rivalled Lake Como in its intensity. The ancient church of Kilmakilloge stands on a rocky eminence a little north of Bunaw, and at it I made my first considerable halt. Its architecture leads me to consider it a twelfth century structure – its medium size, rude masonry, narrow east window, with a smaller one in the south wall, and its round-headed south door, all confirm this view. . . .

From the old church a short walk south to a hollow swamp beside the rocky knoll brought me to the holy lake of Saint Mochionlane, and here was a great concourse of people, although not so many, I was informed, as on the previous day, the first of the Patron. I had heard that there had been some fun the first day and a little fighting, but I was too late for this, and saw none, and no evidence of any save one lad who was being taken to Kenmare on a cart with a very badly smashed face and head. The lake

The ruined medieval church and graveyard at Kilmakilloge near the site of the Lake Fair pilgrimage.

itself is a poor swampy looking place in the middle of soft turfy ground, with the site, now scarcely noticeable, of an ancient cloghaun or hermitage on the east side. Around the edges of the lake are hummocks of grass, which it is said move about in the water in a miraculous way, for what reason I failed to discover. I saw none of this levity on their part, except when I incautiously stepped upon one from the bank, and then something did happen, but it was to myself. . . .

The approach to the lake was lined with beggars who freely offered their prayers for a small gratuity, and seemed to understand that the visitor would derive no benefit until he parted with some of the current coin of the realm as a sort of offering.

I saw very few men at their devotions, but many women and girls travelling around the lake and kneeling on its margins and bathing different portions of their bodies in its waters. The adjoining rocky knoll was much used for going round, some on their feet, others on their knees using their Rosaries. At one side they stopped and knelt, facing the summit in front of them; some poor creatures, women, girls, and children, were extended, as if dead or sleeping, with sores and diseased portions of their bodies displayed to view in the glaring sunlight, a pitiable sight to see. At this place Mass was formerly said.

From the Holy Lake I turned to Bunaw; now Bunaw is a very small place, consisting of a public-house and a small harbour. The latter was the landing place for numerous boats crossing the river from different places, affording a very picturesque sight – the towering mountains and the glistening waters, with the long boats, crowded with occupants bent on piety or pleasure, or a mixture of both. The public-house, owned by an O'Sullivan, had great booths thrown out on every hand, and still seemed unequal to supply the pressing demands for porter. This hostelry was the centre of the Patron; for every one I saw at the holy water I saw ten drinking porter. Along the road were lines of tents with oranges, lemonade, gingerbread and religious articles, with hundreds of people moving about amongst them until the music was started and the dancing commenced. There was also numerous games of chance, thimblerigging, roulette, and card tricks. Many people were drunk, and there was a good deal of fooling and indiscriminate courting.

I was not favourably impressed with a Kerry Patron, and I much fear that if things are now as they used to be, the old romancists only stated facts when describing such scenes.

From *The Lake and Church of Kilmakilloge . . .*

Daniel J. Tallon

1898

DANIEL J. TALLON, lord mayor of Dublin from 1897 to 1900, set up the Mansion House Committee in February 1898 to relieve distress in the west and south caused by potato crop failure in 1897. One of the resulting relief schemes was the construction of the Tallon Road in Castletownbere. In July 1898 the lord mayor, with his secretary, Thomas Kennedy, who was from Castletownbere, and William Field, M.P., paid an inspection visit to Beara. They met members of the local Distress Committee at the Commercial Hotel in Castletownbere, and saw the convent, schools and orphanage. The following excerpt is taken from the official report they wrote of their visit.

We visited the distressed districts of the South of Ireland between the 18th and 24th July. We went through portions of the Cahirciveen and Kenmare Poor Law Unions in the County of Kerry, and the Castletown Bere and Bantry Unions in the County of Cork. We made as exhaustive an examination as the time at our disposal would permit, and, as a rule, we received every assistance from the clergy of all denominations and from the people. The objects of our visit were, first, to ascertain the social and economic condition of the distressed people; second, to examine into the manner in which the funds entrusted to the local committees had been administered; third, to ascertain the prospects for the immediate future; and lastly, to consider how the periodic recurrence of famine might be ended.

The distressed districts of Kerry and Cork are situated amidst some of the most beautiful scenery of Ireland. The bold promontories which stretch far out into the Atlantic, with their magnificent combinations of wood, hill, and water, harbour on their bleak sides and in their craggy glens, a teeming population subject to frequently recurring famines. Visitors from all parts of the world, during the summer season, pass over certain beaten tracks through these promontories. The coach drives over the mountains, through the glens, and along the Atlantic coast, are simply superb, and can scarcely be rivalled. Grand hotels, replete with every modern comfort and convenience, within easy stages of one another, have been erected at Caragh Lake, Waterville, Parknasilla, Kenmare, and Glengarriff. The opening up of these districts for tourists will, to some extent, be an advantage in the summer season, but scarcely affects the economic condition of the distressed people.

For the most part the lands on which the distressed people live are cut away bog, or patches of shallow clay on the mountain side. Both have been won from Nature by hard and continuous labour – the bog land, by cutting away the surface and by drainage; the clay by removing the rocks and boulders. Any cessation in the unceasing work which the peasants bestow on these plots would be followed by their going back to a state of nature. As a rule, these cultivated patches, which swarm with population, are surrounded by large tracts of barren mountain, on which sheep and cattle are grazed. Occasionally, in the midst of these small holdings large pasturage farms exist, from which the people had been evicted in the years subsequent to the famine. The cultivated patches in the possession of each family are small, and in most cases are insufficient for a rotation of crops. The consequence is that potatoes are often grown for years in succession on the same land, with disastrous results. The peasantry are aware of the good effects of rotation, and generally practise it, except where all the arable land in their possession is insufficient. The townlands and districts in which distress prevailed are not all contiguous, but are separated from one another by long arms of the sea and high mountains. The means of communication between them and the outside world are frequently difficult, and the means of inter-communication are often most primitive, and though in both respects there have been remarkable improvements in recent years, yet much remains to be done.

An examination of the houses, or, more correctly, cabins and hovels, of the distressed people showed meagrely thatched roofs, unwhitewashed walls, earthen floors, straw bedding – and little of it – almost entire absence of tables, chairs, plates, cups and saucers, presence of cattle and pigs, close proximity of manure heaps. The poverty revealed by these dwellings was utterly appalling (sodden). There was no trace of the material comforts of the nineteenth century visible. Perennial poverty was only varied by periodic

The Square, Castletownbere, photographed by Robert French towards the end of the 19th century.

starvation. Absence of wholesome food and presence of unsanitary surroundings were accompanied by the terrible scourge of typhus fever. From about a dozen cabins at Cooleragh, near Glengarriff, were thirty-two cases of fever at the same time in the Bantry Hospital last year. . . .

Clothing was scanty and ragged. Many were clad in their own home-made flannel and frieze, but slowly and surely the practice of making these is disappearing. More shoddy is now worn than flannel. Everywhere complaint was made of the absence of able-bodied men. As soon as the young people are full grown they emigrate. The Parish Priest of Adrigole told us that, except in very few cases, there were not two able-bodied men in any of the families in his parish. Though families are large, the available labour is small. In all the distressed districts the people are unable to subsist solely on the small portions of land at present in their possession.

From *Distress in the West and South of Ireland, 1898*

Rudyard Kipling

1898

RUDYARD KIPLING (1865–1936), author of poems, short stories and novels, was born in Bombay, educated in England and returned to India to work as a journalist. He first achieved fame as a writer in 1886, with his *Departmental Ditties*. Kipling went to London, spent some years in the USA and later lived in Sussex. In 1900 he reported on the Boer War in South Africa. His two Jungle Books, *Kim* and *Just – So Stories* established his world-wide reputation, and he won the Nobel prize for literature in 1907. In September 1898 Kipling visited Berehaven as a passenger on HMS *Pelorus* to observe the Channel fleet engaging in naval exercises.

Rudyard Kipling.

Out of the strong-shouldered Atlantic swell – bluer than sapphires – rose the double-fanged rock of the Fastnet. We were close enough to see its steps and derricks and each wave as it shot thirty feet up the rocks – the Fastnet in fair weather. It was like meeting a policeman in evening dress. One does not think of the Fastnet save as a blessed welcoming wink of light through storm and thick weather.

The Irish coast is a never-failing surprise to the big Atlantic rollers. They trip and ground – you can see them check – on the shallows; fling up a scornful eyebrow and then lose their temper and shape in great lashings of creamy foam.

'That's Berehaven,' said the bridge, indicating an obscure aperture in the jagged coastline. 'We shall find the Fleet round the corner. The tide's setting us up a little. Did you ever read 'The Two Chiefs of Dunboy'? We shall open Dunboy House in a minute round the corner.'

'And a half-nine!' sang the leadsman, cursing the long-stocked port-anchor under his breath, for he had to cast to one side of it and it stuck out like a cat's whiskers.

We were between two rocky beaches, split and weathered by all the gales of the Atlantic, black boulders embroidered with golden weed, and beryl bays where the rollers had lost their way and were running in rings. Behind them the green, tiny-fielded land, dotted with white cottages, climbed up to the barren purple hills.

Jaunting cars were a popular form of transport in Beara until the arrival of the motor car.

'Ah! The *Arrogant*'s here anyhow. See her puff!'

A monstrous plume of black, heavy smoke went up to the sky. We whipped round a buoy and came on the Fleet. There were eight battleships alike as peas to the outsider; and four big cruisers. They were not cruising or manoeuvring just then; but practising their various arts and crafts.

The Marines fell in on the poop, and with bugles and all proper observances we paid our compliments as we ran past the sterns of the cruisers, waiting the Admiral's word to moor.

'He's given us a billet of our own. Under his wing too.' An officer shot down on to the fo'c'sle, while the yeoman of signals, whose nose is that of a hawk, kept an unshut eye on the Flag.

'Isn't there a four-foot patch somewhere about here?' said a calm and disinterested voice. The Navigator having brought her in did not need to wrestle with cables; and our anchors with their low, cramped davits are no treat.

'We told 'em about our anchors in the Dockyard,' said the bridge. 'We told 'em so distinctly, and they said: "We're very much obliged to you for the information, and we'll make the changes you recommend – in the next boat of your class." That's what I call generosity.'

'Does that ship always behave like that?' I asked. From all three funnels of a high, stubby cruiser the smoke of a London factory insulted the clean air.

'Oh, no; she's only burning muckings like the rest of us. She's our 'chummy' ship. She's a new type – she and the *Furious*. Fleet rams they call 'em. Rather like porcupines, aren't they?'

The two had an air of bristling, hog-backed ferocity, strangely out of keeping with the normal reserve of a man-of-war.

The *Blake*, long and low, looked meek and polite beside them, but I was assured that she could blow them out of the water. Their own Captains, of course, thought otherwise.

All Ireland was new to me, and I went ashore to investigate Castletown's street of white houses, to smell peat smoke and find Dan Murphy, owner of a jaunting car and ancient friend of the wardroom. In this quest me and the Navigator mustered not less than half the male population of Cork County, the remainder being O'Sullivans; but we found Dan at last – old, grizzled, with an untameable eye, voluble and beautifully Celtic.

'Will I meet ye tomorrow at Mill Cove at nine-thirty? I will. Here's my hand an' word on it. Will I dhrive ye to Glenbeg for the fishing? I will. There's my hand an' word on it. Do I mean it? Don't I know the whole livin' fleet, man an' boy, for years?'

He appeared at the appointed hour with a raw-boned horse and wonderful yarns of trout taken by 'the other gentlemen' in Glenbeg, the lough of our desire, fourteen miles across the hills. It was a cloudless day with a high wind – bad for trout but good for the mere joy of life; and the united ages of my companions reached forty-five. We were quite respectable till we cleared Castletown, and such liberty-men as might have been corrupted by our example. Then we sang and hung on to the car at impossible angles, and swore eternal fidelity to the barefooted damosels on the road, they being no wise backward to return our vows; and behaved ourselves much as all junior officers do when they escape on holiday. It was a land of blue and grey mountains, of raw green fields, stone-fenced, ribbed with black lines of peat, and studded with clumps of gorse and heather and the porter-coloured pools of bog water. Great island-dotted bays ran very far inland, and bounding all to Westward hung the unswerving line of Atlantic. Such a country it was as, without much imagination, one could perceive its children in exile would sicken for – a land of small holdings and pleasant green ways where nobody did more work than was urgent.

At last we came on an inky-black tarn, shut in by mountains, locked and lonely and lashed into angry waves by a downward-smiting blast.

There was no special point in the fishing: not even when the Sub-Lieutenant tried to drown himself; but the animal delight of that roaring day of sun and wind will live long in one memory. We had it all to ourselves – the rifted purple flank of Lackawee, the long vista of the lough darkening as the shadows fell; the smell of a new country, and the tearing wind that brought down mysterious voices of men from somewhere high above us.

None but the Irish can properly explain away failure. We left with our dozen fingerlings, under the impression – Mister Cornelius Crowley gave it – that we had caught ten-pounders.

From *A Fleet in Being*

John Rushworth Jellicoe

1912

LORD JELLICOE (1859–1935) came from a naval background and grew up in Southampton. After entering the Royal Navy in 1872, he served in the Egyptian War of 1882, and survived the sinking of the *Victoria* in the Mediterranean in 1893. Jellicoe also served in the Far East, and with the Atlantic Fleet. He commanded the Grand Fleet during the First World War and was appointed Admiral of the Fleet in 1919. In his memoirs Jellicoe writes of his 1912 visit to Berehaven, which had been chosen as the testing site of a new system for naval gunnery – a system that would soon prove its worth.

Later in the Autumn I took my Squadron to Berehaven and whilst there superintended the trials of a system of firing by Director as proposed by Admiral Sir Percy Scott. The Director system had been fitted to the *Thunderer*, and competitive firings under similar conditions were carried out by the *Thunderer* and the *Orion*, working under ordinary service conditions. Lieutenant E. Altham, the gunnery lieutenant of the *Thunderer*, was helping Sir Percy Scott and was of the greatest possible assistance to him. The trials proved most conclusively the superiority of the Director system, which I strenuously advocated for general adoption in the Navy. There was, however, very strong opposition to this system in the fleet and at the Admiralty, and in spite of all that I could do in urging its adoption, only a small proportion of the capital ships had been fitted with the Director system before the outbreak of war. As soon, however, as I assumed command of the Grand Fleet, I pressed the Admiralty at once to fit all ships with the system; and, by the time that the battle of Jutland was fought, all capital ships had been so fitted for their main armament. I knew that the Germans had an elementary form of Director firing in use, as Sir Percy Scott had visited Kiel a few years earlier and had informed me of the result of his observations there.

From *The Life of John Rushworth, Earl Jellicoe*

Albert Thomas

1921

ALBERT THOMAS started work at fourteen in an Exeter hotel. He went on to become a third footman with the Duke of Norfolk, saw service in South Africa during the Boer War, and worked as a steward in a Dublin club. In 1921 he and his wife were engaged as caretakers for Dunboy Castle. His account of their time there provides a fascinating glimpse of the last weeks before the house was burned down.

Arriving at Bantry, we were taken to the boat, and we looked forward to our trip of thirty-six miles down the Bay. It was a beautiful April day, everything looked so lovely and green, the water blue as the sky, and everything wonderful and peaceful compared to the places which we had just left. But still the tension was there. You could feel it, that under-current of unrest, with the Black and Tans walking about in couples, their revolvers prominently displayed, and bombs bulging from out of their pockets. Some of them boarded the boat, and looked over it; they asked me a few questions, which seemed to satisfy them, and in good time we cast off. The birds going down the Bay were wonderful; I should think that I saw every seabird that I knew, and lots that I didn't. We had a snack at the little bar, and the first twenty miles passed pleasantly enough, but then the wife began to feel the effects of the rough sea a little, and retired, so out of sympathy I retired with her. . . .

We felt quite recovered when we got off the boat and found a car waiting for us at Castletown Bere; and at last we arrived at Dunboy Castle.

It was a good Irish mile and a half from the town (about two English miles), and at the entrance to the drive was a ruined lodge. No one, of course, lived there. The drive itself was quite half a mile long, and such a drive too; beautiful trees lined each side, and then suddenly a glorious view of the sea. It was wonderful, and we were both enraptured with it. Then the castle. It was a noble building, very tall chimneys, turrets as in the olden days, and, in fact, everything that a castle should be. We were met by the two young gentlemen, and made thoroughly welcome; they were naval officers, and very charming, with Irish brown eyes, and every inch gentlemen.

As Madam thought that they would appreciate a good dinner – for they had been there a week on their own and had no doubt roughed it a good deal – she had packed some soup, a leg of lamb, and some sardines. I went to the garden, got some vegetables from one of the men, and then looking through the larder I discovered some tinned cherries, so saying nothing to them I laid the table while the wife prepared the dinner. I asked them what time they would like to dine, suggesting eight o'clock, in order to give us plenty of time, and they agreed. Such beautiful silver, gorgeous glass, and wonderful linen; the wife excelled herself, everything was wonderful, so they said. You see, being so used to messing on board, and especially after roughing it as they had done previous to our arrival, a nicely cooked meal, served properly, appealed to them. With their dinner they had a lovely claret, of which there was quite a lot in the cellar, and they told me that it was a shame that a cook like my wife was to buried down there. It was very nice to be spoken to like that; most employers take it as a matter of course, and are afraid to compliment you for fear that you will ask for an increase in wages. How very silly of them: little do they know that everyone works all the better for an occasional pat on the back.

After dinner, I served coffee in the largest drawing-room that I ever saw. Panelled in really lovely black oak, with pale blue tapestry, it looked truly beautiful when the candles were lit. After we had finished we went into the grounds; it was barely dark, and to hear the younger son playing all the old Irish airs on a fine, grand piano completed one of the most wonderful nights I have ever spent.

The two gentlemen were due to leave the next day, but they did not go, so we gave them another little dinner the following night. One of them had caught some trout, so we served them as they should be eaten – wrapped in buttered paper and put in the oven. An omelette, a Scotch woodcock, and a glorious Hock, the name of which momentarily escapes me, but which tasted like nectar to me, completed the meal. The next day off they went, and the eldest one said that he would see us again in the autumn, as he was getting married then and intended spending his honeymoon there. Oh, how I wished that they had stayed, for they were no trouble, and so kind and considerate. As they were of old Irish blood I found it advisable to agree with everything that they said, and really, after listening to them for a short time they nearly convinced me that they were in the right, no matter what they were discussing; but since then, one wonders. They advised me not to say a word if we saw anything that seemed queer to us, for there were a lot of rebels, as he called them, on the run, and if I encountered any of them I was to do all that they asked me, and give them whatever they should ask for and get a receipt for the things taken away by anyone, especially by the IRA. My instructions were plain, and I could see clearly that if I did not supply their demands they would take what they wanted by force, so I said that I would carry out their instructions to the letter, which I may say I always did, as you will see if you will bear with me for a while.

One day, whilst we were at the extreme end of the castle grounds, a place that we had never visited before, an unknown voice suddenly ordered us to go back to the castle, and not to look around but to walk quickly. He fired a shot in order to let us hear that he was armed, so we walked and walked, and believe me, my neck never ached so much in my life as when we came into sight of the castle. The wife said that she was the same; I often wondered afterwards if it was because our minds were fixed on not looking round, and were much stronger than our curiosity. My wife wanted to pretend to fall down, but I was taking no chances, because I knew that rebels on the run are very funny people to deal with. So we came home.

There was one man on the estate whom everyone knew was a 'Seiner'; they all were, but he was in command of some portion of them. I made a pal of him, and told him that we had no intentions of doing them any harm, but that the least he could do would be to tell us where we were not to go and what not to do, for an experience like the one we had gone through that evening was not playing the game, especially in the castle's own grounds. So a day or two afterwards he told me what had happened. It appeared that a few weeks previously two soldiers had been ambushed and murdered, and one of the rebels, seeing me, had thought that I was searching for their hiding place, but as they had gone now it was quite all right for me to go anywhere on the estate. After having a heart-to-heart talk with the man, and assuring him that they had nothing to fear from us, I clinched matters by asking him if his daughter would like to come up and help us for a day or two. She did come, and a fine, bonny girl she was, too; I paid her five shillings for two days' work, and she was dumbfounded. I firmly believe to this day that she had never possessed five shillings in her life before; at any rate, she ran off and told her father, to make sure that everything was all right and even he said that I had overpaid her. Such was Ireland in those days. . . .

We soon began to feel pretty secure, and to live like human beings. With the lovely grounds and the wonderful bird life down there, we were perfectly happy. There was hardly anything to do excepting on wet days, when we slogged away at things indoors to pass the time away. You see, there were no telephones or front or back door bells to answer, and no one but our two selves to look after; we were surrounded by lovely furniture

Dunboy Castle as it appeared when Albert Thomas came to take up his post as butler and caretaker in 1921.

and beautiful things, and as I could tinker away on the piano life passed very pleasantly. The wife fancied some chicken, so I bought a broody hen from one of the crofters, got some eggs and set the old hen. We named her Sarah; she was a stubborn old bird but in the course of time nine lovely little chicks were in her charge. I decided to make them a nice little run, in order to render them safe from the carrion crows which hung round the castle: my wife liked to dig worms for them for she used to enjoy watching them struggling over them in pairs, until they suddenly fell on their rumps, looking quite scared, when the ill-fated worm parted in the middle. Such then, was the condition of our simple lives when 'it' happened.

I was in the armoury, busily constructing the chicken run, and the wife had gone out into the garden to murder worms, when suddenly I heard a noise. My back was towards the door, and I did not bother to turn, thinking that it was only my wife, so took no notice until the abrupt command, 'Put your hands up,' caused me to take very considerable interest in events behind my back. I swung around and then I saw things. There was the little wife in the midst of nine men, all wearing caps and holding a second cap over their faces so that everything barring their eyes was concealed, and presented a formidable array of revolvers at me. Up went my hands, a hammer in one and a chisel in the other. I must have looked a curious sight, but the wife far outshone me; she was clutching a fork in one hand and a handful of worms in the other. They had surrounded her in the midst of her worm-foraging, and made her put up her hands and some of her captures were beginning to crawl up (or would it be down?) her arms. I could see that she was beginning to feel a bit queer, so I rushed over to hold her; I knew that they would not fire at me, and she quickly recovered.

I asked the men what they wanted and they said: 'Clothes and boots.' I told them quietly how things were and that I was prepared to give them what they fancied if they would give me a receipt. Six of them accompanied me upstairs, leaving three down below with my wife; I showed them some old things that the two gentlemen used to wear, and a lot of old-fashioned stuff which was no good. Then we heard shouting from below; they all rushed to the head of the stairs, but it was only the wife refusing to let the other men enter the room where Sarah and the young chicks were. She had her back to the door, and she would not budge. I explained matters to the one in charge, and they did not go in, revolvers or no revolvers. After packing up what I had let them have they gave me a receipt and left. But they warned me not to leave the castle for at least an hour, or to light the beacon in the tower. I said that I would act on their instructions, for it appeared that my predecessor had built a large sort of beacon in the tower with some shavings, wood and tar, so that if they were in trouble at any time they could light it, the idea being that the flames at night, or the smoke by day, would warn the soldiers on Bere Island, about half a mile away, that they were wanted. It was a silly idea, for the rebels could have hidden safely in the caves about ten minutes walk away; but there you are, Ireland again.

I will say that they were very fair for they asked Rose where the binoculars were that I used in the grounds. Rose said that she had hidden them and would not tell them where; but under pressure, she said that they were in her bed and she knew I valued them as they had been a birthday present from her. When they heard they were mine they refused to take them, saying all they wanted was the Master's things.

The amusing part about the little incident just related is that in spite of their precautions, I knew that four of the men present were our own gardeners. I recognized their clothing, for an Irishman will wear the same clothes until they almost drop off him, also their caps. However, I never let on that I knew them; perhaps it was just as well, for when at the termination of my hour I went to the gardens to see the bailiff, he was worried out of his life. He knew all about it, but was too cute to let me see it. There was nothing in it really; if they had come up openly and asked me, through their leader, I would have given them all that they required. In fact, I told my friend (Ted) so, but no, the Irish must be dramatic.

So the time slipped by, and nothing happened for a month or two with the exception of a carrion crow pinching two of the wife's chickens. She cried and carried on but I could do nothing. So we passed the time away, watching the herons and seagulls fighting, or fishing, for there were heaps of fish there. The local fishermen used to sell me fine, live lobsters for only sixpence each; they could have obtained 2s. 6d. apiece for them from the officers on Bere Island, but they would not sell them to any soldier. So it came to pass that one day two officers came over to the castle to see how things were – one a colonel, the other a captain. I fancied that there was something about the former that I knew, so I asked him if he had been to Exeter lately. He knew me in a minute; it was my benefactor of woodcock fame. We were both delighted at this unexpected meeting, and it was decided that he should bring a boatload of soldiers over on the pretence of searching the castle grounds. The men could bring their grub and the four officers would have a lobster salad and a bottle of the Guv'nor's choice Hock if they would give me a chit for it; it would then be up to my employer whether or not he charged them for it. . . .

We happened one night to be sitting reading; it was about 11.30 and we were just about to go to bed. The wife would not go without me because an old owl was in the habit of hooting at her light in our bedroom; how she hated that owl. At that time of night I was rather surprised to hear a rattle at the door, but I opened it, and ten men walked past me into the room. No masks this time, but all very determined looking men. I could see that something was up so I asked their leader what I could do for him. He replied that they had come to burn the castle down as they had heard that the soldiers had made arrangements to take it over as their headquarters in preference to Bere Island. I told them that this was not true and that if they would only listen to me for a moment I thought that I could convince them how foolhardy it would be for them to carry out their intentions. I asked them quietly if, being local men, it had struck them that without the castle and its grounds there would be no work for six of them; no rates and taxes could be collected, and between £800 and £1,000 a year less would be spent in the town if the castle were no more. They listened, for at least six of them could see my point. The head one was, no doubt, on the run and appeared to be domineering the others, so I suggested putting it to the vote. At this point was almost twelve o'clock, and just on the stroke a most awful, gurgling noise came from the passage, and a hollow rattling of chains. As the wife was still with me, the men could see that we were not responsible for this, and, as the noise drew nearer, they up and ran from the castle as one man, just as if 'Old Nick' had spoken to them.

Then my wife called me 'a cruel, horrible man.' I thought that she had gone crazy for a moment, for to tell the truth, I had the wind up a bit myself, but she led me to the armoury, and there was the ghost, all horrible and ghastly, for I had killed Sarah. She would not mother her chicks, so the wife had condemned her to death; I am afraid that I did not do the job properly, but had hung her up by the legs to bleed. The gurgling noise came from her, and the 'rattling of chains' was caused by the flapping of her wings in her dying struggles; what made her flap them at that particular moment I don't know, but it did happen. . . .

One Sunday morning (I was in town at the time), a large body of soldiers landed from Bere Island, and waited outside the church, which was always well attended *every* Sunday in Ireland. I waited, and whilst the congregation was coming out I saw an officer touch each male worshipper on the shoulder and give one a pick, another a shovel. They waited until they had collected twenty in this manner, and then marched them to a road, across which a huge trench had been dug to stop the traffic. As it was on my way back to the Castle, I followed to see the fun. The officers gave orders for the men to fill in the trench and make good the road – all in their best clothes. I did not stay to see them finish the job, or I should have been late for my dinner, but Ted informed me that some of them did not get their dinner until three o'clock. The road trenching still went on, and so did the refilling, but, you see, the men had to go to church.

But they took their revenge, and that, too, happened on a Sunday a few weeks later. About thirty or forty of the Rebels were, as usual, on the lawn in front of the Castle drilling; and very smart they were at it, all being young, keen and all with a grouse, real or otherwise, mostly otherwise I think. All at once there was a revolver shot; every rebel disappeared in a different direction. What happened was that the one on sentry duty had seen some soldiers leaving Bere Island about a quarter of a mile away and by the time they got to the Castle in about half an hour, everything was quiet and not a soul in sight. Naturally, I had seen nothing out of the way because people used to come out in the Castle grounds every Sunday and walk around the gardens when the owners were not there. But my friend the Colonel knew better and told me if we stayed there our lives would be in danger, for he knew from information he had received that they were going to burn down the Castle and his orders were to take us both back to Bere Island with him and send us back to England. I tried to tell him we were quite safe there, but at last he persuaded us to follow his advice. Rose, being Rose, had always seen that our trunks were packed, in case of a sudden raid by the Rebels, so we were given two hours to put things in order, the soldiers in the meanwhile searching the grounds for rebels, though of course they found none. When everything was ready for our departure and we were waiting for the soldiers to come back, I thought I would let the old gardener Baird know we were going. So I stepped out and began to run to his cottage; as it had begun to rain I took my umbrella with me. I was just turning the corner, when I heard a sharp 'Halt. Who goes there?' Knowing the answer, I stopped and walked towards the soldier. He was very young, about twenty, no more, his rifle at the ready and his finger very shaky, it seemed to me, on the trigger. I told him who I was, but I could not convince him. Rose who had been watching me, came running up, saying: 'Don't shoot him, he is my husband. You ought to know we are English.' But he still pointed his gun and as I had dropped my gamp I was beginning to feel pretty damp. Rose ran back and fetched the Colonel. It seemed hours before he came, but it was really only minutes. The Colonel explained afterwards that this particular soldier had had one of his pals murdered (or killed, which is the right word?) by the Rebels only a short time ago, and his one aim in life was to kill a Rebel. Why Rose thought the soldier ought to have known we were English, and therefore quite all right, is beyond me; but somehow English people are like that. I wonder why?

We were taken to Bere Island, but what I feared happened soon enough. One night I was called up and was shown a very large glow in the sky overlooking the Castle about a mile away. The Rebels had burnt the Castle down as they said they would. I was very, very sorry for all the lovely old silver, the beautiful glass and splendid linen all being burnt, all those gorgeous statues and pictures, the wonderful drawing-room all burning, for what? One can sometimes understand war, with all its horrors, but this seemed to me a very wanton thing to do. I firmly believe that the Rebels were under the impression that the soldiers were going to take the Castle over. If they had, it would have saved it, I think, but either the owners would not give their consent or else the powers that be thought otherwise. I couldn't understand. All I know was no soldier could leave Bere island unless the Rebels knew it, and so promptly that they always had a good half an hour in which to get away. Rose and I often went walking on the shore, when suddenly we used to hear the call of a curlew, a call which was never uttered by a curlew. I know the clear call too well for that, so I knew we were being watched by someone who was warning someone else. We then used to turn round and go back to the Castle.

From *Wait and See*

John O'Donoghue

c.1923

JOHN O'DONOGHUE (1900–1964) grew up on a small farm near Kilgarvan, County Kerry. He served in the Garda Síochána for seven years, then entered a monastery, but left it to work in England. He wrote three books of reminiscences: *In a Quiet Land* and *In Kerry Long Ago* contain memories of the old customs and rural way of life, while *In a Strange Land* describes his experiences as an emigrant in England, employed in the building trade. O'Donoghue also provided material for the Irish Folklore Commission. *In Kerry Long Ago* includes recollections of a cycling holiday one July when he visited his relatives at Garnish in west Beara.

Bidding good-bye to my relatives here I cycled west towards Crow Head. All the way on my left I could see the great expanse of white heaving water which I knew to be the Atlantic. Dark moving shadows swept gently over it here and there as the clouds that made them moved across the sky. Away in the distance I could see the black outline of ships dotting its surface. At the foot of The Hill of The Holy Well where rounds were paid in the past I stopped to admire some of the neatly thatched cottages of the farmers and fishermen. Many of them were very ancient-looking. The walls were built with small dark-grey flagstones and mortar but there was neither plaster nor whitewash on the outside, except on borders round the doors and windows. They looked very picturesque with the brown thatch held down by netted ropes secured by wooden plugs driven into the walls below the eaves. They were single-storey houses and the windows were very small.

Soon I came to Lehanemore and the top of a high cliff called Filebomaleen which was opposite the lovely glen where my special friend, Kenneth O'Hara, lived. I could see his house in the distance and my heart filled up with joy at the thought of meeting him again because his like was hard to find. Most of the houses in his village were quaint in every respect. They were built in funny positions, nearly all of them out of line with the *bohereen* leading through the place, as if they had come there more by accident than design. Some were in sheltered nooks, others nestling against the bare side of the hill. With one or two exceptions, nearly all were single-storey. It was surely such a village as people only find in fairy tales, but to me its principal glory lay in the fact that Kenneth O'Hara lived there in a house which seemed from its position to be in danger of slipping into the green depths of sea below the rocks where I knew the brown snorting seals had their happy-hunting-ground.

The village was well off the main road, however, so I cycled past it through a deep rugged gap in the mountain till I came to Lhaurtheeowen at The Cross of Island View in Annaweelogue where I got the usual welcome from Aunt Kathleen and her family. I was mighty glad to see them. Then I went up the green bank to a romantic little hollow between the rocks where my uncle Walter lived. I was welcomed there also and asked to stay for the night, which I did. I remember well sitting down to tea by the big window that once let light into a shop. It was evening and when I looked out I found the scene enchanting. Kenmare Bay was in front of me like a vast sheet of polished silver; the blue headlands of Kerry making a glorious border in the distance to the north and black islands breaking its surface near the coast. Close at hand were The Three Strands of Annaweelogue with seagulls flying about from place to place, their lonely voices making music in the distance. The sun was sinking in a reddish-gold haze that filled the western sky, its rays reflected in a path of splendour like a fairy highway on the gleaming sea.

'Is it always like that?' I asked Uncle Walter, sitting beside me while his wife Julia poured out the tea and warned me to help myself to home-made cake and butter.

'You may be sure it is not then,' he said, laughing. 'You'd see a change, I'm telling you, if you were here in dark November when wailing winter winds put roaring on the sea and ships come in for shelter in the harbour down below.'

'I meant in summertime alone,' I said, 'because I don't think it could be nice at all in winter.'

'It isn't either then,' said Julia as we left the table.

After a little more conversation I went out along the road to where I expected to see Kenneth. He was there with his companions and gave me a most enthusiastic welcome. He never expected me this evening, so after talking for some time with the others who were also friends of mine, he and I went walking through the glen towards the south. I thought he looked a little sad but his voice was soft and charming as of old. We talked of countless things which never made me tired because I liked his pleasant company so much. He filled my lonely heart with joy and beauty never known before, for he had all the graces of a perfect gentleman. Riches and learning have but little to do with manners or refinement, I thought, as I heard the clatter of his hob-nailed boots beside me on the gravelled road, and the rustle of his home-made oil-skin jacket as he searched for cigarettes.

'Are you going out in the boat tomorrow, Kenneth?' I asked, for I loved being on the summer sea while he and his companions fished for lobsters.

The Calf Rock lighthouse operated from 1866 until it was destroyed by a storm in 1881.

'I am,' he said. 'We're going west to Reen to see if there is anything in the pots.'

'May I go with you?' I asked shyly.

'Of course you may,' he said. 'We'll be leaving Fircale about three o'clock in the evening after my father mows the hay. Mike Dan will be going with us and a few other lads as well.'

I was delighted to hear this, so after we had returned to his companions I said good-night and went back to Uncle Walter's where his mother-in-law, Nell from Killawnmore, told me lots of stories about the district. She was a grand, cheerful woman, somewhat like Maura Nee Lhaera in her manner.

'So you're going to Reen with Kenneth tomorrow,' she said, arranging the grey hair under the little brown shawl she was wearing about her head with the ends tied, first under her jaw and then at the back of her neck. 'A nicer companion you couldn't have, upon my soul. He's a fine fellow surely, and everyone in the place likes him.'

'I'm not at all surprised at that,' said I, feeling that nobody could think otherwise about him indeed.

'He might be going farther back,' she said, 'because his uncle owns the little island at the point of Crow Head. Keep your eyes and ears open as you go along for the place is wonderful and lovely in the sunshine.'

'I have no doubt about that,' said I; 'but I shouldn't like to live there, for it looks so wild and lonely from the slopes of Lehanemore.'

'So it is, to be sure, my love,' said Nell, tapping the toes of her boots on the clay floor; 'very wild indeed. How could it be anything else when 'tis at the end of land that reaches like a great spear into the bosom of the mighty ocean. The little rocky island rises in great black cliffs with a covering of rich red earth on top where grass keeps always green. 'Tis a grand place for sheep. That's why Kenneth's uncle keeps them there. But in olden times it was the home of a fellow called The Gialun Gow.'

'My goodness,' said I in surprise, knowing it was three miles out at the end of a shelterless uninhabited headland covered with heather and ferns, 'how did he manage to get a living there at all?'

'I'll tell you then, my brightness,' said she, 'and it may surprise you to hear it. He was a blacksmith and had a big forge there.'

'A *blacksmith*, is it?' said I in amazement. 'What in the name of heaven made him start his business there, so far away from people wanting shoes put on their horses?'

'God help us, you *glugeen*,' said she, laughing. 'It wasn't horseshoe work he did at all.'

'What the hell did he do then?' I asked, more surprised than ever, for I did not know the customs of the district.

'He did iron work for passing ships,' she said, 'and a big trade it was too in those days by all accounts. He made piles of money out of it and before he died he hid it somewhere on the island where nobody could find it. He was a magician as well, and a few times when some busybodies went to search for it after his death they couldn't do a thing about it, because each time they came, a terrible storm blew with great roaring waves rising like mountains around the island that frightened the lives out of them. I'm telling you they were mighty glad to stop searching and find shelter in a crevasse to save themselves from being thrown like feathers to the yawning waves around them. When the storms died down they were thankful to get away with their lives not to mind the riches of the Gialun Gow.'

I had no doubt about the story because I was after reading in school that long ago the De Danaans had fooled a fleet invading Ireland by asking its leaders to go out nine waves before finally landing in the country. When this was done the De Danaans got up a mighty storm by the power of magic and drowned the strangers near The Bull, Cow and Calf, great black dangerous rocks, rising out of the western sea beyond the headlands here.

'As you go towards the island in the boat,' said Nell, 'look up at the cliffs at the end of Reen and you'll see The Stairs of the Blacksmith's

Cow. A set of benches there is called Bohar Bo Gialun. They look like a real stairway and people say it was up there the blacksmith used to drive his cow to graze on the mainland.'

'It must be a wonderful place,' said I, looking forward eagerly to my visit there.

'It is then, surely,' said Nell, loosening the knot on the shawl at the back of her neck; 'as fine a place as ever human eye could see, but very few will go there for the scenery alone. I must go off to bed now, for God help us, old age puts aching in the limbs.'

'Sound sleep to you, Nell,' said I as she moved towards the bedroom door, 'and pleasant dreams as well.'

'The same to you tonight,' she said, 'and more of them tomorrow.'

Next day I was full of excitement at the idea of meeting Kenneth, and was delighted when at last I saw him come strolling down from the house with his father to the little rocky landing where the boats were tied. I looked into the green water below and saw the brownish-yellow crabs moving slowly along the bottom, feeling glad that I was away from the reach of their vicious claws which they opened and shut as they went from place to place. Nature is a wonder, I thought, as I stepped into the boat with Kenneth who always, from the kindness of his heart, kept warning me about the dangers of the sea he loved so much himself.

''Tis far more treacherous than a faithless friend,' said his father, who was a rather silent man, but had a vivid way for saying things when he spoke; 'but unfortunately we must earn our living on it while we're here.'

'You should come around the time of the *seining*, Brian,' said Kenneth, whose melodious voice made music in my ears no matter what he said. ''Tis then you'd see the real seaman's life. They go in hundreds to the strand before going out at night to do the fishing. Annaweelogue is very busy then with plenty work and money in the place around the end of autumn.'

'I'll come, please God, if I can manage it,' said I, helping him to pull the oar when we got out into the open sea.

Looking back at the land I saw the steep faces of the great black cliffs at Filebomaleen in the east with countless seabirds standing on the verges and flying about in search of food. Here and there a brown seal would stick his head over the water and begin to snort loudly. He looked exactly like a dog in the distance and the older seamen seemed to regard him with awe. They warned the young fellows not to make any frightening gestures towards him.

After rowing close to the land for a few miles we came to the buoys that marked the spots where lobster pots were laid. When these were drawn up I could see the flapping creatures moving quickly about inside. The pots were really wicker baskets shaped like ink-wells so that when the lobsters went in to get the bait they were not clever enough to return by the same way but kept trying to get out at the highest points around the sides of the sunken opening instead until they were caught and put into the boat. Crayfishes went in with them. They were frightful-looking creatures with long tentacles lashing about in all directions. Conger eels went into the baskets as well. These were killed and thrown into the sea. Nobody around the place would eat them, for they had plenty other fish besides.

Rowing is tiresome work, moreover, in the summer, so I can tell you I was glad when we passed the cliffs of Sculla at last and The Stairs of The Gialun Gow came into view. They looked exactly like what Nell had said about them. I tried to picture the blacksmith urging on the cow with a stick as she struggled up the steps like a human being and reached the lovely purple heather on the ground above before going farther inland to the grassy slopes. The sky was clear and blue. The water lapped in gentle waves against the hanging seaweeds on the rocks. Away to the west I could see a tall pointed rock sticking out of the water like a spear. It seemed to grow bigger as we drew nearer until finally it looked like a great tower. No doubt it had some wonderful story following it that I had never heard, for like the valley of Coomlaegill, there was no rock without a romance in the place.

We were right beside the Crow Head Island now. Its rough, grey rocky sides showed many signs of battering from the sea. The grass above them was intensely green. It reminded me of the caps the boys and girls are so fond of wearing on Saint Patrick's Day. A deep narrow slit divided it from the point of the mainland, with water surging through it rather fiercely though the sea outside was calm. I was thinking what a dreadful place it must be in great storms while the boat was rowed beside a flat rock at the foot of the cliffs. The men stepped on to it and I followed them with great caution. We climbed up a sort of secret pathway to the top of the island with a lot of trouble. Then with my feet safely on the soft carpet of grass I looked around me. Away to the west was spread the vast expanse of silvery water, and America was the nearest land beyond the great horizon. To the south lay the blue headlands of Sheep and Mizen while to the north-west I saw the Bull, Cow and Calf rocks, sticking out of the water beyond the point of Dursey Island, itself a scene of beauty that words cannot describe. It lay in front of us to the north, a lovely picture with its brown and purple hillsides and many-coloured fields. Studded among them like gems on setting in a jeweller's window were the neat whitewashed cottages, covered with brownish-grey thatch. Streaks of light-blue smoke were rising from the chimneys, swelling out as they rose higher, then gradually fading away. It was a sight in itself that made a visit to the headland be a pleasure. The Calf Rock was the nearest of the three at present and the sea around it looked quite calm, but I had seen it from Dursey Head some time previously and I'm telling you it was rough enough then. It was a few days after a storm and the sea was still uneasy. Vast white waves rolled up and down its low black sides, sweeping east and west across it, making it look like the eye of some great monster with the sea opening and shutting around it. No wonder people called it The Calf Rock, for the same sweeping waves looked in the distance like the tongue of a cow licking her newly-born calf. It had its history too for there was a lighthouse built on it in the middle of the last century. Part of the tower is still standing there. A mighty storm arose and swept over it at night. The fittings were destroyed and the light-keepers only saved their lives by sheltering under a shelf of rock with the waters pouring over it from the windy side while the storm lasted. When calm returned after a few days they came out and hung their shirts up as a signal of distress. They were rescued after a lot of trouble. I knew one of the survivors, Taid Kelly, who was married to my mother's cousin near Annaweelogue.

While his uncle, Daniel O'Dan of Scrivogue, was counting his sheep, Kenneth and I walked about the island where we saw the ruins of an old building. I was wondering if it was there the Gialun Gow had his forge when Kenneth spoke.

'Do you see the houses over there at the western end of Dursey?' he asked.

'I do,' said I, after lifting up my eyes from the ruin and looking across the little bay that lay between us and the island.

'Taid O'Leary lives in one of them,' he said.

'Is that the man you mentioned the other day when you were warning me about the dangers of the sea?'

'It is indeed. His hand is twisted backwards and he can do nothing about it.'

'The Lord save us, what happened to him? Was he born that way?'

'He was not, but he was out fishing with other men when he was young and a storm came on them suddenly. They could not get back to land and the boat was turned over. All the others were drowned, God rest them, only Taid.'

'How did he escape?'

'He held on to the gunwale and when the boat turned upside-down he was afraid to let go. He kept his hand in one position for hours and hours until the sea got calm at last. It was some time before he was rescued and the sinews were affected so much by having to keep his hand so long in that awkward way that it could never again be put right.'

'He's a lucky man to be alive at all.'

'He is, indeed,' said Kenneth as we walked back to where the others were waiting to get down to the boat again, 'and faith he's a fine, hearty man today in spite of it all, thank God.'

'Amen,' said I, having a final look around me and feeling lonely at the thought of leaving such a lovely spot, because apart from its beauty there was a look of eerie desolation about its peculiar position that filled my mind with awe about the wonders of creation.

Climbing carefully down we went into the boat again and rowed back to Fircale, the little harbour below Kenneth's house. The fishermen transferred the lobsters and crayfishes from the boat to a crate kept floating in the water for storage until the time for sale arrived, and then we all went home.

From *In Kerry Long Ago*

George Bernard Shaw

1923

GEORGE BERNARD SHAW (1856–1950) grew up in Dublin, left school at fifteen, worked in a land agent's office and moved to London in 1876. He wrote novels and criticism before turning his energies to drama. His early plays failed to find an audience, but gradually his genius as a dramatist was recognised. In 1898 Shaw married Charlotte Payne Townshend. They often visited southwest Ireland, and stayed at Glengarriff. In this excerpt Shaw is speaking of *Saint Joan*.

George Bernard Shaw.

During that year, I was at Glengarriff from the 18th July to the 15th August and at Parknasilla from the 15th August to the 18th September, working at the play all the time . . . But the play was neither begun nor finished in Eire. A good deal of it was written in rapidly moving trains between King's Cross and Hatfield.

From *The Oxford Literary Guide to the British Isles*

Harold Speakman

1924

AMERICAN AUTHOR, poet and artist Harold Speakman (1888–1928) saw military service in Italy in the First World War, followed by peacekeeping duties in Montenegro, experiences he describes in *From a Soldier's Heart. Beyond Shanghai, Hilltops in Galilee, Here's Ireland* and *Mostly Mississippi* recount his travels in the 1920s. In the summer of 1924 Speakman embarked on a walking tour throughout Ireland with a donkey called Grania and a cart. Among the notable figures he met were 'A.E.', Lady Gregory, Countess Markievicz, W.B. Yeats, Padraic Colum, Sean O'Casey and Sara Allgood. At the Eccles Hotel in Glengarriff Violet Bryce invited him to Garinish Island.

The following morning was calm, the sea, again at low tide, wore a surface of dark, clouded lacquer. The jade islands were Chinese jewels in their high settings of russet-gold kelp. With oars poised in air, a fishing boat hung beside one of them like a giant dragonfly. A lone duck flew along a vast parabola into the heather. Another group of fishers flung out and hauled in their circles of floats from the top of a small island where sirens should have been.

The lady greeted me cordially. 'I hope,' she said, as we went up a path made rich by the scent of early roses, 'I hope that you haven't heard the ridiculous story about our bringing boatloads of earth here from the mainland!'

'Millions of boatloads . . . ' I quoted.

'Now where could you have heard that!' she demanded with some warmth. 'I never knew anything so stupid!'

'It was an old woman coming over the hill,' I said. 'But it doesn't seem so bad to me. If a place were barren and one wanted to live here, why shouldn't soil be brought from anywhere?'

She looked at me imperiously and a little scornfully. (Evidently this was a subject of long standing and some delicacy.) 'In the first place, there isn't land on the mainland to take away; in the second, the thing is too silly. I can't imagine any one doing a thing like that – except perhaps an American millionaire!'

'Whew! This isn't beginning very well,' I thought. But in another moment she had forgotten her annoyance and was showing me a path so completely carpeted with fallen pink blossoms that in places it was entirely hidden from sight.

Before us, as we turned to the left, lay a formal garden of immediate, compelling charm, with a pool down its length which reflected no end of

Byzantine capitals and antique figures of the East and the ancient West. A pair of Chinese watch dogs stood on guard before the portico of a small classically designed garden villa at the end of the pool.

'This is the bachelor quarters,' said the lady, 'and this is where 'A.E.' stays when he is here.' I looked about the wide room with its fluted marble columns, its chaste, classical decorations, and its stone floors covered by the skins of tiger and bear and deer. Beyond one of the porticos was the beauty of the formal garden. Beyond the other was the beauty of the sea. And I thought to myself, 'If George Russell is the man of his poems, there are times when this spot would suit him very well.'

'Its edges foamed with amethyst and rose
Withers once more the old blue flower of day . . . ' . . .

'He tells me he likes it here,' went on the lady, 'he has painted every nook and corner of the island.'

'And that,' I said, looking at certain indelible marks on the stone floor of the portico, 'is where he cleans his palette.'

She nodded laughing. 'You must see the really lovely places I know so well here. This is the way to the secret garden. Shall I take you to the secret garden?'

As she went on before me raising her skirt a little to avoid the wet grass-tops, I became assured of an unusual phenomenon. The lady was wearing sandals – but no stockings! As I silently pondered this circumstance, with nothing more particular in my mind than the syllable 'Lo!' she spoke again.

'The dew is so bad here on these paths that I wear no stockings – YOU SEE!' Upon which astonishing display of feminine occultism, I blushed an unseen blush, and from that time onward confined my admiration to the charm of columns Byzantine and Ionic. . . .

About us, among colourful rocks, indigenous ferns, grew trees and shrubs of many hundred varieties. Here for more than three years, ninety men had laboured to bring a garden out of the rocky crags of the island, building, planting, transporting – blasting even – but all apparently under such perfect artistry of direction that man's hand had never opposed for a moment the artistry of nature.

When the lady of the island showed me the place where the great hall was to have been built, but which now, after the War, would never be built, it seemed to me that in all this beauty which had been drawn from the rugged rocks and the hidden soil pockets of the island, there was a richer imagery to one who had gone away than a great hall could have held.

No doubt she felt that too, for she told me with a certain pleasure that since the War she had been living with a friend of hers in the gardener's house, like one family with the gardener and the maid. Indeed, when luncheon was ready, we sat down at a long table beside the door of the gardener's simple dwelling – the two ladies, Michael Donohue the gardener, the very pretty, very shy little maid, and I.

'That is Shaw's place where you are sitting,' said my hostess. She went on to tell of the things she had heard him say there, and of the brilliant, fiery play of ideas, rising like a winged flame above certain gatherings in which that astonishing commentator on men and gods (and sometimes women) had struck the first spark; of an actual élan, an almost physical impact of opposing theories and their discharge into verbal flashes of lightning, making for some the chaos less chaotic, but for others, the darkness dark indeed.

He loved the island and knew its moods. Then too, this was a place where an interviewer would not be popping up from beneath every rose bush, or swinging coyly down from every gingko tree. . . .

The luncheon passed very pleasantly, and afterward we walked for an hour down other paths where strange trees and mid-Pacific flowers – thriving wonderfully in the warm, moisture-laden climate of Glengarriff – made frames for blue islands and flying shafts of sunlight which blazed through the steaming mists of sea and shore. At last, with a great bouquet of red and white tubular flowers from the lady of the island for Mrs. Casey of Casey's Hotel, I returned by a small boat to the mainland. As I went across the fields, two old women coming along stopped and looked at the flowers.

'Is it from Garinish Island those flowers are coming?'

'Yes. They are originally from Australia.'

'Australia! Now think of that!' exclaimed one. She came closer and touched the flowers. 'Would I be takin' home a bit of a twig wid me?'

'You would,' I said, and gave her what I thought Mrs. Casey could spare without knowing it.

'I'll be showin' it to himself, just; and won't his eyes be bulgin' out now, wid lookin' at it!'

'Glory be to God,' said the other.

From *Here's Ireland*

Glengarriff Harbour, one of the stopping points for the passenger boats Lady Elsie *and* Princess Beara.

Padraic Colum

1930

BORN IN LONGFORD in 1881, Padraic Colum was one of the first Abbey Theatre playwrights. He was also a poet, whose most famous poems are 'She Moved Through the Fair' and 'The Old Woman of the Roads'. In 1914 Colum went to America, where he spent much of the rest of his life, lecturing and working for publishers. He also wrote several books of travel, including one on Corsica and one on Ireland, from which this excerpt is taken. Colum died in Connecticut in 1972.

An excursion-boat brought me from Cork Harbour to Bantry Bay – a considerable stretch of the coast of Cork. I landed at Glengarriff. To navalists, the bay is one of the best in Europe, sheltered, with deep water, without dangerous rocks or shoals – a bay in which a great fleet could be secure. Mountains close in the sea's long inlet, and an astonishing profusion of vegetation shows itself along the shore. It is a lonely place, too. No town rises beside the bay; no fisherman's boat is on the water; one knows that glens and rough defiles are features of the country that opens to the mountains around. . . .

Glengarriff and the way thence into Kerry is magnificent for scenery of mountain and glen. Around Bantry an enchantment is added to this magnificence: trees and flowers and plants find the atmosphere so kindly that they flourish surprisingly. It looks as if the bounds of gardens had been broken, so much of rare and flowering kind grow amid rocks and by the wayside. This is the place to see that native, the arbutus, with its shining green leaves and its bunches of red berries. The fuchsia has gone native; one has never seen fuchsias unless one has seen them growing around Bantry Bay.

It was the happy thought of a lady living here to make one of the islets off Glengarriff, Garinish, into a garden. This happy thought has been realized in a way that recalls Edgar Allan Poe's 'Landor's Cottage.' Mrs. Annan Bryce has now spent many years collecting and cultivating flowers, trees, and plants that can grow here – and any sub-tropical species can grow here. And she has made her island-garden part of the landscape: one looks down a vista of ilexes to the Kerry Mountains. One walks down an avenue of blooming Mediterranean shrubs to the water of this Irish bay. One sees fantastic orchids close to rocks on which the native heather has been left to flourish. Garinish has been made into a garden of gardens. And it is not merely an enchanting botanic display. There is a home amidst this profusion of trees and plants and flowers – the friendly home of Mrs. Annan Bryce. Painters and writers have been made welcome here. Here is the lovely little house in which Bernard Shaw worked at 'Saint Joan.'

From *Cross Roads in Ireland*

Virginia Woolf

1934

ONE OF THE LEADING LIGHTS of the Bloomsbury group, Virginia Woolf (1882–1941) is renowned for novels that explore the inner life of her characters, with language that is closer to poetry than prose. In late April 1934 she came to Glengarriff during a fortnight's holiday in Ireland with her husband Leonard. This was her first and only visit to the country, though at the time she toyed with the idea of buying a house in Ireland. The Woolfs visited Garinish Island during their two-day stay at the Eccles Hotel, where she wrote the following diary entry.

Glengariff — Monday 30 April 1934

This the 30th April, Monday, so I think, foreign travel not leading to thought. A mixture of Greece, Italy & Cornwall; great loneliness; poverty & dreary villages like squares cut out of West Kensington. Not a single villa or house a-building; great stretches of virgin sea shore; the original land that Cornwall & much of England was in Elizabethan times. And a sense that life is receding. At Lismore the Tchekov innkeeper said Theyre all going away & leaving their houses; nothing's kept up since the war. So the old man on the island here said today – the very sad gentle old man who longed to talk. All gone – What good did the war do anyone? Only the Americans. And crooned & moaned leaning on the rake with which he was heaping up some kind of weed. Yes there is great melancholy in a deserted land, though the beauty remains untouched – miles & miles of Killarney – the water lapping the stones, the butterflies flitting, & not a Cockney there. Today, sitting on the verandah after lunch, the German lawyer having being forced to go to the Island – a string of touts loaf about pressing poetry & boats on one – after they had gone, the invalid, who reminds me of Nelly Cecil began to talk as they all begin to talk; & said she came from Limerick & when we asked if one could get a house there, she said – she laughed a great deal yet seems hopelessly crippled – 'You can get plenty, but its not so nice when you have one.' 'Servant difficulties?' I asked. 'Ah, all that' she said, & one can see, after Bowen's Court, how ramshackle & half squalid the Irish life is, how empty & poverty stricken.

From *The Diary of Virginia Woolf*

Virginia Woolf.

Sean O'Faolain

1939

BORN JOHN WHELAN in Cork, Sean O'Faolain (1900–1991) fought on the Republican side in the Civil War before leaving Ireland to study at Harvard University. After teaching in Boston and London for several years, O'Faolain returned to Ireland. He edited *The Bell* from 1940 to 1946. His first short story collection, *Midsummer Night Madness*, established him as a significant new voice in Irish literature. In addition to short stories, novels, biographies, an autobiography, literary criticism and a play, O'Faolain wrote several travel books.

Bantry is Skibbereen, with the fizz gone. I attribute that to the overwhelming influence of the Big Houses – not but that most of the Big Houses are modestly small houses. All the way from Glengarriff up through the valley of the Bandon River into the city of Cork there is an intrusion of alien influence, starting with the garrisons (now gone) on Bere and the frequent (former) visits of squadrons of the British Navy to Bantry Bay. The modern result is that, as in northern towns like Newry and Strabane and Armagh, where there is also a balance of power, there is here an underlying sectarian self-consciousness and rivalry. I have noticed it repeatedly in Bantry. Maybe it is because Bantry is a kind of frontier town between Catholic and Protestant. Nowhere else have I seen the two come so close together at such a raw stage of development – the moujik natives down from the mountains, the old conquerors entrenched in their forts on the edge of the lovely sea. You cannot be in Bantry for two days before hearing somebody refer to the 'Protestants.' I know no more corrosive futility. It has rotted cities. I once wrote a story about Wicklow which I called *A Broken World.* I have the same feeling about this town. It has no unity. It is a boxing-ring for all West Cork's unresolved prejudices.

It is not a very cheap town to live in. I found this late August that sliced bacon is two shillings a pound, mutton one shilling, beet tenpence, eggs one and four, potatoes eightpence a stone, milk three halfpence. These are not dear prices. (Probably by the time this book sees print they will seem very low.) But Bantry is not a first-class town, and it is remote from a keen city demand. Later in my travels I was to find that such things as position seem to make no difference. The dearest town in Ireland that I noted is Sligo. . . .

Few more lovely seascapes exist in Ireland than that which unfolds itself on the walk to Glengarriff, and beyond. The only rival that I would seriously consider is Clew Bay off Westport. That holds the same sweeping grandeur, the same vast, elemental infinities. But the Glen, as we call it in County Cork, has, in addition, three things peculiar to itself. It has tiny refuges of inlet nooks and coves where the mind can dream itself into a drowsy peace for days on end, hidden low-tide or high-tide lagoons, lovely at any season, little islands where one can bathe and bask, silent but for the cry of a curlew or a gull, or the chattering of herons, or the suck-suck of the seaweed caressing the rocks. It has foliage of a tropical variety and abundance. It has a climate so mild that the place flowers with rare flora, and on the more moist summer days the bay lies heavy as molten metal, and the very rocks seem to melt, and everything swoons in a landlocked sleep. But there is more to say. Look from the terrace of Roche's Head or the Eccles front across at the peaked mountains. It is like a drop-screen scene – a fantasy of fact. Go out from this charmed corner across to the peninsula of those mountains. Go across to the places called The Ranties. You find there the anatomy of bone and muscle and sinew behind what would otherwise seem a mere Glamour Girl appearance of pretty loveliness. If there is in Ireland a harder world than the Bere peninsula, a tougher life, a sterner fight against all that this loveliness of nature means in terms of poverty and struggle and near-destitution, I have yet to find it. Adrigole, some fifteen miles south of Glengarriff, where two old people were found a few years ago, starved to death in their cottage, has given its name to a revealing novel by Peadar O'Donnell. His novels are unrivalled as heart-moving records of life bravely borne in these poorer parts of Ireland.

Few travellers now explore this peninsula, which, since the British left Bere, has sunk back into its own natural primitiveness. If you do not wish to endure or enjoy it, you may drink in the cosy and always sociable bar at Roche's in Glengarriff, and casting an eye around the walls at the mementoes of many a visit from the Royal Navy, imagine the squadrons riding at anchor down in the bay under their lights; think how Castletown must have hummed with blue-jackets on shore-leave; see with the mind's eye the farmers' wives and daughters bringing their butter and eggs, and fowl on market-days down the mountains to the bartering quartermasters on the quays.

The mind cannot stay long with that picture, however; at least no Irishman's mind can. For off Bere on the mainland, he knows, is Dunboy Castle, and Dunboy is one of the reverberations of that awful downfall at Kinsale. In Dunboy O'Sullivan Beare withstood for weeks a terrible siege by Carew, battered by red-hot cannon-ball, withdrawing deeper and deeper into the castle as it crumbled about his men, retreating to the great

View from Roche's Hotel, a popular Glengarriff hostelry from its opening in 1852 until it was demolished in 1958.

hall, to the cellars, finally to the last corner of the basement where the commander, MacGeoghegan, was cut down as he tried to crawl to a store of gunpowder with a torch, ready to blow himself and his men and the enemy to destruction rather than surrender. Carew hanged the survivors. Not a man of the garrison was permitted to live.

The sequel was worse. Still uncaptured and resisting O'Sullivan Beare held out on the mountains until late December, and then, desperate, started a famous and ill-fated march from Glengarriff to the north of Ireland, which still kept on the war. Shamefully he was attacked on the way, not only by the Anglo-Irish but by his own people. They marched in blinding snow and lashing rain for fourteen days. They had to fight a battle almost every day – men, women, and children. They killed their last horses at the Shannon and made canoes out of the skins. Out of a thousand refugees, thirty-five reached O'Rourke's castle in Leitrim. O'Sullivan himself, and his family, later escaped to the Continent – as did the two Earls of Tyrone and Tyrconnell. The name survives in modern Europe – you will find it in Spain, and may run into it in Austria: as with the O'Donnell name which has perpetuated itself among the Spanish nobility.

All over this region tradition keeps alive the events of that fatal opening of the seventeenth century. If the traveller, instead of crossing now over the Kenmare Tunnel road, would go back to Snave Bridge and go up the Baurlinn valley, along the mountain road high over the little Coomhola river purling away down in its lonely glen, he will retrace the reputed course of Carew's march. I heard there, this summer, of a Holland family, said to be descended from one of Carew's men. They possess a little anvil carried by this man. He must have been a farrier or a saddler. It is a small neat affair about a foot in length or less. By the turn of the road, again, at Ballylickey were the gibbets, high on a hill over the inlet, where the Irish were hanged. Across from it is a hill still called Carrignacaoine, where the natives, not permitted to come nearer, could see the bodies silhouetted against the sky. There they raised the *keen* for their dead. The name, Battery Field, not far away, records the place where Carew encamped when first beaten off by the Irish around Glengarriff. It is an awesome district back here in this wild tangle of mountains; Gaelic-speaking; traditional; unforgetting.

From *An Irish Journey*

Kees van Hoek

1945

DUTCH AUTHOR KEES VAN HOEK (b. 1902) began his journalistic career as a parliamentary correspondent at The Hague. Leaving Holland in his early twenties, he worked as a columnist in Paris, Berlin Rome, London, Belgrade, Switzerland and Scandinavia, as recounted in *People and Places.* Van Hoek specialised in interviews with distinguished figures in politics, religion, the arts and philosophy, and he wrote biographies of Pope Pius XII, Paul Kruger and Jan Toorop. He moved to Ireland in the 1930s, and became an Irish citizen in 1946. When he produced *Country of My Choice: An Irish Panorama* in 1945, he was living at Killiney, County Dublin, and employed by the *Irish Independent.*

Spring begins in Ireland at Glengarriff. In the wide bay, against the distant surf of the Atlantic swell, lies the enchanted isle of Ilnacullin, more popularly known to tourists the world over as Garnish Island. The old Martello tower on its highest promontory, built as a signal post against Napoleonic invasions, had been completed by the time the Emperor was deposed. Yet, for ten years a lieutenant and nine men were left on guard, before the island was given over to the goats, great demolishing contractors, as the Bryce family realised when they bought it from the State, many years ago.

With loving care and generous purse they set out to transform it into the truly terrestrial paradise it is to-day. When one has tramped up and down cliffs and rocks, along bays and inlets for a whole afternoon, one fails to grasp how the island can only be fifty acres in area, it seems such a complete world of its own. Harold Peto, of Riviera fame, planned the buildings and laid out the gardens, centred round the charming Casita with its double-decker roofs, its pavement of flagstones from the dismantled forts of Whiddy Island and its stately pillars of creamy Bath stone. Inside it is lined with orange, yellow and brown veined grey marble from the Greek island of Scyros, smooth as satin. Old Italian peasant furniture stands on the floor of Connemara marble.

Outside the Casita spreads a carpet of velvet lawn enclosed by a wall of island stone, through which finely wrought 17th century Seville grilles lead into the other gardens. In summer they are smothered under overhanging wistaria. Yet, almost as colourful is the immense variety of trees and shrubs, now a whole gamut of colours from golden brown to emerald green. The goldfish are deflecting their course in the sunken lily pond, as if escaping the bronze Mercury, a contemporary copy of Giovanni di Bologna's masterpiece. Thrushes and robins are singing for all they are worth to the busts of Homer and Ovid, to the Venetian and Byzantine stone lions, to the Chinese temple dragons and Buddha's disciples in this magic garden. At the end rises the Medici House with its columns of virgin white Carrara marble and of lustrous *rosso antico*.

Past rhododendrons already in bloom, Australian bottle brush, Chilean trees and Cork oaks, past enormous Persian containers, whole stories engraved on their copper, we mount the delicately-curved, stately wide and low steps to the Greek 'Temple of the Winds.' Gulls sail leisurely over the island. The surf makes the only sound over the wide, open bay, as it splashes, deep below, on the island shore. Right in front the mountains which engirdle Glengarriff rise precipitously to the almost two thousand feet of Slieve na Goil, wistfully beautiful in the approaching twilight, strangely reminiscent of Doré's Biblical landscapes. Behind us stretched the broad carpet of lawns to the Martello tower, which dominates in silvern setting the other side of the island. Italian cypresses, Japanese and Scotch pines line the broad avenue. Underneath them the first daffodils and crocuses cheekily raise their yellow, violet, blue and white heads, sudden riots of gay colours on the sedate green of the Happy Valley. But nothing is so startlingly beautiful as the vivid contrast of all this gently reared loveliness and the haughty grandeur of the barren rocks, 'shorn of their whiskers,' as Mr. Bryce calls his elimination of moss and gorse.

Although legend claims Cromwell's Bridge was built on the Lord Protector's orders, there is no record of his ever having visited Beara.

We are sitting in his 'secret garden,' a sheltered nook between the remnants of antediluvian glacier beds. All hothouse plants grow here in the open – South African heather, smelling like spices; flowers from Madagascar and New Zealand, names as exotic as their colours are. He is a big broad-shouldered man, my host, red-haired bushy thickets of eyebrows over his scholarly spectacles, open-complexioned, very Irish – and proud of it. His garden-kingdom is an inherited passion. He took it over from his parents, applied to it study and artistry. His broad, sturdy hands touch a plant with the gentleness of a surgeon – are they not somewhat the children of his mind and imagination, and of his daily care?

Through a narrow path, almost imperceptible from above, we walk back to the bay below, a treasure-island cove for budding Robinson Crusoes, a boyhood dream come true in all its romantic seclusion and wildness. Only the hull of a frigate and the pirates' footprints fail. And so, over steep paths, along bays lined with tall birches and over terraces with fountains smothered under maidenhair, we come back to the little house, so hidden in the foliage that no tourists ever espy it. Electric lights shine over the hundreds of books on the white lacquered shelves. The Squire of Ilnacullin speaks of Oxford, where he studied; of Belgrade where he was *Times* War Correspondent; of Carinthia and Montenegro, where as a diplomat he supervised plebiscites and elections. Tea is poured from a priceless silver heirloom. Fritz, the big silver-haired Schnauzerdog, inspects the home-made cakes. And outside, the evening mists fold gently over the far-wooded shore, leaving Ilnacullin a world of its own.

From *Country of My Choice: An Irish Panorama*

Seán Jennett

1967

SEÁN JENNETT, who was born in 1912, first made his name in the 1940s with two poetry books, *Always Adan* and *The Cloth of Flesh*. Later he became known as a typographer and travel writer, producing more than twenty books. *The Making of Books*, a standard work, strongly influenced the new typography of the 1950s. Jennett was editor of the Crown Classics for Grey Walls Press in the late 1940s, and he edited The Travellers' Guides series (published by Darton, Longman, and Todd) for several years from 1964. Most of his work was in travel writing, with several books about France, England and Ireland, including *The Sun and Old Stones, Deserts of England, Munster, Connacht, The Loire, Paris*, and *Cork and Kerry*.

The road leads through the little village of Durrus to the town of Bantry, whose principal characteristic, on this approach, is an enormous open space covered with asphalt, a place for processions and demonstrations. I came into Bantry one fine day to be stopped here by a Garda while an immense procession passed by. At its head was a pipe band, the men wearing the plain saffron kilts of the Irish kind, and there were other pipe bands at intervals. The rest of the procession was made up of men and women of all ages. There were numerous embroidered banners that gave the names of villages and districts from which contingents had come. I asked the Garda what was going on. 'They are the Sons of Temperance,' said he, and added 'Thanks be to God, they're in the minority.' The Sons eventually gathered into a great mass to be addressed in Irish by a priest. It was a hot and sultry day and every one of them, the pipers especially, looked thirsty.

Bantry is a shopping centre at the head of Bantry Bay. The town stands a little inshore and the bay is blocked by the low mass of Whiddy Island. You might easily come here and idly examine the little shops around the cross roads without ever wandering across that desert of tarmacadam; and if you did not do so, you would never see anything of Bantry Bay at all, at least from Bantry. But you should go to the seaward end of the square, for facing the head of the bay is Bantry House, standing in a demesne, a Georgian house that is one of the very few mansions in Ireland open to the public; the house is, indeed, not large, but it has a good collection of tapestries, paintings, and other works of art, some of which belonged once to Marie Antoinette. The pleasant gardens are a good place from which to have a view of that famous bay, whose name is familiar to many from a haunting, sentimental, nineteenth-century song.

A steep little lane runs up behind Bantry House and near its top a signpost points to 'The Carved Stone'. There is no path through the field, but just pass through the field-gate and go straight ahead and soon you will come in sight of a slender standing stone. This is the Kilnaruane carved stone, set in the middle of other stones that may once have formed a circle round it, with also a faint circular bank of earth. The pillar has an incised cross, but in addition there are carved figures and on one side is a boat sailing vertically towards heaven. One of the stones lying around is a bullaun, that is a stone with hollows in it as though made by grinding with a pestle – these things are common on sites connected with ancient monasteries. The carved stone may belong to the seventh or eighth century and is possibly the shaft of a cross.

From *Munster*

Peter Somerville-Large

1969

PETER SOMERVILLE-LARGE, whose family comes from West Cork, was educated in Dublin. After leaving Trinity College he spent a decade working abroad, with jobs ranging from lecturer in English in Afghanistan, to gold miner in Australia and wharfee in New Zealand. Later he turned to writing and journalism, and has written numerous books of travel, social history and fiction. They include three in which West Cork is featured: From *Bantry Bay to Leitrim, Cappaghglass*, which was short-listed for the Ewart Biggs prize, and *The Coast of West Cork*, based on an exploration of the area by bicycle.

Across the broad sweep of the Kenmare river, the Kerry mountains presented a jumble of peaks capped with cloud, Himalayas to the Alps of Beare. I cycled through barren stretches of hillside on which a few fertile fields were scattered, picked out in dazzling green from the brown wastes of rock and bog. The number of these increased, until I came down to Eyeries, a trim little village set beside the sea in a crescent of rich pasture as bright as rice paddies.

Through Eyeries the road led towards Ballycrovane Bay, bounded by the peninsula of Kilcatherine. Past the ruins of a coastguard station stood the Eyeries pillar stone, seventeen feet high. It was no larger than a young ash-tree, but it dominated sea and mountains, defying the eye to believe that it was not on the same scale. In its beautiful setting it has a grandeur that makes it one of the most marvellous of neolithic monuments. The Ogham on its side looks like an old feather; scratch marks run slantwise or perpendicular off a centre line, or *fleasc*, to make a simple code. 'The grave of the son of Decceda and grandson of Torani.' The stone was quarried from the side of the hill about a mile away, and near the place in the rock from which it was hewn there lies another pillar stone on its side, never moved or erected.

I visited Dan O'Brien in his small house outside the village which overlooks Pallace Strand near the place where Murty Og O'Sullivan was tracked down and killed. (Eyeries was Murty Og's home port, and to reach it from France he would round Dursey or cut through the sound before sailing up the Kenmare river.) A retired bank manager, Dan had settled at Eyeries to indulge in amateur archaeology. He had infected his neighbours with his enthusiasm so that farmers and school-children joined him in searching the fields and mountains for house sites, kernstones and kileens.

The Beare peninsula is particularly rich in traces of Bronze-Age man. As elsewhere in West Cork, there does not seem to have been a classical Iron-Age settlement, and the Bronze-Age cult appears to have continued into early Christian times without a trace of a true iron age. During the early Christian period there was a sharp increase in population, but Beare never became really crowded. Traces of ancient settlements are found everywhere; in the Journal of the Cork Archaeological Society, Dan has produced a massive list of sites which he has noted, west of Glengarriff – a hundred and fifty in all. No guide points out these places in any detail, and many of them are not even marked on the six-inch map. They are all unexcavated; up until 1970 the only site which had been properly investigated by archaeologists was the relatively uninteresting remains of the fortifications of Dunboy.

Dan took me on a swift tour of the local ruins and relics. We went to Caheravart near the Bearhaven-Eyeries road, where there was a fine *cillin*, an early Christian religious settlement, in which a collapsed cell or small church was surrounded by gravestones, many of them the small graves of unbaptised children. The burial ground would have been used a great deal during penal times, when priests were scarce and baptisms infrequent, but the site was much older, probably with a long period of pre-Christian associations. A battered old cross stood among the graves, worn away as if it had been melted, and the whole was surrounded by an earthen ring. The fields round about were studded with house sites, and below them were the traces of an ancient water mill, where an opening had been cut in the rock through which water was conducted to drive the horizontal wheel, now long vanished. Dan was on the lookout for it, and had asked neighbouring farmers to bring him any piece of wood they might dig up. But it was probably long destroyed.

From the settlement, which was situated on a hillside, two standing stones were visible across the valley. On Beare every sixth or seventh field seemed to have the white smudge of a standing stone, sometimes a hefty memorial to the dead or a cult symbol, sometimes a smaller boundary mark, perhaps indicating the division of land. We travelled from Caheravart in a radius of perhaps five miles, viewing a number of these stones, a portal dolmen, a boulder dolmen, a pair of stones that had heeled over in the ground, the ring of an early house, a circle, and a little pile of rocks in the middle of a bog which neither Dan nor any visiting archaeologist cared to commit themselves in identifying.

'It's not a court cairn. At least, it isn't allowed to be one. There are not supposed to be any in the Beare area.'

He hopped from site to site with the enthusiasm of an early Egyptologist journeying up the Nile. He had discovered many of the remains himself, for he had the right sort of eye, and could pick them out, like boys who can find birds' nests. Moreover, this was virgin territory and the six-inch map was by no means inexhaustible, although it was just as necessary to his search as his binoculars. He also required infinite caution to temper his energy. Care was needed before a name was put to a pile of stones on a hillside. It might be something interesting, or a platform for drying turf. A couple of large, oddly angled boulders were perhaps a collapsed dolmen, or merely what the experts termed a 'glacial erratic'. Rough patches of land covered with gorse were perhaps house sites, but they could be the efforts of farmer to clear his fields. A souterrain could turn out to be a henhouse, and a standing stone might have been erected in the last ten years as a scratching post for cattle.

We climbed a mountain to examine a neolithic copper-mine which Dan had found above Eyeries. It seemed obvious that there should be prehistoric mines in the area, but this was the first indication that copper had been exploited thousands of years ago. The climb was long and steep, and halfway up I left Dan sitting in what he called 'the fiddler's field' to tackle the last part of the mountain by myself. The mines were similar to those I had seen on Mount Gabriel, small man-made caves scooped out of the rock. Dan had found a few mauls, the same type of rounded sea stones that I saw lying about on Mount Gabriel. He had wondered where the miners lived, and had been looking for some trace of a house site or ring fort near the mines. When I reached the fiddler's field once more, I found him jubilant; as he rested and waited for my return, he had noticed that the bank beside him had a curve to it, and through the layout of boulders it was possible to distinguish the shape of a large circle smothered in heather and bracken. An obvious place for neolithic miners to have their huts.

I stayed the night in Dan's cottage and set out next morning. At nine o'clock the only inhabitants of Eyeries to be seen were two sad dogs that had stretched out across the road, feeling secure that there would be no danger from passing traffic. Outside the village whirls of mist rose gently from the surrounding hills, but the Kilcatherine peninsula gleamed in the early morning sun. The road curved upwards from Ballycrovane harbour towards Kilcatherine Point and a high place with distant views, which is called Ard Na Cailleach, or the Height of the Hag. In a field below, looking towards the south-west, is the *Cailleach Beara* herself. A slender jagged piece of rock is meant to resemble an old woman with a basket on her back. Sometimes you could catch the glimpse of a beaky profile, at other times she could be anything.

'Christ, man, she's more like a hen,' the farmer who gave me directions to find her had considered. Of all ancient remains she is the most obstinately pagan, although facts about her ancient worship are few. The legend that she was turned from an old woman into a rock by the priest of Kilcatherine church reveals how Christianity finally defeated her powers as the goddess of fertility and witchcraft. She is the Celtic version of Hecate, associated with sorcery and graveyards and darkness. Although she is chiefly remembered as the old woman, the oldest of all, the *Cailleach Beara*, like Hecate, had three manifestations, one of which was that of the beautiful young moon goddess. Directly below the shoulder of the hill where the stone crouches facing out to sea, there are three small oddly shaped narrow fields. One of them is still known as the Field of the Fair Woman.

Kilcatherine used to be known for seine fishing, and twenty boats worked the bay opposite Illaunbesheen island. Today the almost deserted peninsula, which seldom sees visitors or tourists, remains one of the most beautiful places in West Cork with its majestic views of mountains and sea. A few cottages remain, and the ruin of a tenth-century church located above the *Cailleach Beara* further up the hill. Its position perhaps indicates the victory of Christianity over the older forces. Above the door protrudes a little stone head with a gargoyle face which had been found lying in the graveyard, and was set up by the indefatigable Dan O'Brien.

At Ardgroom, the next harbour on the north side of the coast, there is a bar made of shingle, which is called Cois or Leg, because it looks just like a leg with a shoe on the end kicked out from the shore. Above it a small ring fort is full of children's graves, with one stone slab commemorating an English sailor who was buried among them. 'In memory of John Broderick, sailmaker of Gosport, Hants, England, who died on board the R.M.S. *Helen*, and was buried here August, 1869.' The name Broderick curiously repeats itself all over the area. The soldier who led the sack of Dursey was named Broderick; so were some of the followers of Puxley after whom Daphne Du Maurier called her fictitious mine owners in Hungry Hill. In 1969, when Gulf Oil plunged into Bantry Bay, the president of the company was Mr. E. D. Broderick.

Coming into Ardgroom harbour from the Kilcatherine side, the road passes through rich woodland where massive beeches and chestnuts rise above acres of wild rhododendrons. This is a plantation surrounding the ruins of a house built by a Mrs. Puxley shortly after the famine. When the building of the house was in progress, the masons asked her if they might partake of a glass of porter. She seems fully to have shared in the ungracious reputation of her family; refusing their request, she told them briefly: 'Go and drink with the ducks in the stream.' After that the masons did their best to plaster the outside so badly that the water would drown the place out, but she beat their strategy by lining the walls with slate. However, the house was not to last long. Some years afterwards it became the rectory, but around the turn of the century it fell into disrepair. Now only the trees remain.

From *The Coast of West Cork*

Benedict Kiely

1978

BORN AT DROMORE, County Tyrone, in 1919, Benedict Kiely was educated in Omagh and at University College, Dublin. From 1940 to 1965 he worked as a journalist in Dublin, and taught at several American universities in the 1960s. He later lectured at UCD, and has since followed a career as author and broadcaster. Following his first book, *Counties of Contention: a study of Irish Partition* (1945), he has published novels, short-story collections, non-fiction books, a children's story, and has edited several other works. Kiely visited Beara in 1978, while working on a book of travels in Ireland.

This is the road to Seal Harbour. That is the road to Zetland pier. Both names, not lying too easily with the older Gaelic names, are pretty obvious reminders that the British navy and its dependants spent a fair amount of time in the land of Beara who may have been a legendary princess from Spain who married into the people of this place long long before the Normans pushed the Sullivans south-west out of Tipperary. She may also never have existed, or simply have been the king of Spain's daughter who sat in the glow of a thousand hearths, moved through a thousand folk tales from the earliest times down to my late lamented friend, Micí Pháidi, in Rann na Feirsde in the Rosses of Donegal. Gap-toothed Micí could explain in detail how the king of Spain's daughter married a boyo who set out on his travels from Burtonport to the Indiacha Thoir, or East Indies, but who, regardless, ended up in Spain where he did well for himself and where he is to this day. At least he was there in the 1940s when Micí was alive.

Then the wet winding roads,
Brown bogs with black water,
And my thoughts on white ships
And the King of Spain's daughter.

The great tanker across the water is moving seawards – not homing. Does a tanker have a home or just a belly to fill? Whither away, oh splendid ship? Bantry to Bahrain and back again if the Arabs and Israelis don't get in my way. A big belly to be filled and then off sometime to be flushed out, or physicked, in the Gulf of Mexico by men who have to make enough money to be out of the business by the age of 30.

It's a dull thought on a sunny morning by the beauty of Bantry Bay: here, where the Spanish were with guns and gold for O'Sullivan, and the

Main Street, Castletownbere, photographed from the top of the town by Robert French around 1890.

French, 'the tall mast tapering on each gallant ship', and the English, and ourselves, God help us, and whoever came before us.

There between the shore and Beare Island was it that the British fleet mustered before Jutland, a sight to see surely as it set out on that doubtful voyage? Once I talked about that to an American friend of mine and he capped the tale by reminding me that he had been a ship's commander in Nimitz's fleet when it spread out across the Pacific. Which, to judge from what he said, was a real circus: his talk had the last cracked echo of the trumpet men heard when they talked of glory. Now, big bellies are filled with black oil to make the world go round and round and round until the wells run dry.

This must – by the great Donal Cam himself – be the hardest land in Ireland. Nor am I forgetting the Rosses nor portions of Connemara. There are razor edges to the slanting buttresses of Hungry hill which is an angry crouching animal of a mountain even in the morning sunlight. This description of the landscape I take from one of the two novels written about this peninsula. It's the better of the two even if, as Peter Somerville-Large points out in his fine book *The Coast of West Cork*, it is historically inaccurate, and the author was one of the most consistent anti-Irish bigots who ever masqueraded as an historian. But the man, while he wasn't much of a novelist, had an eye for landscape and a pen to follow his eye:

> Leaving Hungry Hill on his right Colonel Goring ascended the brook which fell into the sea behind his house – at Dunboy. After climbing sharply for a couple of miles he reached the cradle of the stream in a wide morass. The peat was dry in the clear autumn weather. The air was fresh and delicious and perfumed with heather. On the banks, between which the tiny rivulet trickled along, were patches of rich, green grass where sheep and cattle ought to have been feeding, but there were no signs of either nor of any human creature. Nature was left alone in her wasteful beauty and, as there was no wind, the silence was unbroken save by the croak of a passing raven, the sharp bark of an eagle, the whirr of some old cock grouse whom the dogs had scented at among the moss hags . . .

That does get something of the great loneliness of the mountain. And here he is, watching the winter morning at Dunboy:

> A warm south-westerly was blowing in from the Atlantic; a swell was breaking on the west end of Beare Island and the clouds hung low on Hungry hill. But the sky was open in the east and the crests of the waves in the bay were sparkling in the sunshine; while mountains and woods were steeped in the soft purple green which makes the winter landscape in the south of Ireland so peculiarly beautiful.

The Colonel Goring that James Anthony Froude put into that novel, *The Two Chiefs of Dunboy*, was (in reality) one of the landed family, the Puxleys of Dunboy. Long after Froude, Daphne du Maurier was to write about them in *Hungry Hill*, a novel that, as Somerville-Large wryly points out, was somewhat unrealistic in that, being about nineteenth-century Ireland, it didn't mention the famine. Although he does add that there is evidence to show that the famine may not have been as bad just here as in other parts of west Cork. But now, looking at those hard rocks, we wonder: and anyway in such matters comparisons may not mean a great deal.

J.A. Froude who, to put it mildly, didn't think much of the Irish except when they were British soldiers, contracted, down in these mountainy places, some sort of half-assed affection for the shadow or memory of the historic Morty Og O'Sullivan, the other chief of his novel: wandering soldier and privateer whose dead body was hauled at the stern of an

English ship all the way from here to Cork harbour. The tanker would now be ploughing across the path followed by that eighteenth-century ship and the corpse of one of the last of the great O'Sullivans.

The tanker is still very big in the bay as we come down the road into Castletownberehaven. Nearly 35 years ago, and in the middle of a tempest, I came here for the first time and a young woman who had been talking to one of the Puxleys told me, among other things, the story of the four wild brothers from Adrigole.

What I remember most about that visit is (i) that it rained for three days and three nights (ii) that I was reading Maxim Gorki and (iii) that one of the two girls in the post-office had worn her way with her toenail through the toe of her right shoe. It was that girl or, perhaps, the other one who told me about the four wild brothers from Adrigole and this was how I afterwards used what she told me in a short story:

> Once upon a time there lived four brothers in a rocky corner of Adrigole in west Cork, under the mountain called Hungry hill. Daphne du Maurier wrote a book called after the mountain but divil a word in it about the four brothers of Adrigole. They lived, I heard tell, according to instinct and never laced their boots and came out only once a year, to visit the nearest town which was Castletownberehaven on the side of Bantry Bay.
>
> They'd stand there backs to the wall smoking, saying nothing, contemplating the giddy market-day throng.
>
> One day they ran out of tobacco and went into the local branch of a certain bank to buy it, and raised havoc because the teller refused to satisfy their needs. To pacify them the manager and the teller had to disgorge their own supplies. So they went back to Adrigole to live happily without lacing their boots, and ever after they thought that in towns and cities the bank was the place where you bought tobacco.

It rained, as I've said, for three days and three nights and the dark sky, driven like mad by a gale that came up and down the mountains from Kerry and Kenmare Bay, was so low you could have touched it if you cared to take the risk of bringing down worse on your head. Nor could my companion on that journey nor myself move out of the place until the rain stopped and the sky cleared. This was why.

He was a photographer and a very good one. The late Aodh de Blacam had just written for the late Fr. Senan Moynihan a study of that marathon march of O'Sullivan Beare from Glengarriff to Leitrim.

The photographer was there to begin the photographs to illustrate the article. The skies did not favour photography. As for myself I was there because I was doing an article on Daniel O'Connell's Darrynane House then about to be converted into a museum and a monument. The photographer had just finished the Darrynane pictures and I was going the rest of the way for the fun and the curiosity.

Howandever there we were in Castletown and in the downpours of rain. Thirteen trawlers from Bilbao were blown in out of the storm. The streets were crowded with little brown men, holy medals around their necks, deeply religious oaths on their lips, merriment and good nature in their eyes, bundles of silk stockings and bottles of quite lethal Iberian brandy under their oxters. The stockings and the brandy they would barter for anything available. The dances in the hall beside the hotel were a sight to see. You wouldn't know under God what country you were in. And the rain rained and the wind blew and the sky licked the roofs of the houses: and I was reading Maxim Gorki.

It's quite simple how I remember that I was reading Gorki. It was that bit in his memoirs where he describes how the wooden houses went on fire in Osharsk Square in Nijhni Novgorod now known as Gorkigrad. The fire crackled like an animal chewing bones. It made real comic reading when there you were and the heavens urinating on you at the far end of west Cork. The one thing Castletownberehaven was not going to do that season was bloody well go on fire.

One evening when the rain was drawing its breath a bit I walked up and up the slope behind the church, up and up until I was out there on my own and the town well below me. The clouds came at me like buffaloes. To my right hand what would normally have been a simple mountain stream went down like Niagara towards the bay. It was a wonder all out that it didn't take the town with it. Oh far away was that animal of a fire in Osharsk Square, and I thought of Standish O'Grady and a little poem he had written about a mountain stream. After all, that was O'Grady's town, so I quoted him out loud to the torrent to remind it and the weather how they should behave themselves:

Cloud-begot, mountain-bred,
Heather-nursed child,
Innocent, beautiful,
Winsome and wild:
Here she comes dancing
O'er boulder and rock,
And in many a waterfall
Shakes her white frock.

A day and a half later the rain eased off: poetry is a slow-working charm.

And one of the two girls who worked in the post-office had worn her way with her toenail through the toe of her right shoe.

She told me about this when she told me how she had been honoured to talk to one of the Puxleys of Dunboy when Brian Desmond Hurst and the actors and cameraman were there, briefly before, working on the movie based on the Du Maurier novel. There she was, she said, ashamed of her life, talking to Miss Puxley and her toe peeping out like a rabbit. So she put her left foot over the toes of her right foot and stood like that, balancing as well as she could until she noticed that the lady was balancing in the same way, except that her right foot was hiding the toes of her left foot: and the girl didn't know and never would whether there was or was not a hole also in the lady's shoe, or whether that was just the way the gentry stood, like herons, you know, or storks or flamingoes.

She was a lively west Cork brunette and I'll never know whether or not she was making it all up. The other girl was blonde. It was a long time ago and, as I've said, you wouldn't have known, what with the rain and the men from Bilbao, what country you were in. Nor can I recall for certain which of the girls told me about the four wild brothers who lived according to instinct in the rocky wilderness of Adrigole.

From *All the Way to Bantry Bay*

Chris Duff

1996

BEFORE TAKING TO the waters in his kayak, Chris Duff worked as a navy diver. He has become one of the world's top names in sea kayaking, clocking up 14,000 miles since 1983. On one trip he kayaked from New York, up the Mississippi, through the Great Lakes, down the St. Lawrence and back to New York. On another journey he circumnavigated England, Scotland and Wales. In June 1996, Duff set off from the mouth of the Liffey on his 1,200 mile solo kayak trip that would take him around Ireland. It also took him to Beara.

After an hour of getting tossed around like a cork, I entered the narrows between Dursey Island and the mainland. I was drained and it felt good to close my eyes and let the current gently spin me in a circle. Rough water paddling was exhausting. The physical exposure seemed to strip away all the protective emotional layers, and I felt as worn as the rocks on the outer coast. In the thick of big breaking waves, it was a constant measure of controlling the flight or fight instinct: too little adrenaline and I won't be aggressive enough, too much and I'll burn up energy too fast. The inclination is to pour on the power and try to get through the rough stuff fast. It doesn't work. The boat charges ahead, then plows into the oncoming wave or crashes into a trough. The only way is to slip into low gear and grind it out. Slow and steady, not fighting the power of the waves but letting them set the pace and hopefully missing the ones that fold over and break on themselves. Dig in, a brace or back stroke here or there, then dig in again. It can be frustratingly slow and fatiguing.

After a brief rest in the channel, I turned and headed back out. Moments after leaving the calm, I almost went over. An inflamed tendon in my right wrist made gripping the paddle shaft with my thumb impossible and I couldn't control the angle of the blade. I had ignored the pain in the rough waters on the outside of the island. Now, without the distraction of breaking waves and a pitching boat, I was keenly aware of it. A wave tossed the boat over on its side and I sliced the edge of the paddle, rather than the back of it, into the water. A last-second hip flick with my right knee jammed against the inside of the cockpit kept me from going over. Despite the tendinitis and the near capsize, I was encouraged by my reaction time. It was instant and automatic, the way it had to be.

Getting thrown over and hanging for that millisecond on the edge of the boat was a reminder of just how tenuous my grasp on the trip was. I had to be 'on' one hundred percent of the time and it was wearing me down. It hadn't been a massive wave that had almost upended me. In fact, it had been a ridiculously small one that I hadn't been paying attention to. I had come down off the adrenaline high of an hour earlier and was focused on a cove a quarter mile in front of me, looking forward to getting out of the boat, into warm clothes, and already thinking about how much food and water I had in the rear compartment. I hadn't been attentive to the moment – the worst mistake I could make. It wouldn't have been a big deal to have gone over, but it was a reminder of how much a month of paddling had both honed my reactions and also begun to take its toll.

I paddled into the tiny harbor of Garnish, a naturally protected cove that looked as if it would dry out at low water. A couple of thirty-foot fishing boats were anchored at the mouth, their lines hanging loose between bow and buoy. Next to the government pier was a boat ramp piled high with lobster traps and three dinghies pulled above the highest line of seaweed. I landed and walked up to the bigger of two buildings near the water's edge. In the corner of one window was a post office emblem and a stained piece of cardboard with STORE hand-lettered on it. I needed bread and jam, the basics for lunch, and knocked on the open door. An Irish lass with a tangle of red hair, a baby in her arms and another at her feet, greeted me with a smile.

'Hi,' I said. 'I saw the sign and was hoping to buy some soda bread, if you have any.'

'Oh, that's an old sign,' she answered. 'My mum has some sweets for the kids but I wouldn't know about any bread. Come inside and I'll ask her.'

She disappeared into the house, the little guy at her feet hesitating, struggling to keep his balance and staring up at me with huge blue eyes and a dirty, chubby face. We looked at each other for a few seconds, me the giant in the doorway, he the little Irish cherub. I waved my fingers at him and he bolted.

From the doorway and in through another that led to the kitchen, I followed the bare feet and fat little legs. At the far end of the kitchen was a simple table, chairs pulled out as if everyone had just gotten up, and a picture of Jesus on the wall above. A sea breeze ruffled the curtains over the sink and a lady looking just old enough to be a grandmother was stirring something on the stove. 'If it's soda bread you're looking for, I haven't got any. But come in and sit down. I'll make ye a sandwich. There's salmon in the fridge and it'll take only a minute.' Then as if everything was decided she said, 'Yer from America, are ye?'

'Yes, from Washington, on the West Coast.'

'And ye here on holiday, are ye?'

'Well, it's a sort of holiday. I left Dublin a month ago and I'm trying to paddle a kayak around the coast. I should be back in Dublin . . .'

The stirring of the pot stopped. She turned, looked me over head to toe, then straight in my eyes, and said, 'Ye mean to be telling me ye rowing a canoe right round Ireland?'

'Well, we call them kayaks, but, yes, that's what I'm hoping to do.'

The pretty lady with the flaming copper hair came through another doorway with her husband, the babe still in her arms, the toddler clinging to her leg and staring at my feet. The dad, in his mid-twenties, smiled, nodded, and shyly said hello. I suddenly felt like I was on stage, everyone looking at me with expectation. It felt awkward. These people not believing what they were hearing and me still feeling the rush of the morning paddle and the salt drying stiffly on my face.

It was the little guy in diapers who broke the spell and made me smile. I wondered why it was always children that saw the obvious. He didn't care where I had come from or where it was I was going. He was staring at my sandaled feet, my toes covered in sand.

'Are ye alone?' His mother's puzzled question brought me back to the world of adults.

'Yes.'

'Ye came through the channel and not the outside, I hope,' the older lady scolded.

The spoon was poised over whatever was in the pot and no one moved an inch. Oh boy, I knew where this was going, but there was no backing out of the kitchen, especially since there was the offer of a salmon sandwich.

'No, I wanted to see what the outside looked like.' Then, as a quick diversionary tactic, I said, 'But I did paddle into the narrows and saw the cable car over the channel.' As if that would somehow excuse me from being a fool and paddling around an island with an easy inside passage. My diversionary tactic didn't have the effect I had hoped. In fact, it sounded pretty weak under the scrutiny of her gaze.

'Ye came around Dursey Head on a day the likes of this?' She paused a second, then pronounced the verdict, 'Ye must be mad!'

There it was again. I knew it was coming and thought how I should be counting the number of times I had heard it. The salmon fisherman pulling nets, the shopowners adding sums of penciled figures, the fellow in the pub pulling a pint of Guinness. They each had the same reaction: a look of disbelief, hands frozen in space, and when they saw I wasn't 'having them on,' the inevitable: 'Yer mad. Ye know that, don't ye?'

I had little defense to fall back on. I was hoping the baby might cry or the pot boil over, anything to release me from center stage. But no such luck. The verdict was in and I had the right to a final word.

I nodded and with resignation admitted, 'Yes, I've actually heard that before.'

The woman shook her head, stirred the contents of the pot once again, then dried her hands on her apron. 'Ye must be hungry after such a foolish thing. Pull up a chair and I'll make you a sandwich.'

In her eyes maybe I was mad, but if it's one thing the Irish are famous for, it's their hospitality – even to madmen. Despite my obvious instability, everyone I met wanted to help in whatever way they could. This time it was salmon, mayonnaise, and lettuce. A sandwich and strong tea heavily sweetened never tasted so good. We sat and talked. Mostly about fishing: lobster, mackerel, and of course the weather. I heard again how the summer before had been the finest in twenty years. Seven weeks and not a day of rain. The seas smooth as glass and everyone had color in their faces. The little beach had been filled with locals and tourists alike.

A Dutch couple, or maybe they were German, were cycling through Ireland and camped on the knoll above the pier. Good thick grass – I could stay there if I wanted to. . . .

Two or three cups of tea, maybe an hour of sitting and chatting. An old dog wandered in through the open door, took a look at the stranger, and stiffly walked out again. Life was slow and easy when the road ended at the lobster pots sitting idle on the pier.

I was beginning to like the lazy pace. The sea could wait for tomorrow. I needed a day to rest my arm and the offer of the grassy knoll sounded like a good place to hang out. I camped that evening above the quiet of the moored boats. The smell of the sea, a pile of nets outside the tent opening, and the grass beneath my head assured me that all was right in this little corner of the world.

The next morning, I set out with the wind raising whitecaps on the open water. Looking back at the protected cove, I could see someone standing on the knoll, hands held to their eyes. I remembered seeing an old pair of binoculars sitting on the windowsill near the kitchen sink. I held the paddle on end and waved an arc of farewell, then let the seas surf me over to Allihies – a wild ride across three miles of dancing waters. To the north was Cod's Head, then five miles of open water that was too rough for a safe crossing. The mouth of the Kenmare River would have to wait for calmer winds. I decided to land and walk into the village of Allihies.

I left the boat upside down on the beach and headed up the one-lane road. Out of the wind the sun was warm and there wasn't anyone in sight. A perfect day for a walk. Halfway to town, I passed a gray burro sleepily walking in the opposite direction. He stopped, let me scratch him between the ears, then continued on his way.

A whitewashed cottage with a sign on the stone wall offered tea and scones and a place to sit in the sun. I stepped through the low door and asked for a pot of tea and two scones, lots of butter, then returned to the courtyard to chat with an old man leaning against the warm rock of the house. He must have been at least eighty, tall even in his old age, big hands slightly trembling and folded half on his lap. He wore a dark suit jacket, buttoned and covering shoulders that were still wide but stooped. A white shirt and tie, and eyes that closed in warm, safe sleep in the middle of a sentence. He would awaken and ask if I was staying in town. I would explain again that, no, I was just traveling through. Just in town for the day. And again he would doze off.

I wondered who he was. How he had spent his life and what I would be like when I reached his age. Was I his past and was he my future? In that courtyard the same sun warmed us both and so little time separated our ages. I wanted to know him. I drank my tea while he slept.

When he awakened again, I gently asked, 'Have you lived here all of your life?'

There was a pause and he answered, 'No, no.'

I could see his eyes trying to reach back through either sleep or confusion of time, maybe both.

'Where did you live?'

He turned his head slowly to the west and pointed a shaking hand in the general direction of where I had paddled from that morning. Toward the hills that climbed above the bay and looked down on the single lane coast road.

'Three miles from here. A little farm.' His hand came down, found its folded position on his lap, and his eyes closed again.

The day before, I had spent a few hours following the road that cut over the headland and looked down on the island narrows. I thought of the crumbling buildings I had seen. Four walls open to the sky, doorway and windows filling with brambles and making a home for the birds singing in the safety of wild roses and bracken. Maybe one of those houses had been his? Where I had spent a few hours, he had lived most of his life. One old man had lived his life above a small bay looking out on the sea. A young man travels the world looking for adventure and maybe the sense of place that the old one has known. I paid for the tea and scones and left him sleeping in the sun.

Allihies, after Mass outside the church, around the turn of the 20th century.

Sources

John Janes John Janes, 'Cavendish's Last Voyage, 1591' in *Hakluyt's Voyages*, ed. Richard David, Chatto & Windus, London 1981, p. 596.

Thomas Stafford Thomas Stafford, *Pacata Hibernia, or a History of the Wars in Ireland*, ed. Standish O'Grady, 2 vols., Downey & Co., London 1896, pp. 190–209. (First published London 1633.)

Thomas Dineley Thomas Dineley, *Observations in a Voyage through the Kingdom of Ireland*, University Press, Dublin 1870, pp. 83–84.

John Stevens John Stevens, *A Journal of My Travels in Ireland since the Revolution* in John P. Harrington, *The English Traveller in Ireland*, Wolfhound Press, Dublin 1991, p. 131.

Dive Downes T. A. Lunham, 'Bishop Dive Downes' Visitation of His Diocese' in *Journal of the Cork Historical and Archaeological Society*, vol. 15, 1909, pp. 163–168.

Jaques Fontaine Francis Joseph Bigger, 'A Huguenot Hero of Berehaven in 1704' in *Journal of the Cork Historical and Archaeological Society*, vol. 4, 1898, pp. 289–292.

Charles Smith Charles Smith, *The Antient and Present State of the County and City of Cork* (2 vols. 1750), vol. 2, pp. 291–298.

Arthur O'Neill 'The memoirs of Arthur O'Neill' in D. O'Sullivan, *Carolan: The Life, Times and Music of an Irish Harper*, Routledge & Kegan Paul, London 1958, pp. 147–148.

Richard Pococke John McVeagh, ed., *Richard Pococke's Irish Tours*, Irish Academic Press, Dublin 1995, pp. 160–164.

Arthur Young Arthur Young, *A Tour in Ireland*, George Bell & Sons, London 1892, pp. 343–345. (First published 1780.)

Theobald Wolfe Tone Theobald Wolfe Tone, *The Autobiography of Theobald Wolfe Tone 1763–1798*, ed. R. Barry O'Brien, Maunsel & Co., Dublin 1910, vol. 2, pp. 165–176.

Jacques Louis de Bougrenet de Latocnaye, *A Frenchman's Walk through Ireland 1796–7*, trans. John Stevenson, Hodges Figgis & Co., Dublin 1917, pp. 95–99.

Isaac Weld Isaac Weld, *Illustrations of the Scenery of Killarney and the Surrounding Country*, Longman, Hurst, Rees, Orme & Brown, London 1812, pp. 280–293. (First published 1807.)

Edward Wakefield Edward Wakefield, *An Account of Ireland, Statistical and Political*, Longman, Hurst, Rees, Orme & Brown, London 1812, vol. 1, pp. 60–63.

Horatio Townshend Horatio Townshend, *Statistical Survey of the County of Cork*, Dublin, 1810, pp. 387–397.

Anne Plumptre Anne Plumptre, *Narrative of a Residence in Ireland*, Henry Colburn, London 1817, pp. 257–259.

Caesar Otway Caesar Otway, *Sketches in Ireland*, William Curry, Dublin 1827, pp. 376–392.

Thomas Crofton Croker T. Crofton Croker, *Researches in the South of Ireland*, John Murray, London 1824, pp. 313–314.

Hermann von Pückler-Muskau H. von Pückler-Muskau, *Tour in England, Ireland and France in the Years 1826, 1827, 1828 & 1829*, trans. Sarah Austin, Massie Publishing Co., Zurich 1940, pp. 304–307.

Georgiana Chatterton Lady Chatterton, *Rambles in the South of Ireland during the Year 1838*, Saunders & Otley, London 1839, vol. 1, pp. 56–69, 73–79, 81–84.

John Windele John Windele, *Historical and Descriptive Notices of the City of Cork*, Cork 1839, pp. 273–275, 287–289.

Mr & Mrs S.C. Hall Mr & Mrs S.C. Hall, *Ireland: Its Scenery, Character, etc.*, Hall, Virtue & Co., London 1848, pp. 143–157. (First published 1841.)

William Makepeace Thackeray W.M. Thackeray, *The Irish Sketch Book* in *The Works of William Makepeace Thackeray*, vol. vii, Smith, Elder & Co., London 1877, pp. 342–349. (First published 1843.)

Johann Georg Kohl Johann Georg Kohl, *Ireland, Scotland, and England*, Chapman & Hall, London 1844, pp. 85–92.

Asenath Nicholson Asenath Nicholson, *The Bible in Ireland*, Houghton & Stoughton, London 1926, pp. 182–197. (First published as *Ireland's Welcome to the Stranger*, 1847.)

Anthony Trollope N. John Hall, ed., *The Letters of Anthony Trollope*, Stanford University Press, California 1983, vol. 2, p. 1008.

F.F. Trench W. Steuart Trench, *Realities of Irish Life*, Macgibbon & Kee, London 1966, p. 244. (First published 1868 by Longmans, Green & Co.)

Alfred Tennyson Alfred Perceval Graves, *Irish Literary and Musical Studies*, Elkin, Matthews, London 1913, pp. 7–8.

Rose Trollope Frances Eleanor Trollope, *Frances Trollope: Her Life and Literary Work from George III to Victoria*, Richard Bentley & Son, London 1895, vol. 2, pp. 32–33.

Charles Kingsley Frances Kingsley, *Charles Kingsley, His Letters and Memories of His Life*, Henry S. King, London 1877, pp. 108, 295.

James Anthony Froude James Anthony Froude, 'A Fortnight in Kerry' in *Short Studies on Great Subjects*, Longmans, London 1871, pp. 180–193, 210–213.

Richard McMullen R. T. McMullen, *Down Channel*, George, Allen & Unwin, London 1931, pp. 74–87. (First published 1869.)

John Skelton John Skelton, *The Table-Talk of Shirley*, William Blackwood, Edinburgh and London 1895, pp. 145–147.

Marie-Anne de Bovet Marie-Anne de Bovet, *Three Months Tour in Ireland*, trans. Mrs. Arthur Walter, Chapman & Hall, London 1891, pp. 139–144. (First published as *Trois mois en Irlande*, Hachette, Paris 1891.)

David McArdle David McArdle, 'A Visit to Castletown-Berehaven' in *Irish Naturalist*, vol. 3, 1894, pp. 190–192.

Francis Joseph Bigger Francis Joseph Bigger, 'The Lake and Church of Kilmakilloge, the Ancient Church, Holy Well, and Bullán-stone of Temple Feaghna, and the Holy Well and Shrine at Saint Finan's, County Kerry' in *Royal Society of Antiquaries of Ireland Journal*, vol. 28, 1898, pp. 314–515, 319–320.

Daniel J. Tallon Daniel Tallon, William Field and Thomas Kennedy, *Distress in the West and South of Ireland, 1898*, Dublin 1898, pp. 14–16.

Rudyard Kipling Rudyard Kipling, *A Fleet in Being: Notes of Two Trips with the Channel Squadron*, Macmillan, London 1916, pp. 46–50. (First published 1898.)

John Rushworth Jellicoe Sir Reginald Bacon, *The Life of John Rushworth, Earl Jellicoe*, Cassell, London 1936, p. 179.

Albert Thomas Albert Thomas, *Wait and See*, Michael Joseph, London 1921, pp. 75–80, 82–83, 85–86, 89–90.

John O'Donoghue John O' Donoghue, *In Kerry Long Ago*, B. T. Batsford, London 1960, pp. 128–136.

George Bernard Shaw Dorothy Eagle and Hilary Carnell, eds., *The Oxford Literary Guide to the British Isles*, Oxford University Press 1977, p. 115.

Harold Speakman Harold Speakman, *Here's Ireland*, Robert M. McBride, New York 1925, pp. 53–58.

Padraic Colum Padraic Colum, *Cross Roads in Ireland*, Macmillan, New York 1930, pp. 312–314.

Virginia Woolf Anne Olivier Bell, ed., *The Diary of Virginia Woolf*, Hogarth Press, London 1980, vol. 3, pp. 209–210.

Sean O'Faolain Sean O'Faolain, *An Irish Journey*, Readers Union with Longmans Green, London 1941, pp. 109–116.

Kees van Hoek Kees van Hoek, *Country of My Choice: An Irish Panorama*, The Kerryman, Tralee 1945, pp. 77–80.

Seán Jennett Seán Jennett, *Munster*, Faber, London 1967, pp. 99–100.

Peter Somerville-Large Peter Somerville-Large, *The Coast of West Cork*, Victor Gollancz, London 1972, pp. 203–207.

Benedict Kiely Benedict Kiely, *All the Way to Bantry Bay*, Victor Gollancz, London 1978, pp. 186–191.

Chris Duff Chris Duff, *On Celtic Tides: One Man's Journey around Ireland by Sea Kayak*, St Martin's Press, New York 1999, pp. 77–82.

Picture Credits

By courtesy of the National Library of Ireland: p.15 Bantry, on beach, 4862WL; p.55 Hungry Hill, Adrigole, 7551WL; p.109 Suspension Bridge, Kenmare, 1863WL; p.136 Kenmare, 2748WL; p.157 Castletownbere, Square, 7540WL; p.165 Dunboy, Castletownbere, 4856WL; p.181 Steamboat Pier, Glengarriff, 8865WL; p.197 Castletownbere, Main Street, 7551WL.
By courtesy of John Eagle: p.29 Mare's Tail Waterfall.
By courtesy of Kilkenny College: p.32 Portrait of Richard Pococke.
By courtesy of the National Maritime Museum, London: p.36 Berehaven, by J.R. Wells in *London Illustrated News*, 11.8.1888.
By courtesy of the National Portrait Gallery, London: p.38 Arthur Young, by George Dance; p.131 Charles Kingsley, by Adriano Cecioni; p.132 J.A. Froude, by Harry Furniss; p.177 George Bernard Shaw, by Harry Furniss; p.183 Virginia Woolf, by Francis Dodd.
By courtesy of Madame Mollie O'Grady: p.42 Ardnagashel House, 1826, by S.M. Derinzy.
By courtesy of the Royal Dublin Society: p.51 Isaac Weld, by Martin Cregan.
By courtesy of the Ulster Folk Museum: p.52 The Kerry bull Rory O'More.
By courtesy of Ian Vickery: p.91 Donemark Falls, by an unknown artist.
By courtesy of the *Belfast Telegraph*: p.153 F. J. Bigger.
By courtesy of the Commisioners of Irish Lights: p.172 Calf and Heifer Rocks, from Robert Callwell's original ms, 1869.
By courtesy of the Irish National Picture Co.: p. 206 Allihies, postcard view.

Acknowledgements

We are grateful to the following for granting permission to quote from their works: Irish Academic Press and John McVeagh for *Richard Pococke's Irish Tours*; B.T. Batsford Ltd for *In Kerry Long Ago* by John O'Donoghue; Curtis Brown and Peter Somerville-Large for *The Coast of West Cork*; A.P. Watt Ltd and Benedict Kiely for *All the Way to Bantry Bay*; Random House Group Ltd, with acknowledgements to Hogarth Press, the Executors of the Virginia Woolf Estate and Anne Olivier Bell (editor) for *The Diaries of Virgina Woolf.*

Our thanks to everyone who helped us in the compilation of this book:

Beara Historical Society, Josette Cadoret and Simon Prichard, Joe Coencas, David Durell, Mary Kelly, Patrick Kelly, Delia Kelly, Henk Aben, Jeremy Addis, Sue Booth-Forbes, Rachel Boydell, Barbara Bray, Trish Caffrey, Paul Cudahy, Mario Haas, Gerdie Harrington, Lyn Herring, Douglas Keating, Connie Murphy, Diarmuid Murphy, Ann O'Connor, Paddy O'Conor, Fachtna O'Donovan, Dianne Ressinger, Donal O'Sullivan, John Finbar O'Sullivan, Gillian Sheehan, Barbara Simon, Amanda VanDoorene.

Sarah Ball, National Botanic Gardens Library; Kieran Burke, Cork City Library; Tim Cadogan, Cork County Library; Michael Costello, Kerry County Library; Mary Kelleher, Royal Dublin Society; Bríd Leahy, Dublin City Archives; Gerard J. Lyne, Genealogical Office; Siobhan O'Rafferty, Royal Irish Academy; also staff of the following institutions: *New York* Brooklyn Public Library, French Institute, Goethe Institute, New York Public Library, New-York Historical Society. *Dublin* National Library of Ireland, Trinity College, Irish Architectural Archive, Alliance Française. *Cork* Boole Library, University College. *London* National Maritime Museum Library, Guildhall Library.

A Beara Bibliography

Non-fiction

Bennett, William, *Narration of a Recent Journey of Six Weeks* in Ireland, Gilpin, London 1847.

Boland, Rosita, *Sea Legs: Hitch-Hiking the Irish Coast Alone*, New Island Books, Dublin 1992.

Bradley, Brendan P., *Bantry Bay*, Williams & Northgate, London 1931.

Brady, William Mazière, *Clerical and Parochial Records of Cork, Cloyne and Ross*, Thom, Dublin 1863–4.

Brehony, Tony, *West Cork, 'a kind of history like . . . '*, Bray 1997.

Brewer, James Norris, *The Beauties of Ireland*, 2 vols., Sherwood, Gilbert & Piper, London 1826.

Brody, Hugh, *Inishkillane*, Allen Lane, London 1973.

Carroll, Michael J., *Wolfe Tone and The French Invasion of 1796 – A Brief History of Events*, Bantry 1995.

Carroll, Michael J., *A Bay of Destiny*, Bantry 1996.

Clements, Paul, *Irish Shores: A Journey round the Rim of Ireland*, Greystone, Antrim 1993.

Colquhoun, Ithell, *The Crying of the Wind: Ireland*, Peter Owen, London 1955.

Coyne, J. Stirling, *The Scenery and Antiquities of Ireland*, vol. 2, George Virtue, London 1842.

Cusack, Mary Francis, *A History of the City and Cork*, Kenmare Publications, Dublin and Cork 1875.

De Selincourt, E., *The Letters of William and Dorothy Wordsworth: The Later Years, 1821–1853*, rev. Alan G. Hill, Oxford 1978–88, vol. v, pt. 2.

Duquet, Alfred, *Irlande & France*, Maunsel, Dublin and London 1916.

Durell, Penelope, *Discover Dursey*, Ballinacarriga Books, Allihies 1996.

Floyd, M., *The Face of Ireland*, B.T. Batsford, London 1937.

Froude, J.A., *The English in Ireland in the Eighteenth Century*, Longman's, Green & Co., London 1872–74.

Gibson, Charles Bernard, *The History of the County of Cork*, Thomas Newby, London 1861.

Graves, Alfred Perceval, *To Return to All That*, Talbot Press, Dublin 1930.

Gwynn, Stephen, *The Charm Of Ireland*, Houghton Mifflin, Boston and New York 1930.

Harrison, Richard S., *Bantry in Old Days*, Bantry 1992.

Harrison, Richard S., *Beara and Bantry Bay: A History of Rossmacowen*, Rossmacowen Historical Society, Rossmacowen 1990.

Healy, James N., *The Castles of County Cork*, Mercier Press, Cork and Dublin 1988.

Heyward, Richard, *In the Kingdom of Kerry*, Dundalgan Press, Dundalk 1946.

Hogan, Edmund, *Description of Ireland*, M. H. Gill, Dublin and Bernard Quaritch, London 1878.

Holland, W., *History of West Cork and the Diocese of Ross*, Southern Star Ltd., Skibbereen 1949.

Inglis, Henry D., *Ireland in 1834. A Journey throughout Ireland during the Spring, Summer and Autumn of 1834*, Whittaker, London 1834.

Jennett, Seán, *Cork and Kerry*, Batsford, London 1977.
Johnson, James, *A Tour in Ireland, with Meditations and Reflections*, S. Highley, London 1844.
Jones, E.H. Stuart, *An Invasion that Failed – The French Expedition to Ireland 1796*, Blackwell, Oxford 1950.
Joynes, J.L., *The Adventures of a Tourist in Ireland*, Kegan Paul Trench, London 1882.
Keogh, T.M., *A Short Account of the History and Antiquities of Bere Island and Berehaven*, Pardy & Son, Bournemouth 1913.
Knox, Thomas W., *The Boy Travellers in Great Britain and Ireland*, Harper, New York 1891.
Lansdowne, H.W.E, *Glanerought and the Petty-Fitzmaurices*, Oxford University Press 1937.
Lewis, Samuel, *Topographical Dictionary of Ireland*, London 1837.
McCarthy, Jennie, *A History of Derrycreha National School and Its Area*, Glengarriff 1995.
McCarthy, Philomena, *Kenmare and Its Storied Glen*, Kenmare 1993.
McVeagh, John, *Irish Travel Writing: A Bibliography*, Wolfhound Press, Dublin 1996.
Mandat-Grancey, E. de, *Chez Paddy*, E. Plon, Nourit et Cie., Paris 1887.
Manning, Olivia, *The Dreaming Shore*, Evans Brothers, London 1950.
Mansfield, M.F., *Romantic Ireland*, L. C. Page & Co., Boston 1905.
Marmion, Anthony, *The Ancient and Modern History of the Maritime Parts of Ireland*, London 1858.
Mersey, Richard, *The Hills of Cork and Kerry*, Gill & Macmillian Dublin 1987.
Murphy, John A., ed., *The French Are in the Bay*, Mercier Press, Cork and Dublin 1997.
Newby, Eric, *Round Ireland in Low Gear*, Collins, London 1987.
O'Brien, Daniel, *Beara: A Journey through History*, Beara Historical Society, Castletownbere 1991.
O'Callaghan, John Cornelius, *History of the Irish Brigades in the Service of France*, Irish University Press, Shannon 1969.
O'Dwyer, Liam, *Beara in Irish History*, Vantage Press, New York 1977.
O'Dwyer, Riobard, *Who Were My Ancestors?* series of 4, Astoria, Ill., 1987–89: Genealogy of Eyeries, Allihies, Castletownbere and Bere Island parishes.
O'Grady, Standish, *Selected Essays and Passages*, Talbot Press, Dublin 1917.
O'Leary, Con, *A Wayfarer in Ireland*, R.M. McBride & Co., New York 1936.
O'Mahony, Jeremiah J., *West Cork and Its Story*, 2nd ed., Tower Books, Cork 1975.
O'Sullivan, Ted, *Bere Island: A Short History*, Inisgragy Books, Cork 1992.
O'Sullivan Beare, Philip, *Historiae Catholicae Iberniae Compendium* (Lisbon 1621); trans. Matthew J. Byrne as *A History of Ireland under Elizabeth*, Sealy, Bryers & Walker, Dublin 1903.
An Oxonian, *A Little Tour in Ireland*, Edward Arnold, London 1859.
Potter, George W., *An Irish Pilgrimage*, Providence Journal Company, Providence 1950.
Ressinger, Dianne W., ed., *Memoirs of the Reverend Jaques Fontaine 1658–1728*, New Series No. 2, Huguenot Society of Great Britain and Ireland, Tinsley Brothers, London 1992.
Scott, Clement, *Round about the Islands, or Sunny Spots near Home*, London 1874.
Seward, William Wenman, *Topographia Hibernica*, Dublin 1795.
Shoemaker, M.M., *Wanderings in Ireland*, Putnam, New York 1908.
Shine, John, ed., *Bonane, a Centenary Celebration*, Bonane 1992.

Somerville-Large, Peter, *From Bantry Bay to Leitrim*, Victor Gollancz, London 1974.
Stark, Archibald G., *The South of Ireland in 1850,* James Duffy, Dublin 1850.
Stevenson, Burton Egbert, *The Charm of Ireland*, John Murray, London 1915.
Sullivan, T.D., *Bantry, Berehaven and the O'Sullivan Sept*, Sealy, Bryers & Walker, Dublin 1908.
Tietzch-Tyler, Daniel, *The Geology of Allihies Mines*, Geological Survey of Ireland 1996.
Tuosist History & Newsletter Committee, *Tuosist 6000*, Tuosist, 1999.
Verling, Martin, *Gortbroc*, Coiscéim, Dublin 1996.
Walford, Thomas, *The Scientific Tourist through Ireland*, London 1818.
Williams, R. Alan, *The Berehaven Copper Mines*, Northern Mine Research Society, Sheffield 1991.
Woodham-Smith, Cecil, *The Great Hunger*, Hamish Hamilton, London 1962.
Wright, G.N., *Ireland Illustrated*, Fisher, London 1831.

Fiction

Birch, Carol, *Songs of the West*, Heinemann, London 1994.
Colum, Padraic, *Adrigoole*, Jonathan Cape, London 1929.
DuMaurier, Daphne, *Hungry Hill*, Victor Gollancz, London 1943.
Froude, J.A., *The Two Chiefs of Dunboy*, Longman's, Green & Co., London 1889.
Hopkin, Alannah, *A Joke Goes a Long Way in the Country*, Hamish Hamilton, London 1982.
O'Brien, Conor, *The Runaways*, Harrap, London 1941.
O'Grady, Standish, *Lost on Du Corrig*, Cassell, London 1894.
O'Grady, Standish, *The Chain of Gold*, Unwin, London 1895.
O'Grady, Standish, *In the Wake of King James*, Dent, London 1896.
O'Grady, Standish, *Ulrick the Ready*, Downey, London 1896.
Phipps, John-Francis, *New Times*, New Millenium, London 1999.
Purcell, Deirdre, *Falling for a Dancer*, Townhouse, Dublin 1993.
Purcell, Deirdre, *Francie*, Townhouse, Dublin 1994.
Tremayne, Peter, *The Subtle Serpent*, Hodder Headline, London 1996.
Wassell, Elizabeth, *The Honey Plain*, Wolfhound, Dublin 1997.

Index